Changes in the Market Structure
of Grocery Retailing

WILLARD F. MUELLER
LEON GAROIAN

Changes in
the Market Structure
of Grocery Retailing

THE UNIVERSITY
OF WISCONSIN PRESS
Madison, 1961

Published by the University of Wisconsin Press
430 Sterling Court, Madison 6, Wisconsin

Printed in the United States of America

Library of Congress Catalog Card No. 60—11444

TO SHIRLEY AND BETTY

Preface

THIS study deals with recent changes in the industrial organization of grocery retailing. We make no pretense at taking the full measure of all changes which are relevant to the performance of this dynamic industry. Rather, we have concentrated our efforts on two major tasks. First, we have attempted to measure certain market characteristics which economic theory and empirical studies suggest as being important determinants of competitive behavior. This involved the often tedious task of compiling data necessary to understand the nature and to measure the magnitude of these changes. Second, we attempted to interpret the probable implications of these changes for the market performance of grocery retailing and related industries.

After this study was begun in March, 1958, the Federal Trade Commission initiated on October 9, 1958, an economic inquiry into food marketing. The first aspect of the FTC study deals with concentration and integration in the grocery retailing field. On June 30, 1959, it released a short interim report, "Economic Inquiry into Food Marketing." Some of the data from this report we incorporated into this study. However, when this study was accepted for publication in January, 1960, the final FTC report had not been completed. It was released on May 22, 1960. Consequently, none of its contents is included in this book. The FTC inquiry and this study may therefore be considered as independent treatments of recent market changes occurring in grocery retailing.

Much of the FTC study is based on original sources and is for the period from 1948 to 1958. The present study is based primarily on secondary sources and covers primarily the period from 1940 to 1958. Much of the material of the two studies covers essentially the same ground, for example, the extent and impact of mergers. The most distinctive feature of the present study is its attempt to analyze some of the market implications of the structural changes it measures; the FTC inquiry is content to stop with a description of these changes.

Research planning, funds, and personnel for this study were provided jointly by the Marketing Economics Research Division of the Agricultural Marketing Service, U.S. Department of Agriculture, and the University of Wisconsin. Professor Garoian was stationed at Madison and served as co-author with Professor Mueller of the University of Wisconsin.

Professor Garoian was employed jointly by the Marketing Economics Research Division, USDA, and the University of Wisconsin during the course of this study.

We express our gratitude to the following persons for their generous assistance in contributing to the conception and completion of this study: Professor Harlow Halvorson of the University of Wisconsin for his generous assistance in working up the data on the nature of grocery operations in various cities and his many helpful suggestions on many other phases of the study; Messrs. Winn Finner, Alden Manchester, Paul Nelson, Kenneth Ogren, Allen Paul, and Willard Williams, all of the Marketing Economics Research Division of the U.S. Department of Agriculture, for their many suggestions and thoughtful criticisms of a preliminary draft of the study; Professors Reuben Buse, Robert Clodius, Peter Dorner, and Mr. Russell Parker of the University of Wisconsin, for their helpful criticisms of a draft of this study; Messrs. M. V. George and Jerry Gunnelson for their diligent aid in gathering and working up many of the data used herein; and finally Mrs. Lucille Copas and Miss Judy Karnes for typing the various drafts of the manuscript.

We have considered all and adopted many of the suggestions of the critics. They may not agree with some of the inferences drawn by us, and possible errors of fact presented herein are our own.

Willard F. Mueller
Leon Garoian

Contents

List of Tables

List of Charts

Changes in the Market Structure
of Grocery Retailing

CHAPTER ONE

Introduction

FOOD retailing occupies a strategic position in the American economy. Its sales—currently over $50 billion annually—are greater than those of any other American industry. Nearly one of every six dollars spent by American consumers is spent at food stores. Food processors depend largely upon food retailers as outlets for their products. Over two-thirds of all farm products ultimately are channeled through food stores.

In the past few decades vast and significant changes have occurred in food retailing as in other parts of our economy. These changes have apparently been generated by a complicated admixture of technological and economic factors which in turn have induced marked changes in industrial structure. Because the farming, processing, and distributing industries are integrally related, changes in one necessarily induce changes in the others. And because of the strategic position of food retailing in the distribution process, consumers, processors, and farmers, as well as food retailers themselves, have a vital interest in the way in which it performs its functions, both in terms of operating and pricing efficiency.

It is not surprising, therefore, that the recent changes in food retailing have attracted the attention and concern of diverse interests in the U.S. economy. But unfortunately, reliable knowledge of the nature, extent, and causes of these changes is scarce. For example, George

Mehren concluded an analysis of some aspects of the changing food market structure by saying, "I would like to know what the changes have been and are—their causes, interrelationships, effects, and susceptibility to control. These questions are not presently answered."[1] This study was undertaken to answer some of these questions, especially as to the major changes which have occurred in the market structure of food retailing and the probable impact of these changes on firm behavior and industrial performance.

NATURE OF STUDY

The basic assumption of this study is that market structure is a strategic variable determining firm conduct and industrial performance. Bain defines market structure as "those characteristics of the organization of a market which seem to influence strategically the nature of competition and pricing within the market."[2]

The factors responsible for the market behavior or decisions of firms are elusive and multidimensional quantities. Cochrane has grouped the factors affecting decisions of firms into three convenient categories: "(1) Those external to the market (e.g. national income, war), (2) those internal to individuals operating in the market (e.g. the state of a buyer's ulcers, or the whimsey of a seller's wife), and (3) those *peculiar* to and *significantly* influential in the market itself."[3]

Market structure theory is concerned only with isolating the third kind of factors. Economic theory and industrial experience suggest that among the leading market structural characteristics affecting firm behavior are: (1) the degree of buyer and seller concentration—described by the number and size distribution of sellers or buyers operating within the relevant market, (2) the extent to which firms sell identical or differentiated products, (3) the ease with which new firms can enter the relevant market, and (4) the extent to which firms are or may become vertically integrated. In practice, these structural characteristics often are intricately interrelated. For example, high barriers to entry are likely to restrict the number of firms in a particular market; also, a high degree of successful product differentiation tends to raise the barriers to entry which in turn tends to limit the number of firms in the market. But casting attention on each of these factors tends to provide more meaningful insights into the likely long-run structures of an industry rather than simply into those existing at a particular time. For example, although an industry may have very few firms at a particular time, if technology is such that there are no significant barriers to entry, future, and possibly current, behavior is likely to be more competitive than market concentration alone suggests.

Focusing attention on market structure in a research study does not imply that the analysis is not interested in the technological or other factors responsible for particular market structures. On the contrary, a firm's growth methods and the underlying motives for growth are necessarily of interest in market structure analysis because they explain why a particular structure exists. This explanation in turn is crucial in matters of public policy concerned with questions of whether particular market or industrial structures perform in a socially acceptable manner.

Nor is market structure analysis uninterested in market conduct or performance. As already indicated, the very essence of market structure analysis is the assumption that firm conduct and long-run industrial performance are in large part a function of certain isolable elements of market structure. This is not to imply that market behavior can be induced precisely from a particular set of market elements. But empirical investigations have demonstrated that decisions of firms on pricing and other policies are influenced very directly by the market structure within which they operate. Some of Bain's early work is very enlightening as to the relationship between industrial profits and market concentration,[4] as is his recent study of the effects of barriers to entry on a firm's behavior and profits.[5]

Similarly, a number of studies in the agricultural industries have demonstrated the relevance of market structure analysis in interpreting the market behavior of firms.[6]

The reader should be cautioned that the final judgment as to whether an industry performs in a socially acceptable manner cannot be deduced from structural elements alone. This is true because the relationships between structure and performance are not precisely correlated; thus some economists have developed the concept of "workable" or "effective" competition. This concept was developed because nearly all modern industrial markets seriously violate the assumptions of pure competition—infinite numbers, free entry, and homogeneous products—and because they contain elements of both monopoly and competition. Consequently, some economists[7] advocated what they considered the more realistic but less precise norm of workable competition.

Since J. M. Clark's pioneering work on this concept, economists have developed a variety of criteria an industry must possess for it to pass the test of being "workably"—although not perfectly—competitive. The suggested criteria can be placed into three categories: (1) market structure, (2) firm conduct, and (3) industrial performance.[8]

The primary purpose of this study is not to determine whether or not the retail grocery industry is workably competitive. Rather, our objective is a more limited and less difficult one. It is to attempt to

(1) measure the broad changes which have occurred in the market structure of food retailing since 1940, (2) study some of the methods of growth involved in bringing them about, (3) draw some theoretical inferences as to the impact of these changes in market structure on current and prospective competitive behavior and performance in food retailing and allied industries. Because market structure and industrial performance are not correlated in a precise fashion, this study should be viewed primarily as a pioneer work directed at making a first approximation of actual performance. Other more intensive industry studies are currently underway aimed at analyzing the impact of these changes on market conduct and industrial performance in particular agricultural processing industries.[9]

Sources of Data

Secondary sources used to obtain most of the data on which this study is based include investment manuals, trade journals, house organs, annual reports of concerns, government investigations of food retailing, and to a limited extent personal interviews. Hence, the method employed was largely an indirect one. An alternative approach would have been to contact through direct interviews or questionnaires a sample of firms which would have served as a miniature image of the total universe.[10] Presumably, the direct method would have provided more complete and reliable data for those firms contacted, thus permitting accurate generalizations for the entire universe. But because of the nature and objective of the study, the direct method of inquiry was not used for the following several reasons.

1. Reliable information is available from published sources of many of the broad structural changes analyzed herein.

2. Because most of this study is concerned with changes occurring since 1940, it seemed that information gained from direct interviews or questionnaires would be quite inaccurate for the earlier years.

3. The direct method of inquiry based on confidential information often places serious limitations on the usefulness of a study of this kind. Readers and other researchers are interested in learning the growth patterns and market behavior of particular, identifiable firms, as well as broad patterns of change and behavior. By relying on published sources for the basic data, we can provide such information.

After this study was begun the Federal Trade Commission initiated an inquiry into the food industry. The FTC's study attempts to measure some of the same structural variables as this study does. Some of the data from its Interim Report[11] released June 30, 1959, have been incorporated in this report. However, the final draft of this study was completed before the FTC released its final report on May 22, 1960.

The FTC study and this study should provide those interested in grocery retailing with alternative sources of information on a number of aspects of market structure, for example, the role which mergers have played in transforming the structure of grocery retailing.

CHAPTER TWO

Current Importance and Historical Origins of Grocery Retailing

Place of Grocery Retailing in the U.S. Economy

In 1954 sales by all retail stores came to about $170 billion. Food retailing, with sales of nearly $40 billion, constituted the largest part of the total retail trade (Table 1). Its 384,616 stores employed slightly over 1,000,000 persons or roughly one out of every seven persons employed by all kinds of retail stores.

The Bureau of the Census classification of food stores includes retail establishments primarily engaged in selling food for home preparation. It divides retail food establishments into seven classifications according to the types of commodities sold (Table 2). *This study is concerned mainly with grocery and combination stores.*

Grocery retailing constitutes the most important segment of the retail food business. In 1954 there were 279,440 grocery stores with combined sales of $34,420,764,000 (Table 2). These stores constituted 73 per cent of all retail food stores and accounted for 87 per cent of all retail food-store sales. When sales are used as the measure of size, grocery retailing is America's largest industry.

Moreover, grocery-store sales are growing more rapidly than total food-store sales. Whereas in 1929 grocery stores accounted for about 66 per cent of food-store sales, their share expanded to 77 per cent in 1939, 85 per cent in 1948, 87 per cent in 1954, and 88.6 per cent in 1958. This increasing relative importance of grocery-store business is due to its expansion into a wide assortment of food and nonfood items.

Evolution of the Modern Food Store

The modern food store is the product of a long and interesting evolution. Its development may conveniently be divided into five stages.[1]

8

TABLE 1
Retail Trade

Kinds of business	Number of establishments		Total sales (000 omitted)		Total paid employees	
	1939	1954	1939	1954	1939	1954
Food stores	560,549	384,616	$10,164,967	$39,762,213	814,746	1,025,849
Eating and drinking places	305,386	319,657	3,520,052	13,101,051	830,063	1,352,828
General merchandise group	50,267	76,198	5,665,007	17,872,386	965,884	1,258,990
Apparel group	106,959	119,743	3,258,772	11,078,209	417,396	607,340
Furniture, home furnishings, appliance dealers	52,827	91,797	1,733,257	8,619,002	220,950	351,772
Automotive group	60,132	85,953	5,548,687	29,914,997	400,166	710,802
Lumber, building materials, hardware, farm equipment dealers	79,313	100,519	2,734,914	13,123,528	257,641	446,690
Drug stores, proprietary stores	57,903	56,009	1,562,502	5,251,791	192,296	300,435
Other retail stores	196,337	408,650	3,634,444	26,730,696	386,576	869,748
Retail trade total		1,721,650		$169,967,748		7,124,331

Source: U.S. Department of Commerce, Census of Business, 1954.

9

TABLE 2
Characteristics of Retail Food Trade

Kind of store	Number of establishments		Sales (000 omitted)	
	1948*	1954	1948*	1954
Grocery and combination	350,754	279,440	$ 24,729,717	$ 34,420,764
Meat markets	23,920	22,896	1,641,087	1,943,969
Fish markets	4,517	4,458	132,331	184,148
Fruit and vegetable markets	13,482	13,136	394,602	484,503
Candy, nut, confectionery	27,165	20,507	586,592	567,955
Bakery products	19,500	19,034	722,761	862,290
Delicatessens	7,917	8,132	308,336	479,787
Food stores, NEC	13,658	13,777	692,438	752,439
Total	460,913	381,380	$ 29,207,864	$ 39,695,855

*Adjusted to 1954 census basis of classification.

Source: U.S. Department of Commerce, Census of Business, Retail Trade, 1948 and 1954.

10

The general store with its stocks of hardware, leather harnesses, farm tools, mercantile goods such as ready-to-wear clothing and sewing materials, and staple foods can be considered the antecedent of the modern grocery store. Characteristic of the era of the potbellied heater and the cracker barrel, the general store embodied many of the traditions of the trading posts from which it evolved.

After the general store came the specialized grocery stores and meat markets which carried forward many of the characteristics inherent in the general stores. Like the general stores, grocery store operations involved personal clerk service, customer credit, and often the exchange of home-produced items for store items, much as in barter. Merchandise was stocked on shelves which approached the ceiling and were intentionally made inaccessible to customers by placing them behind the counters. The distinguishing characteristic of the grocery store and meat market was its specialization in merchandising food items.

By 1912, a few southern California food retailers were referring to their stores as "self-service" operations, introducing the third and most significant innovation leading to the modern food market.[2] While cautious southern California proprietors experimented by operating self-service and clerk-service sections in the same stores for a few years, by 1920 self-service had been established as an improved means of food retailing, apparently appealing to customers and proving satisfactory to proprietors.[3]

By the early 1920's a fourth major step had been taken toward the modern grocery store—the combination store. Perhaps not basically as significant as the innovation of self-service, the combination store brought together under one roof—but not necessarily under one management— departments which sold fresh meats, fresh fruits and vegetables, and dairy products, in addition to groceries. The introduction of the combination food store doubled store size.[4]

The combination of the self-service and combination store into one retail unit resulted quite naturally in the supermarket by the 1930's. The early supermarkets were four to five times larger in floor space than the earlier grocery stores.

The origin of the term "supermarket" is more obscure than are the economic forces and personalities associated with it. Several theories have been advanced about its origin, but the first use of the word supermarket in a corporate or firm name is associated with Albers Super Markets, Inc., which started operations in Cincinnati under this name in November, 1933.[5]

In an early definition, a "supermarket" is described as "a highly departmentalized retail establishment, dealing in foods and other merchandise, either wholly owned or concession operated, with adequate parking space, doing a minimum of $250,000 annually. The grocery department, however, must be on a self-service basis."[6]

The supermarket embodied the accumulation of previous innovations in food retailing and quickly supplemented them with the opportunities offered from technological advances in other segments of the nation's economy. As a native institution, the supermarket marks the effective utilization of numerous external scientific advances whose effects cannot be viewed in isolation from those internal to the food-retailing industry. Improvements in communication, refrigeration, and transportation made possible the physical existence of modern supermarkets, influencing not only distribution functions but also customer shopping habits.

Most supermarkets presently stock 5,000 or more different items including an increasing number of nonfood items. In this respect supermarkets are reverting on a grander scale to one characteristic of the

TABLE 3
Percentage of Supermarkets Operating Various Departments

Department	Per cent of markets with departments		
	1950	1955	1957
Drugs and cosmetics	89.1	99.0	97.7
Wines	23.4	27.4	33.8
Magazines	38.0	67.7	74.6
Housewares	45.1	88.4	92.3
Stationery	33.7	79.8	91.5
Toys	14.1	68.7	74.6
Beer	37.5	46.1	52.3
Liquor	8.2	n.a.	n.a.
Hardware	23.4	57.6	72.3
Sundries	38.6	n.a.	n.a.
Fountain lunch	13.0	6.2	n.a.
Store baked goods	n.a.	58.7	65.4
Dietetic foods	n.a.	95.6	96.9
Soft goods	n.a.	52.4	64.6
Children's books	n.a.	73.5	76.1
Cooked foods	n.a.	59.6	63.8
Greeting cards	n.a.	59.1	53.1
Garden supplies	n.a.	57.2	62.3
Appliances	n.a.	33.1	29.2

n.a.: Not available.

Source: Super Market Merchandising, various issues.

general stores of past generations. Table 3 indicates the relative increases in sales of certain nonfood items by food stores. Cosmetics and housewares are almost universally found in today's supermarket.

By 1958 nonfoods constituted a significant part of total sales in the typical supermarket, amounting to about 5.2 per cent of total sales (Table 4).[7]

TABLE 4
Nonfood Sales in a
  Typical Supermarket, 1958

Item	Per cent of total sales
Health and beauty aids	2.30
Housewares	.92
Magazines and books	.58
Soft goods	.54
Toys	.35
Phonograph records	.30
Stationery	.23
All nonfoods	5.20

Source: Facts in Grocery Distribution
(Progressive Grocer, 1959).

From the standpoint of manufacturers, food stores have become important outlets for several nonfood items. Of the total national sales in 1953, 32 per cent of all razor blades, 43 per cent of dentifrices, 41 per cent of baby powders, and 37 per cent of aspirin were made by food stores.[8]

The growing significance of the supermarket in modern food retailing is demonstrated by the fact that in 1932 there were 300 supermarkets and by 1958 there were 29,920 (Table 5). Even more striking is the growing share of total food sales accounted for by supermarkets. Whereas in 1953 supermarkets accounted for 48 per cent of all food sales, by 1958 they accounted for 68 per cent (Table 6).

While originated by independent food retailers, the corporate chain was largely responsible for the rapid spread of the supermarket in food retailing. In 1939 the chains were credited by one source with operating 1,443 supermarkets compared to only 217 operated by independents. But in subsequent years independent food retailers built super-

markets at a more rapid pace than the chains did. By 1958 they operated 14,600 compared to 15,400 operated by chains (Table 6).   *step*
    A final innovation in the modern retail-food market worthy of com-
ment is the development of the "superette." A superette is essentially a
cross between the small corner grocery and the modern supermarket.
Like the corner grocery, it retains the smaller staff and handles fewer
items; but it is geared to self-service although rendering fewer services
than the supermarket. The result is a unit large enough to operate with

TABLE 5
Growth of Supermarkets

Year	Number of supermarkets
1932	300
1936	1,200
1937	3,066
1940	6,175
1945	9,575
1950	14,217
1955	20,537
1957	24,336
1958	29,920

Annual sales of $375,000
or more.

Source: 1932-57 based on
M.M. Zimmerman, "Super
Market Boom," Super Mar-
ket Merchandising (April,
1957), p. 131; 1958 based on
Facts in Grocery Distrib-
ution (Progressive Grocer,
1959), p. F-8.

lower unit costs than the corner grocery, but small enough to be operated by one or a few individuals. The growing importance of superettes
relative to small stores suggests that in the future practically all food
distribution will be done through supermarkets or superettes. By 1958
superettes (stores with sales of between $75,000 and $375,000) were
doing over three times as much business as small stores (Table 6).

TABLE 6
Size and Sales of Grocery Stores

Size of stores	Number of stores (thousands)		Per cent of stores		Total sales (millions)		Per cent of sales	
	1953	1958	1953	1958	1953	1958	1953	1958
Small (under $75,000)								
Chain	1	0.4	0.3	0.1	$ 70	$ 25	0.2	0.1
Independent	272	195.0	75.0	68.4	6,785	3,500	19.5	7.2
Total	273	195.4	75.3	68.5	6,855	3,525	19.7	7.3
Superettes ($75,000 to $375,000)								
Chain	8.6	3.7	2.5	1.3	2,345	1,100	6.8	2.3
Independent	62.0	56.0	17.1	19.6	8,755	10,750	25.2	22.2
Total	70.6	59.7	19.5	20.9	11,100	11,850	32.0	24.5
Supermarkets (over $375,000)								
Chain	10.3	15.4	2.8	5.4	10,060	15,400	29.0	31.9
Independent	8.6	14.6	2.4	5.1	6,700	17,500	19.3	36.3
Total	18.9	30.0	5.2	10.6	16,760	32,900	48.3	68.2
Grand total	362.6	285.0			$34,715	$48,300		

Source: Facts in Grocery Distribution (Progressive Grocer, 1954 and 1959).

Types of Retail Food Firms

To this point we have discussed only the evolution of the food store without distinguishing between types of organization of firms owning these units. Much of the remainder of the study analyzes the relative size and growth of different types of retail firms. However, it will be helpful at this point to describe briefly the various kinds of business organizations existing in grocery retailing today.

A single person or firm may operate one or several retail store units. Customarily when firms own three or less stores they are called *independent* food retailers, and when they operate more than this they are referred to as *chain* retailers. In recent years some sources, including the Bureau of the Census, have defined independents as firms with under 11 stores and chains as firms with 11 or more stores.

In this study, a chain is defined *as a firm operating four or more stores, except when specifically stated otherwise.*

In addition to the above distinction between types of food retailing firms, independent firms are further identified as to whether or not they are *affiliated* in certain respects with other independents. Affiliated independents, in turn, are further divided into *cooperative* and *voluntary* chains of independents.

RETAIL GROCERY CHAINS

The Great Atlantic and Pacific Tea Company was America's first food chain. It began in 1859 as a tea store and by 1865 had added a line of groceries and was operating 25 stores. In 1880 A & P opened its 100th store.[9]

Another early food chain was the Jones Brothers Tea Company, organized in 1872; it later was succeeded by the Grand Union Company, which today is the country's 10th largest food chain.

In 1882 B. H. Kroger initiated the Great Western Tea Company, which subsequently became the Kroger Company, which today is the 3rd largest food chain in the country. In 1887 H. C. Bohack started what later became the H. C. Bohack Company, the 17th largest food chain operating today. Many others of today's largest chains or their predecessors were organized around the turn of the century.

By 1929 there were 693 food chains operating 52,514 stores.[10]

INDEPENDENT FOOD RETAILERS

Independent grocery stores make up the second broad class of grocery stores. In this study an independent is defined as a grocery firm operating fewer than four stores.

Independent stores are not homogeneous in terms of sales volume, variety of goods sold, services performed, or in their procurement policies. They range from small, family-operated stores to huge supermarkets.

Within the independent group, two important trends are especially worth noting. The first is the increasingly large size of store units. The second is the growing importance of affiliations of independents.

Small stores continue to decline in relative importance. Between 1953 and 1958 alone, the sales by independent stores with annual sales under $75,000 dropped from 31 per cent to 11 per cent of total sales by independents (Table 6). During the same period sales by independent supermarkets increased from 30 per cent to 55 per cent of total sales by independents. As a result of this size transformation within the independent group, sales are becoming concentrated in relatively fewer stores. Whereas in 1958 there were 265,000 independent stores, the 14,600 independently owned supermarkets, which constituted only 5.1 per cent of all independent stores, accounted for 55 per cent of total sales of independents (Table 6).

The second trend within the independent group especially worthy of note is the increasing affiliation of independents in order to achieve some of the advantages of integrated operations enjoyed by the chains.

Affiliations of independents are of two general types. The *cooperative retail chain*[11] is an organization of independent retailers which advertises, functions as a wholesaler, or performs other merchandising functions cooperatively. These organizations are owned and run for the benefit of their independent retailer-owner-patrons and constitute forms of horizontal and vertical integration. Some organizations are much more closely integrated than others. The cooperative retail chain is sometimes referred to as a cooperative group or a cooperatively owned wholesale unit.

The *voluntary retail chain* is a group of independent retailers affiliated with a wholesaler for buying, advertising, or other merchandising activities. Such an organization is initiated or sponsored by an independent wholesaler in contrast to the cooperative chain in which independent retailers are the initiators and owners of the organization. Voluntary chains are not operated on a nonprofit basis as are cooperative chains, but are based on the mutual benefits resulting from operating certain retailing and wholesaling functions in an integrated manner. Hence, voluntary chains represent a form of vertical and horizontal integration based entirely on contracts and informal agreements among the various participants. This type of organization is sometimes referred to as a voluntary group, and the wholesaler initiating such groups or chains of independents is sometimes referred to as a voluntary wholesaler.

CHAPTER THREE

Horizontal Integration and Market Concentration

INTRODUCTION

By *horizontal integration* is meant that a firm increases in size by selling an increased volume of its existing product lines.[1] In grocery retailing this can be done by increasing the size of a grocery store or by increasing the number of stores owned by one firm. The replacement of a small store by a supermarket is an example of the former and the grocery chain is an example of the latter. The extent to which a firm is horizontally integrated is one measure of its absolute size.

Market concentration refers to the extent to which sales in a particular market are channeled through a certain firm or number of firms. It is obvious that there is a relationship between market concentration and the degree of horizontal integration of firms in the market. However, the two concepts are not identical. Strictly speaking, horizontal integration is solely an indication of the absolute size of firms. Since it is possible for a firm to be large in an absolute sense yet constitute only a small part of a particular market, the two concepts must not be interchanged indiscriminately.

Relative firm size and market concentration are studied because economic theory and industrial experience suggest that they are significant variables conditioning competitive behavior. The degree to which sales are concentrated through a few firms is considered to be economically significant because of the assumption that when sellers are few, they have an incentive to follow an interdependent pricing policy. In other words, each firm comes to recognize that its selling—or buying—policy affects the entire market because the firm is such a large part of the market. Hence, relative fewness of sellers encourages concerted behavior, even in the absence of collusion, with the result that such industries behave less competitively than when numbers are larger.

But while most students of industrial structure agree that there is a relationship between market concentration and firm behavior, there is less agreement as to the exact nature of this relationship. Some economists suggest that other factors are more important determinants of firm behavior.[2] And the reader should not infer that we intend to imply that the relative size of firms or the degree of market concentration are the only, or necessarily even the most important, factors determining firm conduct in all markets. But we do believe that market concentration and firm conduct are sufficiently related to warrant careful study of changes in market concentration in food retailing. Significant changes in market concentration are especially important in industries which have many firms. The transformation of an industry from many to relatively fewer firms almost certainly affects the competitive conduct of the remaining firms more than any other conceivable factor, except price controls or similar institutional restraints on the conduct of firms. Consequently, because food retailing traditionally has been one of America's least concentrated industries, current and prospective changes in market concentration almost certainly are among the key variables influencing competitive behavior therein. In the following pages we shall measure the actual changes in market concentration which have occurred in recent years.

MARKET CONCENTRATION: THE RELEVANT MARKET

Measurements of market concentration always implicitly or explicitly involve certain basic assumptions about the character of the market studied. Defining the relevant market is not a simple matter. This is especially true when the measure is used to reveal the relative importance of particular firms in both buying and selling, as in food retailing where firms sell in essentially local markets but buy in regional or national markets. Moreover, in buying, the relevant market varies from one commodity to another. For example, a retailer may buy its canned vegetables in primarily a national market but its newspaper advertising copy in an entirely local market. Hence, no single measure of market concentration serves all purposes. Therefore, a variety of measures have been used here, ranging from those based on the assumption that food retailers operate in national markets to the other extreme that they operate in a number of local markets as defined by the various cities in which they operate.

CHANGES IN NUMBERS AND SIZES OF STORES

The broadest possible definition of the structure of the retail grocery industry is one assuming that all grocery stores compete with one another within the same market. According to such an aggregate view of the market, market concentration increased appreciably since 1940. The total number of grocery stores declined from 444,950 in 1940 to 285,000 in 1958, or about 36 per cent (Table 44).

Another measure of over-all store concentration is to compare changes in the average number of persons served per grocery store. Using this as an index, we find that whereas in 1940 each grocery store served an average of just under 300 persons, by 1950 this number had grown to about 380, and by 1958 to 615 (Table 7). Expressed in these terms, grocery-store concentration nearly doubled between 1940 and 1958.

TABLE 7
Number of Grocery Stores and U.S. Population

Year	Population (millions)	Grocery stores (thousands)	Population per store
1940	132.1	444.9	297
1945	139.9	397.0	352
1950	151.7	400.7	378
1958	175.4	285.0	615

Source: U.S. Department of Commerce, Statistical Abstracts.

Still another broad measure of the concentration of grocery-store sales is to compare the volume of sales accounted for by various numbers of stores. In 1958, 30,000 supermarkets, constituting only 10.5 per cent of all grocery stores, accounted for 68.2 per cent of all grocery-store sales; 59,700 superettes, constituting 20.9 per cent of all grocery stores, accounted for 24.5 per cent of sales; the remaining 195,400 small stores, constituting 68.5 per cent of all stores, accounted for only 7.3 per cent of all sales (Table 6).

This concentration of sales in large stores has proceeded at a rapid pace in recent years. Between 1953 and 1958 alone, the concentration of grocery-store sales in supermarkets increased from 48 per cent to 68.2 per cent.

The preceding comparisons are solely in terms of concentration of sales in grocery stores. They show nothing of the concentration of sales by firms. Let us therefore turn to the changes in the concentration of grocery sales by various numbers of firms.

CHART I

PERCENTAGE CHANGE IN SHARES
OF GROCERY SALES BY MAJOR CHAINS

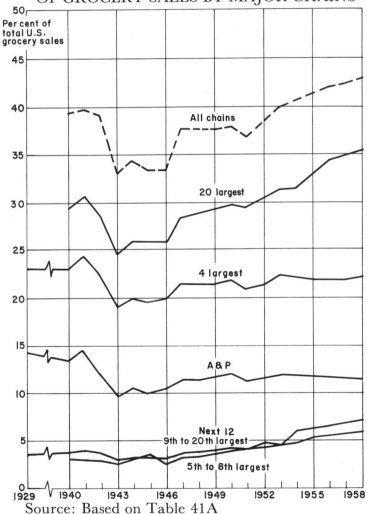

Source: Based on Table 41A

National Concentration of Sales by Large Chains

In 1958, grocery chains (defined as firms with four or more stores) did about 43 per cent of the grocery-store business (Chart I). This represented an all-time high of the chains' share of total grocery-store sales. From 1929 until 1951 the chains' share of total grocery-store sales was very stable, except for the war years, at about 38 per cent of the total. Since 1951, however, their share has increased quite regularly (Chart I and Table 8).

The share of grocery sales accounted for by chains of over 10 stores has increased more rapidly than for all chains. Between 1948 and 1958 their share increased from 34.4 per cent to 41.7 per cent.

Although chains as a group have not greatly increased their share of total grocery-store sales, there have been significant increases in the share of total grocery business done by large chains.

One indication of the over-all increase in concentration within the chain sector of grocery retailing is the decline in the number of chains in recent years. Between 1953 and 1958 the number of chains with 4 or more stores decreased from 866 to 790, and the number of chains with 10 or more stores declined from 279 to 247 (Table 9). Practically all of this decline has occurred in the last three years.

The most significant structural change within the chain sector of grocery retailing has occurred in a group of between 20 and 30 large chains. Because data are readily available for only the largest chains, we shall analyze in detail the growth since 1940 of the top 20 chains and its impact on the structure of national, regional, and local markets.

market concentration of top 20 chains

In 1958, the 20 largest grocery chains[3] accounted for 82.8 per cent of grocery-chain sales (Tables 41A and 41B). This has represented an increase of about 4 percentage points since 1940 when they did 78.2 per cent of grocery chain sales. During World War II their share of chain sales dropped to a low of 74.8 per cent in 1942; not until 1951 did they fully regain the significant loss in share they sustained during the war years.

The share of total grocery-store sales by the 20 largest grocery chains increased from 29.3 per cent in 1940 to 35.6 per cent in 1958. They reached a low of 24.6 per cent in 1943.

We estimate that in 1958 the 21st to 50th largest chains accounted for about 7.2 per cent of all grocery-chain sales and 3.1 per cent of total grocery-store sales. Hence, by 1958 the country's 50 largest grocery chains were doing about 90 per cent of the grocery-chain business and about 39 per cent of the total grocery-store business.

TABLE 8
Total Sales of Grocery and Combination Stores and Chain Stores
(In Millions of Dollars)

Year	Total grocery and combination sales*	Grocery chains of over 3 stores	Per cent of total grocery sales	Grocery chains of over 10 stores¶	Per cent of total grocery sales¶
1929	$ 7,353	$ 2,833	38.53	...	...
1935	6,352	2,466	38.82	...	...
1940	8,317	3,113	37.43	...	...
1941	9,604	3,734	38.88	...	...
1942	12,141	4,551	37.48	...	...
1943	13,276	4,357	32.82	...	...
1944	13,662	4,710	34.48	...	...
1945	14,330	4,769	33.28	...	...
1946	18,477	6,291	34.05	...	...
1947	22,364	8,436	37.72	...	...
1948	24,770	9,319	37.62	$ 8,532	34.44
1949	24,800	9,609	38.74	...	...
1950	26,412	10,140	38.39	...	...
1951	30,346	11,569	38.12	...	...
1952	32,238	12,089†	37.50	...	...
1953	33,623	13,113	39.00	...	...
1954	34,993	13,997	40.00	13,553	38.73
1955	36,919	15,137	41.00	14,222	38.53
1956	39,180	16,456	42.00	15,894	40.57
1957	42,444	17,826	42.00	17,377	40.94
1958	$ 44,546	$ 19,155	43.00‡	$ 18,590	41.73

*U.S. Department of Commerce, Statistical Abstracts (various editions).
†Sales for 1952-58 were estimated by assuming chain grocery store sales were the same percentage of grocery-store sales as food chain store sales were of all food-store sales, as estimated by the Bureau of Census of the U.S. Department of Commerce.
‡Estimate.
¶Federal Trade Commission, Economic Inquiry into Food Marketing, Interim Report, June 30, 1959.

TABLE 9
Number of Food Chain Companies

Year	2-3 stores		4-9 stores		10-15 stores		16-25 stores		26 or more stores		Total*	
	Chains	Stores	Chains	Stores	Chains	Stores	Chains	Stores	Chains	Stores	Chains	Stores
1953	2,013	4,654	587	3,040	95	1,136	76	1,484	108	17,564	2,879	27,878
1954	2,234	5,122	592	3,109	92	1,103	71	1,378	112	17,279	3,101	27,991
1955	2,301	5,235	587	3,033	97	1,155	70	1,382	108	16,795	3,163	27,600
1956	2,464	5,560	598	3,116	88	1,052	65	1,296	103	16,703	3,318	27,727
1957	2,508	5,652	568	2,942	87	1,018	62	1,215	106	16,774	3,331	27,601
1958	2,335	5,207	543	2,848	88	1,043	58	1,153	101	16,848	3,125	27,099

*Totals include Canadian stores operated by U.S. companies.

Source: Compiled by Business Guide, Inc., publisher of Chain Store Guide Directories (New York), and published by National Association of Food Chains (Washington, June, 1958).

24

Even more significant than the increase in share of total sales accounted for by the top chains is the change in market shares by chains of various sizes within this group.

The Share of the Top Four Chains Declines.—In 1940, the country's four largest chains accounted for 61.5 per cent of chain sales and 23 per cent of total grocery-store sales (Tables 41A and 41B). From the low of 19.1 per cent in 1943, the share of this group gradually increased to 22.4 per cent of total grocery-store sales by 1958. However, A & P is the only chain in this group to experience a decline in its share of grocery sales during this period; and although its share has continued to decline in recent years, since 1951 the growth of the other three top chains has more than offset A & P's decline.

The Share of the Fifth to Eighth Largest Chains Rises.—Between 1940 and 1958 the fifth to eighth largest chains increased their share of grocery-store sales from 3.2 per cent to 6.1 per cent. During the same period their share of the chain-grocery business grew from 8.6 per cent to 14.1 per cent (Tables 41A and 41B). Since 1950 alone, the share of chain-grocery sales by this group increased by 3.4 percentage points.

Of this group in 1958, the most active growth in share of chain sales was made by Winn Dixie, which increased its share from .4 per cent to 3.3 per cent, and Food Fair, which increased its share from .9 per cent to 3.7 per cent (Table 10).

The Share of the Ninth to Twentieth Largest Chains Doubles.—The most striking changes in relative market shares occurred in the ninth to twentieth largest chains. Between 1940 and 1958 this group's share of total grocery-store sales increased from 3 per cent to 7.2 per cent (Tables 41A and 41B); and its share of chain sales increased from 8.1 to 16.6 per cent. Nearly three-fourths of this increase in relative share occurred since 1950.

The accuracy of the preceding estimates of changes in concentration is affected somewhat by the growing importance of nonfood items in modern supermarkets. However, we do not believe that the increasing share of total grocery sales accounted for by chains can be explained by the growing volume of nonfood sales by chains. First, nonfood sales averaged only 5.2 per cent of all supermarket sales (Table 4).[4] Hence, even if chain supermarkets handled these nonfoods and independent supermarkets did not, and if chains handled none of these nonfoods before 1940, the introduction of nonfoods would explain less than half of the increase in the share of total grocery sales of all chains and less than one-third of the increased market share of the top 20 chains. Of course, most nonchain supermarkets also handle a considerable number of nonfoods. For example, in 1957, 97.7 per cent of all supermarkets—independent and chain alike—had drug and cosmetic departments, and 92.3 per cent had houseware departments (Table 3). Items sold in these departments account for over half of all nonfood sales. Moreover, some independent supermarkets enjoy much higher nonfood sales than do many chains.

MARKET CONCENTRATION ON REGIONAL BASIS

While concentration in grocery retailing at the national level is a significant measure of market structure for some purposes, especially in defining the structure of the buying side of grocery-store retailing for products sold in national markets, it is also important to consider concentration on a regional basis. This measure is relevant because most chains are essentially regional in character and hence have their operations concentrated in relatively few states, sometimes in only a few cities. Even A & P with its over 4,000 stores, in 1958 did not operate in 11 states, and the country's second largest chain, Safeway, operated in only half of the 48 states.

All but one of these chains on which estimates are available accounted for over 5 per cent of all grocery-store sales in the regions in which they operated (Table 10). On the other hand, only A & P accounted for over 5 per cent of national sales in 1958. In fact, nine of these chains do over 10 per cent of the grocery-store business in their operating regions. These data illustrate clearly that while most of the top 20 chains do one per cent or less of the national grocery-store business, all are relatively large in the regions in which they operate. Even such a relatively insignificant chain nationally as Weingarten, which accounts for .3 per cent of national grocery-store sales, does 14.4 per cent of the business in its operating area (Table 10).

CONCENTRATION IN LOCAL MARKETS

Although chains buy most of their products in virtually national markets, and to some extent in regional markets, they sell in essentially local markets. Here we shall consider city boundaries as defining the relevant local market. Actually, of course, in large cities location factors prevent all grocery stores from being in direct competition with one another for their customers' patronage. Moreover, some kinds of grocery stores have so differentiated themselves from other grocery stores in the same city that they are really in a different market. Especially important in this respect are the small grocery stores—and increasingly superettes—located in the heart of the city which stay open long hours and every day of the week. Of course, differentiation of this sort does not insure large profits or even survival unless the unique demand function created thereby is sufficient to warrant profitable operation. But the important point is that such stores may have considerable control over their pricing, service, and product policies. Hence, we might generalize that in many cities not all stores are within the same economic market. But for our purposes we shall define the market structure of local markets as being co-extensive with city boundaries.

TABLE 10
Percentage of Sales by the 20 Largest Chains

Chain	Average per cent of food sales in operating cities*		Per cent of sales in areas operating†	Per cent of U.S. chain grocery sales		Per cent of U.S. grocery store sales	
	1942	1957	1956	1940	1958	1940	1958
A&P	12.0	15.6	13.8	35.8	26.6	13.4	11.4
Safeway	25.0	22.6	11.3	12.8	11.6	4.8	5.0
Kroger	11.0	15.7	10.5	8.3	9.3	3.1	4.4
American	12.7	19.6	9.6	4.0	4.6	1.5	2.0
National Food	4.3	9.1	8.6	2.0	4.1	.7	1.8
Food Fair	4.6	18.1	7.8	.9	3.7	.4	1.6
Winn-Dixie	9.6	22.9	16.3	.4	3.3	.2	1.4
First National	12.2	18.2	13.6	4.6	2.9	1.7	1.2
Grand Union	6.9	17.4	6.0	1.1	2.6	.4	1.1
Colonial	12.7	14.4	12.3	1.5	2.3	.6	1.0
Jewel Tea	8.2†	24.6†	13.8†	.9	2.3	.4	1.0
ACF-Wrigley	n.a.	12.9	12.4	.07	2.0	.02	.9
Loblaw	7.9	12.7	9.4	.7	1.5	.3	.6
Stop & Shop	2.8	13.7	6.1	.7	1.0	.3	.4
Penn Fruit	n.a.	n.a.	8.3	n.a.	.8	n.a.	.4
Thriftimart	n.a.	n.a.	n.a.	.2	.9	.1	.4
Red Owl¶	6.0	11.3	11.3	.4	.9	.2	.4
Bohack	n.a.	n.a.	7.3	.8	.8	.3	.4
Lucky	n.a.	13.3	3.4	.2	.7	.1	.3
Weingarten	n.a.	14.4	n.a.	.4	.7	.2	.3
Average (unweighted)	9.7	16.3	10.1	4.0	4.1	1.5	1.8

n.a.: Not available.

*These are the cities in Table 42 in which these chains operated in 1942 and 1957. See footnote †, Table 42, for description of method used to compute these estimates.
†Chains (This Week, 1957).
‡These comparisons exclude the sales of Jewel's home service routes.
¶These comparisons exclude Red Owl's wholesale sales.

IMPORTANCE OF LARGE CHAINS IN LOCAL MARKETS

As shown above, in the aggregate the top 20 chains command a significant position in the national market, and individually all are of quite significant size in their operating regions. Unfortunately, completely accurate information is not available on the relative importance of these chains in the cities in which they operated. However, we have made estimates of the average market shares of 17 of these chains in those of the country's 258 largest cities in which they operated and for which the necessary data were available. The results are shown in Table 10.

The following procedure was used to make these estimates. The only information available was the number of stores a chain operated in each city. By assuming that each of the stores it operated in the city had sales equal to the average sales of all its stores, we estimated the sales of each chain in each city.[5] We then computed that chain's share of the total sales in the city by dividing its estimated sales by the city's total food sales.

This method is subject to considerable error. Most important, there may be wide variation in the size of a chain's stores. Consequently, estimated market shares in particular cities may greatly overstate or understate actual concentration. Of course these errors tend to cancel out to some extent. This error is least important for chains which are concentrated in a few cities.

Another point to be noted is that this is an estimate of the average share of total *food* sales of each chain in the cities in which it operated, not an estimate of its share of total *grocery*-store sales which is the measure used elsewhere in this study. Thus, the estimate tends to understate each chain's share of total *grocery*-store sales.

Although this method does not provide a precise indication of the average market share of these chains in their local markets, comparisons with estimates made by another source suggest that our procedure provides a fairly accurate measure of local concentration.[6]

On the basis of this procedure, in 1957 all but one of the 17 chains for which such estimates could be made, averaged[7] over 10 per cent of the sales in the cities in which they operated (Table 10). Over half accounted for over 15 per cent of the sales in the cities in which they operated, and three did over 20 per cent of this business. Jewel Tea, which is concentrated largely in the Chicago area, averaged 24.6 per cent of the sales in the cities in which it operates.

Moreover, in the cities studied, between 1942 and 1957 these chains increased significantly their average share of grocery sales. For example, whereas in 1942 A & P averaged 12 per cent of the grocery business in the cities in which it operated, in 1957 it averaged 15.6 per cent (Table 10). In fact, of the chains for which we could make such estimates, only Safeway's average share of sales in the markets in which it operated declined between 1942 and 1957. All chains for which such comparisons could be made, on the average increased their share of local sales from 9.7 per cent to 16.3 per cent during this period.

These are only rough estimates of the market shares of these chains in local markets. Further study is needed to obtain precise information on this score.

INCREASE IN THE SHARE OF LOCAL MARKET SALES OF THE TOP 20 CHAINS

In 201 cities studied, the combined average share of city sales of the top 20 chains increased from 22.3 per cent in 1942 to 38.9 in 1957 (Table 42). That is, together these 20 chains averaged (unweighted) nearly 40 per cent of the business done in these cities in 1957.[8]

The increase between 1942 and 1957 resulted because more of the top 20 chains operated in these cities in 1957 than in 1942 and because

TABLE 11
Operations of the 20 Largest Chains
in the 258 Largest Cities*

Chains	1942	1957	1942 per cent of total cities	1957 per cent of total cities	Per cent change 1942–57
A&P	212	200	82.2	77.5	−5.7
Safeway	75	79	29.1	30.6	5.3
Kroger	78	100	30.2	38.8	28.2
American	32	35	12.4	13.6	9.4
First National	18	18	7.0	7.0	0
National Food	19	58	7.4	22.5	205.3
Colonial	16	37	6.2	14.3	131.3
Jewel Tea	1	8	0.4	3.1	700.0
Grand Union	13	21	5.1	8.1	61.5
Food Fair	18	35	7.0	13.6	94.4
Bohack	4	4	1.6	1.6	0
Loblaw	7	13	2.7	5.0	85.7
Stop & Shop	5	10	1.9	3.9	100.0
Weingarten	1	9	0.4	3.5	800.0
Red Owl	5	14	1.9	5.4	180.0
Winn-Dixie	6	29	2.3	11.2	383.3
Lucky	2	10	0.8	3.9	400.0
ACF-Wrigley	-†	14		5.4	
Penn Fruit	1	5	0.4	1.9	400.0
Fitzsimmons	1	4	0.4	1.6	300.0

*These cities are the 258 largest in 1942. The smallest of these cities in 1942 had a population of 18,000.
†Not reported in any of the cities in 1942.

Source: Computed from Editor and Publisher, Market Guides, 1943 and 1958 editions.

chains already in some of these cities in 1942 increased their share during the next 15 years.

These chains enjoyed the greatest relative increase in concentration in cities under 100,000 (Table 42). This reflects the fact that most large chains started in large cities, but in recent years have been expanding into smaller cities as well. But in 1957, these chains still had larger market shares in large cities than in smaller ones.

In addition to city size, the rate of population growth also affects the degree of market concentration by particular firms. It was hypothesized that rapidly growing cities attract new entrants and hence make it more difficult for existing firms to expand their share of the market. To test this hypothesis, we analyzed the growth history of A & P, Safeway, and Kroger in those cities in which they operated in 1942 and 1957.[9]

These comparisons reveal that for cities of all sizes, these three chains increased their average share of sales in the slowest-growing[10] cities by 27.7 per cent, whereas they actually experienced an average decrease of 2 per cent in the faster-growing cities (Table 43). Similarly, in each population class these chains as a group experienced greater average increases in market shares in slow-growing cities than in fast-growing ones. Of course, there were exceptions to this over-all performance. For example, Kroger's share of sales in cities of between 60,000 and 249,000 increased 53.4 per cent in slow-growing cities contrasted to 73.9 per cent in fast-growing cities. But the over-all experience of these firms indicates that population growth, which is the main determinant of retail food market expansion, has an important bearing on the rate with which a grocery firm expands its share of a particular market. Apparently, markets experiencing rapid increases in demand create an environment more conducive to entry by new firms and/or survival by smaller independents.

GEOGRAPHIC EXPANSION OF THE TOP 20 CHAINS DURING THIS PERIOD

As mentioned above, the increase in the share of sales of the top 20 chains in the over 200 cities studied was due partly to their expansion into more of these cities from 1942 to 1957. Here we shall trace the extent of their geographical expansion.

No chain stores operated in all 258 cities studied[11] in any of the years analyzed. A & P came closest; it operated in 212 cities in 1942 (Table 11). Between 1942 and 1957 all chains except A & P and First National increased the number of cities in which they operated.[12] In many cases their actual increase as well as percentage increase was sizable. National Food experienced the greatest absolute increase by virtue of its expansion from operating in 19 cities in 1942 to 58 in 1957. Many of the small

TABLE 12
Frequency Distribution of the 20 Largest Chains of 1957 Operating in 211 Cities*

Number of chains operating in city	Number and per cent of cities									
	1942	Per cent	1945	Per cent	1950	Per cent	1955	Per cent	1957	Per cent
1	56	26.5	45	21.3	41	19.4	33	15.6	33	15.6
2	117	55.5	127	60.2	115	54.5	73	34.6	50	23.6
3	35	16.6	36	17.1	47	22.3	87	41.3	81	38.5
4	3	1.4	2	0.9	8	3.8	12	5.7	42	19.9
5	0	. . .	1	0.5	0	. . .	6	2.8	5	2.4
Total	211	100.0	211	100.0	211	100.0	211	100.0	211	100.0

*In addition to these 211 cities, there were 47 cities among the country's 258 largest cities for which data were not available for at least one of the years. In these 47 cities, the frequency distribution in the last year for which these data were reported was as follows: One chain (11 cities); two chains (12 cities); three chains (11 cities); four chains (9 cities); five chains (3 cities); and seven chains (1 city).

Source: Computed from Editor and Publisher, Market Guides, 1943, 1946, 1951, 1956, and 1958 editions.

31

chains experienced large percentage increases in the number of cities in which they operated because they operated in so few cities in the early 1940's.

One means of measuring the impact of the above geographic expansion of these chains on the structure of local markets is to compare over a period of time the number of these chains operating in each of the cities studied. Table 12 summarizes these comparisons. It indicates the intensity with which the top 20 chains operated in the 211 cities studied.[13] For example, in 1942 in about 82 per cent of these cities there were only one or two of these chains. But by 1957 only about 40 per cent of these cities had only one or two chains. On the other hand, in 1942 only 1.4 per cent of these cities had four of these chains and none had five, but by 1957, 19.9 per cent had four chains, and another 2.4 per cent had five.

TABLE 13
Average Number of Chain Retail
Grocery Firms in Cities of Various Sizes

Population	No. cities in each group		Average No. chain firms		Average top 20 chains	
	1942	1957	1942	1957	1942	1957
Under 35,000*	33	6	3.2	4.7	1.8	2.2
35,000–59,999	52	58	3.0	5.3	1.8	2.5
60,000–99,999	45	46	3.4	6.1	1.9	2.6
100,000–249,999	42	54	3.3	5.8	1.8	2.7
250,000–499,999	17	19	3.1	8.0	1.8	2.8
500,000 and over	11	17	6.4	9.6	2.2	3.1
Total	200	200				

*The smallest city in 1942 had a population of 18,000; the smallest in 1957 had a population of 31,000.

Source: These are the 200 largest cities in 1957 on which the necessary data were reported for both 1942 and 1957 in Editor and Publisher, Market Guides, 1943 and 1958 editions.

These data indicate that these chains increasingly expanded into one another's markets from 1942 to 1957.

Table 13 illustrates the change which occurred in the number of chains operating in cities of various sizes between 1942 and 1957. For example, whereas in 1942 cities with populations of between 35,000 and

59,999 averaged 3 chains, by 1957 they averaged 5.3 chains. In 1942, these cities had an average of 1.8 of the 20 largest chains and by 1957 they had 2.5. Comparable increases also occurred in cities of other size classes during this period, although the total number of grocery retailer firms operating in these cities generally decreased about 20 per cent.

CONCENTRATION OF SALES OF FOUR LARGEST GROCERY RETAILERS
OPERATING IN 133 CITIES

The preceding comparisons dealt solely with the shares of sales in local markets accounted for by the nation's top 20 chains. In many cases, however, chains not significant nationally or even regionally account for a significant proportion of the grocery-store sales in their local markets. For example, in San Antonio, Texas, Handy Andy Stores reportedly account for 31 per cent of sales and H. E. Butt stores for 26 per cent.[14] No national chain supplies a significant share of this market.

Because of the importance of small chains in local markets and often even large independents operating fewer than four stores, local concentration ordinarily is much higher than the above data on only the top 20 chains might suggest. Unfortunately, it was impossible to make such estimates from the data used above in tracing the growth experience of the largest chains in the over 200 cities studied. Other sources permit us to obtain such estimates for 133 cities in 1958.

According to a *Supermarket News* study of grocery sales in 133 cities, the largest grocery retailer operating in each of these cities averaged 25.4 per cent of total grocery sales, the two largest retailers averaged 42.2 per cent, and the four largest averaged 58.3 per cent (Table 14).[15]

There is a tendency for sales concentration to be highest in the smallest cities. In cities with populations of between 35,000 and 74,999, the largest grocery retailer averaged 30.6 per cent of sales and the four largest averaged 61.6. In cities with populations over 1,000,000, the largest chain averaged 16.8 per cent of sales and the four largest averaged 40.5 per cent.

Thus, although the 20 largest chains do a smaller share of business in small cities than in large ones (Table 42), sales concentration is actually higher in small cities than in large ones. This reflects the fact that chains which are relatively unimportant nationally often are very important in their local markets. In fact, independent retailers were among the four largest retailers in some cities summarized in Table 14.

Table 15 illustrates the wide differences in market concentration found in these 133 cities. In 40 (30 per cent) of these cities, the largest retailer did less than 20 per cent of the grocery business, whereas in 10 (7.5 per cent) it did over 40 per cent. In 89 cities (72 per cent) the four largest did over 50 per cent of the grocery business and in 29 (24 per cent) they did over 70 per cent.

These data clearly indicate that grocery-store sales are very concentrated at the local level. And although we are unable to compare concentration changes over a period of time in these cities, the preceding analysis of the growing share of local sales accounted for by the 20 largest chains from 1942 to 1957 suggests that the chains' share of local sales has increased significantly since the early 1940's. Moreover, data presented below on the rapid growth of voluntary chains in recent years suggest that their share of local market sales also has increased since the early 1940's.

Legal Relationship among Top Chains

In the preceding discussion all chains have been treated as separate legal entities. While this may be an appropriate assumption for some purposes, it should be noted that a number of the top chains have certain direct or indirect legal ties which may encourage them to behave in an interdependent manner when making certain decisions. Here we shall mention the cases of such interfirm relationship identified in the course of this study.

LEGAL TIES BETWEEN BOHACK AND COLONIAL

National Food Products Corporation is a holding company whose principal assets, as of December 31, 1957, consisted of a 31.4 per cent common stock interest in Colonial Stores and a 21.1 per cent interest in H. C. Bohack Company.[16]

Mr. R. B. Stearns of National Food Products is also on the board of both Colonial and Bohack. The other seven board directors of National Food Products are also on Colonial's board. None is on Bohack's board.[17]

In 1958, Colonial had sales of $437 million and was the country's 9th largest chain; Bohack had sales of $161 million and was the country's 17th largest chain (Table 71). Their combined sales of $598 million were greater than those of all but six other chains.

We have found no evidence of concerted behavior between these firms. It should be noted that these chains operate in different areas, Bohack in New York and Colonial mainly in the South, Ohio, and Indiana. Thus any joint action probably would have involved their buying efforts.

LEGAL TIES BETWEEN NATIONAL FOOD, LOBLAW, AND GEORGE WESTON, LTD.

In 1953, George Weston, Ltd., acquired control of Loblaw, Inc., and in 1955 it acquired a 37 per cent interest in National Food.[18] George Weston also controls Loblaw Groceteria of Canada and many baking and some other food-processing plants in Canada and the United States.

In 1958, National Food had sales of $794 million, which made it the country's 5th largest chain. In 1958 Loblaw had sales of $285 million, which made it the 13th largest chain. These two chains had combined sales of over $1 billion, which were exceeded by only three other chains.

It is not known to what extent these chains may make decisions jointly. However, National is primarily a midwestern chain and Loblaw an eastern chain. In 1957 the only state in which they both operated was Ohio, and here National Food operated only two stores.

CHAINS AFFILIATED WITH TOPCO ASSOCIATES

A recent development of considerable potential significance for the market structure of food retailing is the affiliation of a group of chains for buying purposes. Although there may be other instances where chains combine for this purpose, or are members of groups sponsoring independent retailers, the leading example is Topco Associates, Inc. Topco, organized in 1948, is a cooperative association of 29 chains

TABLE 14
Average Share of Grocery-Store Sales
by the Largest Grocery Retailers in 133 Cities in 1958

Population of cities (000 omitted)	Number of cities	Average per cent of grocery-store sales		
		Largest retailer	Two largest retailers	Four largest retailers*
35–74	17	30.6	48.7	61.6
75–99	22	22.4	38.7	55.6
100–199	43	25.9	42.6	60.6
200–499	26	26.4	44.8	60.2
500–999	20	24.0	39.8	55.4
1000 and over	5	16.8	26.8	40.5
Total	133	. . .	. . .	. . .
Average . . .		25.4	42.2	58.3

*Eight cities listed fewer than four retailers. These cities are not included in the averages appearing in this column.

Source: Computed from Distribution of Food Store Sales in 133 Cities (Supermarket News, 1958).

located throughout the country. It is reported to be the "only organization serving retail food chains in the purchasing, packaging, and distribution of . . . private brand products. . . . "[19]

Among Topco's membership in 1957 were many of the nation's
largest regional food chains, including from among the 20 largest food
chains, Penn Fruit, Weingarten, and the three operating divisions of
ACF-Wrigley.[20]

Organized on a cooperative basis, Topco's membership requirements
preclude membership by small chains by specifying that members have
annual retail sales of $15 million.

TABLE 15
Frequency Distribution of Market Shares
of the Largest Grocery Retailers in 1958

Per cent of grocery sales in cities	Number of cities		
	Largest chain	Two largest chains	Four largest chains
Less than 20	40	2	0
20–29	50	20	4
30–39	33	41	11
40–49	8	31	19
50–59	1	26	34
60–69	1	11	26
70–79	0	2	19
80–89	0	0	10
Over 90	0	0	0
Total cities	133	133	123*

*Ten cities did not give information for four chains.

Source: Computed from Distribution of Food Store Sales
in 133 Cities (Supermarket News, 1958).

Topco serves as a buying agent for its chain members and buys
supplies for members directly from processors.[21] Topco labels are used
on 600 different products. In addition, in 1958 Topco initiated arrangements to buy fresh produce directly from growers and packers in the
producing areas.

Topco brands account for an average of approximately 10 per cent
of the members' retail sales, or about $150 million.[22]

By 1958 Topco's chain members operated 777 supermarkets and 3,000 smaller stores with a combined retail volume of over $1.5 billion.[23] This amounted to nearly 3 per cent of total grocery-store sales and over 7 per cent of chain-grocery sales. This amount was exceeded by only three corporate chains.

Topco members apparently operate in different local markets, and therefore do not compete with each other in selling. However, since the specific purpose for organizing Topco was to increase its members' buying power, it can be assumed to have eliminated competition among its members in the purchase of some products.

SUMMARY OF IMPACT ON MARKET STRUCTURE OF CHAIN LEGAL TIES

Apparently the above instances have not affected significantly the structure of food retailing at the retail level since the firms involved do not compete in the same local markets. Consequently, their only effect could have been in the purchasing of products sold in national or regional markets. While Topco apparently has eliminated competition in buying among its members in the purchase of some products, we could not determine the effects of the other cases cited above.

Insofar as these firms also act jointly in making some purchases, structure of the national market is somewhat more concentrated than that represented in Table 41A.

Market Structure of Independent Grocers

To this point we have dealt mainly with the concentration of grocery-store sales among corporate chains. Actually, however, in some important respects the structural changes within the independent (firms with fewer than four stores) grocery-store segment have had a greater impact on the market conduct of food retailers than changes in the corporate chain sector. These structural changes have been of two main types: (1) the number of independent grocers has declined appreciably with a concomitant increase in the average size of the remainder, and (2) there has been an appreciable increase in the share of independents affiliated with so-called cooperative and voluntary chains. Because in some respects these organizations operate like corporate chains, their impact on market structures will be analyzed here.

DECLINING NUMBER OF INDEPENDENT GROCERS

Between 1940 and 1958 the number of independent grocery stores dropped from 405,000 to 266,000 or over 30 per cent (Chart II). Most of this decline occurred since 1950 when 375,000 independents were still operating. By 1958 the number of independents had declined by

CHART II

ESTIMATED NUMBER OF GROCERY STORES

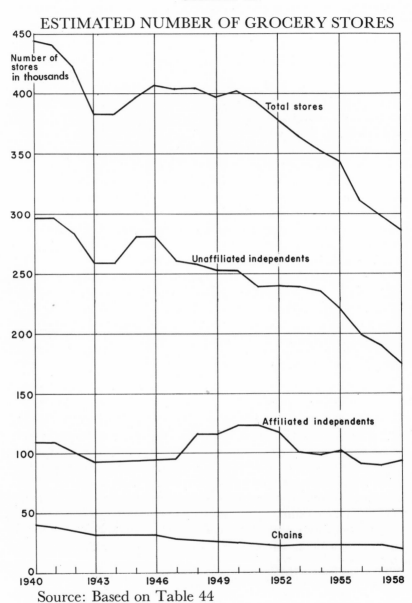

Source: Based on Table 44

about 110,000 stores or nearly 30 per cent in just seven years (Table 44).

Unaffiliated independents experienced the most significant decrease. They dropped from 296,250 in 1940 to 173,600 by 1958, or over 40 per cent (Table 44).

RELATIVE GROWTH OF AFFILIATED INDEPENDENTS

In 1936 there were 81,242 independent grocers affiliated with 534 voluntary chains (Table 16). By 1956 the number of voluntary chains had increased slightly, but the number of independents affiliated with voluntaries had declined.

Cooperative chains have experienced a considerable expansion both in numbers of groups and of retailers affiliated with them (Table 16).[24]

Although between 1940 and 1958 sales of all independents fell from about 63 per cent to 57 per cent of total grocery-store sales, cooperative and voluntary chains increased significantly their share of independent grocery-store sales during this period. Whereas affiliated independents did about 46 per cent of the independent grocery-store business in 1940, by 1958 they did about 73 per cent (Chart III).

Thus, the over-all market structure of the independent segment of food retailing may be characterized as consisting of about 800 voluntary and cooperative chains of independents which account for about 73 per cent of independent volume, and 173,600 unaffiliated independents which do the remaining 27 per cent.

CONCENTRATION WITHIN THE INDEPENDENT GROUP

Data are scarce on the relative sizes of various affiliated independent groups. Moreover, it is difficult to measure the structural characteristics of these groups because it is not always clear to what extent the so-called overhead or national organizations—such as Independent Grocers Alliance or Cooperative Food Distributors of America—actually participate in buying or in providing other relevant functions for members and the extent to which they simply assume the role of trade associations.[25] But since these national organizations do provide their members with some significant functions, as a minimum the national promotion of the names of their organizations and brands, their relative size is of some significance in determining the relative market structure affecting behavior of independent grocery retailers.[26]

Available data indicate that the three largest national groups are:

1. Cooperative Food Distributors of America, with 1956 retail sales of about $6 billion.[27] This represents 15.3 per cent of national grocery-store sales and 26.4 per cent of the retail sales of all affiliated independents. This was one-third greater than A & P's sales in that year.

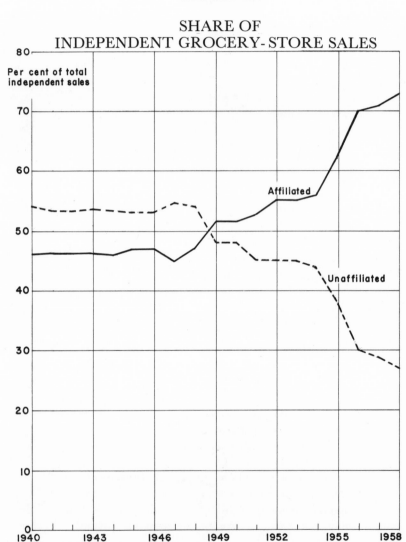

CHART III

SHARE OF
INDEPENDENT GROCERY- STORE SALES

Source: Based on Table 45

40

TABLE 16
Number and Membership
of Voluntary and Cooperative Chains

Year	Voluntaries		Cooperatives		Total	
	Groups	Retailers	Groups	Retailers	Groups	Retailers
1936	534	81,242	166	24,849	700	106,091
1939	521	81,081	161	25,042	682	106,123
1950	456	89,513	234	37,708	690	127,221
1956	584	66,877	240	38,526	824	105,403

Source: Index to Voluntary Chains and Retailer Cooperatives
(New York: American Institute of Food Distribution, 1957).

41

2. Retailers affiliated with Independent Grocers Alliance (IGA.) had estimated sales of $3 billion in 1956.[28] This represented 7.7 per cent of grocery-store sales and 13.2 per cent of affiliated independent sales. This was larger than all corporate chains except A & P.

3. Members of Red & White Corporation had estimated retail sales of $1.25 billion in 1956.[29] This represented 3.2 per cent of grocery-store sales and 5.5 per cent of affiliated independent-store sales. This was larger than all but the top three corporate chains.

Thus, estimated sales of retailers affiliated with these three national organizations totaled $10.25 billion in 1956, or 26.2 per cent of total grocery-store sales and 45.1 per cent of affiliated independent sales.

SALES OF INDIVIDUAL AFFILIATED GROUPS

As indicated elsewhere, apparently most buying, merchandising, and other important functions of affiliated groups of independents are made by the individual sponsoring groups. Consequently, the relative sizes of these individual groups are more important indications of their implications for market structure than are data of the size of the national organizations.

In 1955 there were at least 16 groups which had retail sales exceeding $100 million and 9 groups with sales of $50 million or over (Table 46).[30]

The largest group in terms of retail sales is Certified Grocers of California. In 1955 Certified's approximately 1,350 affiliated stores had sales of $1.4 billion. Only two corporate chains had sales greater than this in 1955. Moreover, since over 80 per cent of Certified's retailers are concentrated in Los Angeles County,[31] its members' share of local sales is considerable. Many other voluntary and cooperative chains are very important in their operating regions. Super Valu's affiliates, with retail sales of around $250 million in 1955, constituted only .7 per cent of all grocery sales; but Super Valu is very important in its operating area. In 1957, 14.8 per cent of all Minnesota consumers reportedly did most of their shopping in Super Valu stores.[32]

Similarly, whereas affiliates of Fleming's IGA. had only .4 per cent of national grocery-store sales in 1955, in the Wichita, Kansas, area they did 27.4 per cent of the business, second only to Safeway.

As a group, the independent retailers affiliated with the 20 largest voluntary and cooperative chains listed in Table 46 accounted for 15.1 per cent of all grocery-store sales. Significantly, this was only 3.7 percentage points more than A & P's share of grocery sales in 1955.

Retailers belonging to these 20 voluntary and cooperative chains did 22.7 per cent of the independent grocery-store business in 1955. The 20 largest corporate chains made about 81 per cent of all corporate chain sales. These comparisons indicate that the largest voluntary and cooperative chains do a much smaller share of the grocery business than do the largest corporate chains.

These 20 large voluntary and cooperative chains had approximately 12,000 affiliated retailers.[33] This represented about 15 per cent of all affiliated independents.

The recent FTC Food Inquiry provides some valuable data on the structure of these groups. Table 18 classifies the 319 voluntary and 144 cooperative groups operating in 1958 which reported to the FTC survey.

Most of these groups operated in only one state (54.5 per cent of the voluntaries and 58.3 per cent of the cooperatives), had fewer than 100 stores (72.1 per cent of the voluntaries and 35.7 of the cooperatives), and had wholesale sales of under $10 million (74.6 per cent of the voluntaries and 67.4 per cent of the cooperatives). In fact, fully 95.9 per cent of the voluntaries and 95.8 per cent of the cooperatives had wholesale sales of under $50 million.

These comparisons indicate that the great majority of these groups were quite small in terms of wholesale sales. For example, in 1958 the country's 20th largest corporate chain had sales with a wholesale value of about $100 million. There were only five voluntary[34] and three cooperative groups with wholesale sales of over $100 million.

We may gain a further insight into the relative importance of affiliated groups by comparing the proportion of total wholesale purchases of affiliated independents which actually are channeled through these groups.

TABLE 17
Per Cent of Sales by the 20 Largest
Cooperative and Voluntary Chains in 1955

Size group	Total sales (millions)	Per cent of total grocery store sales	Per cent of total of independent store sales
4 largest	$ 2,718	7.4	12.5
5–8 largest	890	2.4	4.1
9–12 largest	615	1.7	2.8
13–20 largest	715	3.6	3.3
Total	$ 4,938	15.1	22.7

Source: Based on Table 46.

TABLE 18
Classification of Voluntary and Cooperative Groups, 1958

States served	319 voluntary groups		144 cooperative groups	
	Number of wholesale sponsors	Per cent of total	Number of cooperatives	Per cent of total
One	174	54.5	84	58.3
Two	86	27.0	34	23.6
Three	39	12.2	19	13.2
Four	12	3.8	2	1.4
Five or more	8	2.5	5	3.5
	319	100.0	144	100.0
Affiliated stores:				
1–50	143	44.8	17	11.9
50–100	87	27.3	34	23.8
100–500	79	24.8	80	55.9
500–1,000	7	2.2	8	5.6
1,000–2,000	3	.9	2	1.4
2,000–2,400	. . .	. . .	2	1.4
Not reporting	. . .	. . .	1*	. . .
	319	100.0	144	100.0
Annual sales size volume: (millions of dollars)				
Under 1	15	4.7	8	7.8
1–5	154	48.3	54	38.3
5–10	69	21.6	30	21.3
10–25	45	14.1	28	19.9
25–50	23	7.2	12	8.5
50–100	5	1.6	3	2.1
100–350	5	1.6	3	2.1
Not reporting	3	.9	3	. . .
	319	100.0	141	100.0
Total sales	$ 3.5 billion†		$ 2.0 billion‡	

*Total membership of 143 cooperatives, 34,230. Correspondence pending with one cooperative re membership.

†This includes sales of $2,088.2 million to affiliated retailers and $1,405.6 million to unaffiliated retailers.

‡All but $22.5 million of this figure were to members. This was for 141 cooperatives.

Source: Federal Trade Commission, Economic Inquiry into Food Marketing, Interim Report (1959), Voluntary Group, Table 4, Cooperatives, Table 4.

We estimate the total 1958 wholesale value of sales of all affiliated independents at $16.4 billion.[35] Thus the 319 voluntary groups and 141 cooperatives reporting to the FTC supplied only about 20.5 per cent[36] of the wholesale business of all affiliated retailers. These comparisons reveal that while affiliated independents do about 73 per cent of the retail business of all independents, those reporting to the FTC buy only about 20 per cent of their total products through their voluntary and cooperative groups. We estimate that retailers affiliated with the 20 largest cooperative and voluntary chains buy about 44 per cent of their products from their affiliated wholesalers.[37]

Perhaps the leading structural characteristic to be inferred from the preceding facts is that many so-called independent grocers increasingly are channeling their purchases through a relatively few voluntary and cooperative chains and are performing various merchandising functions on a group basis instead of operating completely independently. Recent trends in this direction suggest that within the next decade practically all independents will be affiliated with such groups.

Accompanying this trend toward increased affiliation of independents is the equally important trend of increasing functions performed by these groups. While few groups approximate the closely integrated operations of corporate chains, many apparently are striving for this objective.[38] But to date, these groups account for only about 20 per cent of the total purchases of all affiliated independents. This means that on the buying side, at least, affiliated independents have failed to concentrate their buying power to the same degree as corporate chains.

On the selling side, such groups may result in a tendency toward concerted action resulting from joint and uniform advertising and promotion programs. Such practices tend to bring about greater uniformity in selling policies than if independents were unaffiliated. But since the degree of coordination or integration among most of these groups is considerably less than in corporate chains, we would expect them to behave in a more independent manner than the various stores of a corporate chain.

OWNERSHIP OF RETAILERS BY SPONSORS OF VOLUNTARY CHAINS

Some sponsors of voluntary chains actually seem to be transforming their operations into corporate chains by developing or acquiring their own retail units. This development is so important that it warrants separate attention as a precursor of future developments.

We have not attempted an exhaustive study of this development. However, Consolidated Foods Corporation, Chicago, seems to have gone furthest in this respect. Consolidated is a food manufacturer-distributor sponsoring several voluntary chains with combined retail members of about 2,600 in 1956. Beginning with the purchase in 1956 of Klein Super Markets which had 23 stores and the Piggly Wiggly Midwest Company which had 34 stores, Consolidated has expanded rapidly into food retailing. In 1958 it acquired the Lawson Milk Company which operated 175 small retail stores in Ohio, and in 1959 acquired Quality Food Stores which operated 12 supermarkets in Minnesota.

By 1959 retail operations accounted for slightly over one-third of Consolidated's total annual sales of about $360 million;[39] wholesaling accounted for another third and processing for the remainder. Thus in just four years Consolidated's retail grocery operations have grown to a point where today it is about the 21st largest corporate grocery chain, as well as being the sponsor of the 2nd largest group of voluntary chains.

Super Valu Stores, which sponsored a voluntary chain of around 700 stores in 1956, also has entered food retailing recently through its subsidiary, Super Valu Markets, Inc. Its acquisition in 1959 of five retail stores of Piggly Wiggly Midland Company, with annual sales of $7 million, brought to 11 the number of stores which it owned outright. These stores have annual sales of about $14 million.

The Godfrey Company, a Milwaukee-located sponsor of a voluntary chain of between 201 to 225 IGA. stores,[40] in 1954 entered food retailing through its subsidiary, Sentry Markets, Inc. By 1959 Godfrey was operating eight of its own large Sentry supermarkets.

The FTC Food Inquiry reported that between 1948 and 1958 sponsors of voluntary chains acquired 131 retail units with combined sales of $63 million.[41] It is not possible to determine which of the acquisitions discussed above were reported to the FTC since it only identifies such acquisitions by states. However, the report shows that 73 stores with sales of $38 million were acquired in states other than those in which the acquisition discussed above occurred.

Available data do not permit a very accurate estimate of the extent to which sponsors of voluntary chains have entered food retailing. But the preceding findings suggest that in recent years sponsors of voluntaries have acquired retailers with sales of near $150 million. Since it is likely that they have grown at least as much through internal growth, it appears that voluntaries are becoming quite integrated into the field of food retailing. This may well mark the next step in the evolutionary development of many voluntary chains. In a sense, this development may be viewed as an indication of the failure of voluntary chains to compete effectively with corporate and cooperative chains. The wholesale sponsors of such chains apparently feel that their profit position is best promoted, or at least made more secure, by ownership integration into food retailing rather than integrating solely on a nonownership basis through the voluntary chain technique. At this time, however, it is still too early to predict whether the above cases are exceptions to the rule or presagers of the future. We are inclined to the latter view.

CHAPTER FOUR

Effect of Horizontal Mergers on Market Structure

Internal versus External Growth

FIRMS may grow horizontally either through internal expansion or by external expansion which involves acquiring of, merging with, or consolidating with other concerns. Most often large firms grow *externally* as well as *internally* during some period of their growth history.[1]

In this chapter we shall analyze the extent to which grocery chains have employed mergers in their horizontal expansion and the extent to which growth achieved through mergers has changed the market structure of food retailing.

The terms *merger, acquisition,* and *consolidation* will be used interchangeably, although they have specific legal meanings. We are concerned only with their economic effects.

Growth by Mergers

It is necessary to recognize that there are two levels of causes for mergers: (1) reasons for a firm's wishing to grow, and (2) factors which make mergers the best means of growing. We shall consider each of these briefly. The following discussion is not a quantitative analysis of the importance of these factors in promoting mergers in food retailing. Rather, they are presented to clarify the nature of external growth motives without measuring their precise relevance.

REASONS FOR GROWING

Economic theory assumes that firms grow because by doing so they increase or secure their profit position. Growth may influence the level

48

and security of profits in a number of ways. Here we shall cite several reasons associated with increased horizontal integration which seem to have a bearing on the profits of grocery retailers.

Economies of Horizontal Integration. — Horizontally integrated food retailers have a number of distinct advantages over others. At the local market level, the chain with several stores in the same city enjoys distinct economies in advertising and merchandising. Regional and national chains also enjoy advantages of specialized management, large-scale procurement of supplies, and greater ease in obtaining equity and loan capital.

Geographic Diversification. — Horizontal integration over a wide geographic area increases a firm's security or survival power. Unsatisfactory operating conditions in one area may be counterbalanced by more satisfactory ones elsewhere. Hence, the geographically diversified grocery retailer is likely to possess more potential survival power in the event of price wars and the like, than the local chain or independent.

Prestige. — If there are no significant diseconomies of large-scale operations, management of large firms may desire to grow ever larger in order to enjoy the prestige associated with operating one of the country's largest firms. The extent to which this motive underlies growth in the U.S. economy is not measurable; yet it seems to permeate many growth decisions, and in some cases may well be as important as the other motives mentioned above.

Market Power. — Increasing horizontal integration may proceed to the point where it results in a high degree of market concentration; then the remaining firms may have some control of their selling and/or procurement policies. Of course, even if growth is not originally motivated by a desire to attain market power, it may eventually result in sufficient market concentration to confer market power on firms.

INCENTIVES FOR GROWTH BY MERGER

Firms do not merge for the sake of merging. Rather, they merge because, first, they have a need or desire to grow for any of the above reasons, and second, they believe that growth by merger is the most desirable or efficient means of attaining such growth. There are several basic factors which make growth by merger preferable to growth through internal expansion.

Market Structure Considerations. — Because grocery retailers do not operate in a perfectly competitive market structure but in markets of relatively few grocers where nonprice considerations are often important in getting patronage, they may have considerable difficulty in rapidly expanding their share of the market. Even severe price cutting will not affect sales greatly because rivals likely will match the lower prices and therefore few patrons will switch from one concern to the other.

Under these market conditions, growth by merger is often the most economical means of growing. By acquiring a going concern, a firm can increase its size by about the amount of the acquired retailer's volume.

Market structure considerations are especially important when retailers desire to enter a new market. As mentioned above, grocery retailers enjoy important advertising economies by operating several stores in the same area. But since it may be extremely difficult to open a number of stores in a new market in a relatively short period, a firm desiring to enter a new market has an important incentive to do so through the merger route. Thus we would expect many chains to make their initial entry into a new market via merger.

Financial Considerations. — Buying a going concern often is easier to finance than is internal growth on a comparable scale. First, lenders may be more prone to make loans for growth by this means because they can better gauge the future success of the venture. Second, the persons selling a going concern are often willing to work out special purchase plans or are willing to accept securities of the acquiring concern in exchange for the assets of the acquired concern.

Economy of Buying Facilities. — Sometimes the market price of a firm offered for sale is lower than the cost (less depreciation) of replacing the facilities. Then another firm may have an incentive to acquire the discontinuing firm quite apart from any of the preceding incentives for merging.

Tax Incentives. — The popular literature on mergers often cites the tax structure as an important incentive for mergers. Taxes generally are cited as motivating mergers in two ways.

First, spokesmen for independent retailers criticize the corporate income tax as being too severe at the lower income levels to permit independent food retailers to accumulate enough earnings to finance expansion.[2] Associated with this is the alleged problem of gaining access to favorable financial markets by independents seeking loan or equity capital with which to finance expansion.

A second tax reason often cited is the impact of estate taxes on closely held retail organizations.[3] Estate taxes are the same whether the estate consists of stock or an equal value in cash or its equivalent. However, heirs may be forced to liquidate their holdings in a closely held corporation to pay these taxes. Consequently, they may decide that the most convenient way to get these funds is to sell their interest in such a corporation to another firm.

Another tax reason for mergers is that under certain conditions an acquiring firm gets not only the assets of another concern, but its tax losses as well. Hence, even if a firm had no assets, it might still be valuable to an acquiring concern if it had incurred large losses prior to its acquisition.

It should be emphasized that the first two tax considerations mentioned above are reasons why some firms are offered for sale. They do not explain why other concerns are interested in acquiring them. On the other hand, the third reason cited—the carry-over of losses for tax reasons—is definitely a reason why both the acquiring and acquired concern desire to merge.

The preceding discussion has indicated, first, various reasons firms have for growing, and second, reasons why they may prefer growing by merger rather than internally. This discussion has not attempted to exhaust these reasons. Rather, it has mentioned a number of motives which may be most important in food retailing. Thus these motives should essentially be considered as hypotheses.

Although the main purpose here is to analyze the effects of mergers rather than their causes, the data presented below do permit us to test some of the hypotheses presented above.

Sources of Data on Horizontal Mergers

The collection of reliable data on mergers and acquisitions for the 18-year period encompassed in this research posed methodological problems. Several alternatives were considered, including the direct method of contacting food chains. But because the project had no legal authority requiring compliance with this request, and because the chains might not wish to divulge such data or incur the expense and give the time necessary to provide it, the indirect method of using secondary published sources was employed.

Moody's Industrials was the basic source for information on the number of horizontal and vertical acquisitions. This source was supplemented by *Chain Store Age* and *Progressive Grocer,* two monthly food retail trade publications. Each monthly issue of these publications was examined, commencing with January, 1940, through January, 1958. Beginning with the January, 1953, issue, *Supermarket News,* a newspaper of food retailing published twice monthly, served as an additional source. In addition, merger data were provided from several miscellaneous secondary sources. The Appendix shows the net number of mergers reported in each of these sources.

Fortunately, in all but a few instances, these sources provided information of the number of stores operated by acquired retailers. Sales were given for about 45 per cent of the acquired stores. This information revealed that the great majority of acquisitions involved stores of supermarket size. Consequently, it was assumed that all acquired firms for which sales data were not given had sales per store equal to average supermarket sales in the year of the acquisition. By applying this assumption to those acquired stores for which sales data were given, we can obtain an estimate of average sales per store within 5 per cent of their actual average sales. Thus, it appears that this assumption results in a fairly accurate estimate of the size of acquired stores. Comparison of our merger statistics for the years 1949–58 with those reported in a recent FTC study suggests that the secondary sources used in this study provide quite complete information on grocery mergers.[4]

It should be noted, however, that the data are more complete for the years 1953–58 than for previous years because additional sources were used beginning with 1953 (Appendix). We estimate that the data on the number of firms acquired are 57 per cent less complete for 1940–52 than for 1953–58. However, this underreporting for 1940–52 involved mainly small firms. We estimate that the data on the number of stores (as contrasted to firms) reportedly acquired were 13 per cent less complete for 1940–52 than for 1953–58 (Appendix).

Comparison of our merger data for 1952–57 with data collected by the Bureau of the Census indicates that our sources reported 2.4 per cent fewer retail mergers and 9.4 fewer acquired stores than did Census.[5] On the basis of this comparison and the above estimates of the extent to which our sources underreported mergers prior to 1953, we estimate that for the entire period 1940–58 there actually were 420 retail mergers involving 4,685 stores (Appendix). This suggests that our sources understate the number of actual retail firms acquired by at least 20 per cent and the number of stores operated by the acquired firms by 13 per cent.

In the following discussion of the effects of mergers on firm growth and market structure, we shall deal only with the impact of mergers recorded in our sources. It should be kept in mind that the estimates are likely to understate somewhat the impact of mergers. This understatement is least important in the case of acquisitions by the 20 largest chains. It is our judgment that the data on these firms understate their mergers (measured in store numbers) by less than 10 per cent.

Extent of Horizontal Merger Activity, 1940–58

According to the sources used herein, from 1940 to 1958, 342 American retail grocery firms, operating 4,061 stores and having sales of $2,896,135,000, were acquired by other American retail grocery firms.[6]

Total merger activity in food retailing proceeded at a relatively low rate until the early 1950's. In every year from 1940 to 1952, less than 10 retail firms were acquired, according to our data. However, in terms of the number of stores and sales involved, merger activity in 1941 was as great as or greater than in all years but 1955 (Chart IV).

The most significant characteristic of over-all retail grocery merger activity from 1940 to 1958 is the accelerated rate it has followed since

CHART IV

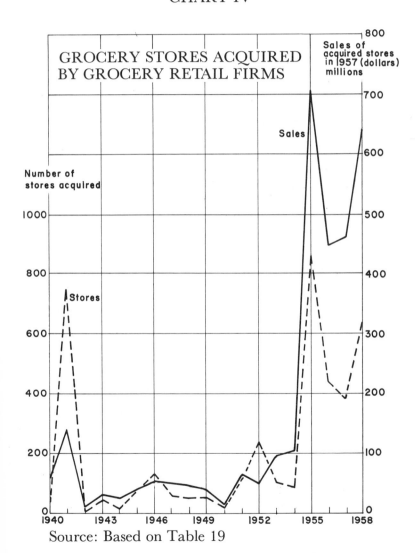

Source: Based on Table 19

TABLE 19
Retail Grocery Firms and Stores Acquired by Grocery Retailers

Year	Number of acquired firms	Number of acquired stores	Sales of acquired firms (current dollars) (000 omitted)	Sales of acquired firms (1957 dollars) (000 omitted)
1940	8	22	$ 26,083	$ 61,033
1941	6	745	112,083	238,431
1942	1	6	2,633	4,777
1943	3	47	20,438	33,212
1944	1	17	15,429	25,425
1945	3	40	18,799	30,548
1946	3	135	37,171	53,362
1947	4	62	40,529	47,184
1948	3	52	35,792	38,775
1949	4	49	35,267	39,890
1950	2	10	7,210	8,150
1951	6	97	63,816	64,926
1952	7	234	49,649	49,020
1953	26	103	93,526	95,568
1954	25	89	99,816	102,443
1955	61	876	674,528	701,542
1956	59	435	431,925	447,144
1957	47	387	458,544	458,544
1958	73	655	672,897	662,313
Total	342	4,061	$ 2,896,135	$ 3,162,287

1950. The volume of mergers, measured in terms of sales of acquired firms, was greater from 1955 to 1958 than during the entire preceding 15 years.

It should also be noted that during the period studied, merger activity in food retailing did not parallel closely the pattern of over-all merger activity in manufacturing and mining. The economy experienced a definite merger cycle from 1940 to 1947. From a relatively low level of 140 mergers in 1940, over-all merger activity increased significantly during World War II and reached a high of 419 in 1946; then merger activity subsided until it reached a low point in 1949. Thereafter, the pace of merger activity again quickened and has continued on a relatively high plateau since the middle 1950's.

There was no merger movement in food retailing comparable to the 1940–47 merger cycle in the rest of the economy. This fact suggests that the special conditions of wartime did not promote horizontal mergers in food retailing. It is significant, however, that vertical acquisitions of

TABLE 20
Number of Retail Grocery Firms and Stores Acquired by Chains, 1940-58

Stores of acquired firms	20 largest chains		Other chains		Total all chains			
	Firms* acquiring	Stores acquired	Firms acquiring	Stores acquired	Firms acquiring	Per cent	Stores acquired	Per cent
1	15	15	93	93	108	31.6	108	2.7
2-3	16	39	38	99	54	15.8	138	3.4
4-9	40	259	57	338	97	28.4	597	14.7
10-15	10	123	16	198	26	7.6	321	7.9
16-25	8	163	8	151	16	4.7	314	7.7
26-50	22	762	2	76	24	7.0	838	20.7
51-99	4	327	...	...	4	1.2	327	8.1
100 and over	6	1237	1	175	7	2.0	1412	34.8
Not disclosed	3	...	3	...	6	1.7	...	...
Total	124	2925	218	1130	342	100.0	4055†	100.0

*A&P, First National Stores, and Penn Fruit of the top 20 were not reported as making acquisitions during these years.
†Not included in this final total are six firms acquired but for which the number of stores was not disclosed.

food processors by food retailers (Chapter V) did follow the over-all merger trend of the 1940–47 movement. As discussed below, many such vertical mergers were motivated by special wartime conditions.

Since 1948, however, grocery merger activity has paralleled quite closely the merger activity of the economy as a whole, suggesting that during this period some common causes underlie mergers in retailing and other segments of the economy.[7]

SIZE DISTRIBUTION OF ACQUIRED RETAILERS

Of the 342 retail mergers reported in the data used in this study, 108 (32 per cent) acquired firms operated only 1 store and 162 had 3 or fewer (Table 20).

At the other extreme, only 7 acquired firms operated over 100 stores. But while these 7 constituted only 2 per cent of all acquired retailers, they operated 35 per cent of all the stores of the acquired firms reported here. Moreover, the 32 acquired retailers operating over 25 stores accounted for 64 per cent of all stores operated by acquired retailers.

These data indicate clearly that although most acquired retailers involved quite small firms, the largest 32 acquisitions were more important in terms of number of stores operated than the 310 other acquisitions reported here.

CHARACTERISTICS OF ACQUIRING FIRMS

The 342 retail grocery acquisitions reported here were acquired by 165 grocery retailers (Table 21). Fifty-five (33.4 per cent) of the acquiring firms made only 1 acquisition and 123 (74.6 per cent) acquired 10 or fewer stores. Only 7 chains acquired firms operating a total of over 100 stores.

Seven grocery retailers with 1958 sales of over $500 million made 81 acquisitions or 23 per cent of the total reported here. These 81 firms operated 2,484 stores, or 61 per cent of all acquired stores (Table 22).

Nineteen chains with 1958 sales of over $100 million acquired 3,219 stores, or 79 per cent of all stores operated by all acquired retailers. This indicates that while 165 grocery retailers made acquisitions from 1940 to 1958, the 19 largest acquiring chains played the dominant role in grocery retail merger activity from 1940 to 1958.

IMPACT OF HORIZONTAL MERGERS ON MARKET STRUCTURE

EFFECT ON STORE NUMBERS

The 4,061 stores reported in our sources as being acquired from 1940 to 1958 (Table 19) were less than one per cent of the average number of stores operating during this period (Table 47). Even the 876 stores

TABLE 21
Distribution of Acquiring Chains, 1940-58

Total number of stores acquired*	Number and per cent of acquiring firms					
	20 largest chains in 1958†		Other chains‡		Total acquiring chains	
	Number	Per cent	Number	Per cent	Number	Per cent
1	. . .	. . .	55	37.16	55	33.35
2	. . .	. . .	19	12.84	19	11.52
3	. . .	. . .	8	5.41	8	4.84
4	. . .	. . .	10	6.76	10	6.07
5	1	5.88	10	6.76	11	6.66
6−10	1	5.88	19	12.84	20	12.12
11−25	4	23.54	18	12.16	22	13.34
26−50	1	5.88	6	4.05	7	4.25
51−100	1	5.88	2	1.35	3	1.82
101−250	5	29.42	1	.67	6	3.63
251−500	2	11.76	. . .	. . .	2	1.20
Over 500	2	11.76	. . .	. . .	2	1.20
Total	17	100.00	148	100.00	165	100.00

*Six acquisitions for which number of acquired stores was not given were counted as operating only one store each.

†A&P, First National Stores, and Penn Fruit of the 20 largest chains in 1958 were not reported as making acquisitions during this period.

‡All acquiring concerns were assumed to be chains although a few mergers undoubtedly involved acquisitions by single-store firms.

TABLE 22
Retail Grocery Firms and Stores
  Acquired by Grocery Retailers, 1940-58
  (Sales in Millions of Dollars)

1958 sales of acquiring firms	Number of acquiring firms	Number of firms acquired	Stores acquired	Average number of firms acquired	Average number of stores acquired per firm
Over 1,000	2	14	775	7.0	387.5
500−999	5	67	1,709	13.4	341.8
250−499	4	24	310	6.0	77.5
100−249	8	38	425	4.8	53.1
50−99	6	17	164	2.8	27.3
25−49	5	12	71	2.4	14.2
Under 25 or not known	135	170	607	1.3	4.5
Total	165	342	4,061	2.07	24.61

acquired in 1955 represented only .255 per cent of all stores operating in that year.

As shown earlier (Table 20), 94 per cent of all acquired stores were operated by chains with four or more stores. Hence, we may expect that the main impact of grocery-store mergers has been upon the chain sector of food retailing. This is borne out by the comparisons made in Table 47. The number of grocery stores acquired each year averaged .06 per cent of the total number of grocery stores operating each year and .88 per cent of the total number of chain stores operating each year. In 1955 alone, stores of acquired retailers were 3.9 per cent as great as the total number of stores operated by grocery chains in that year.

EFFECT ON OVER-ALL SALES CONCENTRATION

Another broad measure of the impact of mergers on market structure is a comparison of the sales volume of acquired stores with total grocery-store sales. Such a comparison indicates that in only five years — 1941, 1955, 1956, 1957, and 1958 — did the sales of acquired firms exceed one per cent of total grocery-store sales (Table 48). For the whole period they averaged about .5 per cent per year. This fact suggests that mergers in food retailing have not induced any drastic transformation in industrial structure comparable to that occurring in some other American industries. However, mergers by the 20 largest chains have been relatively much more important than these over-all comparisons suggest. From 1940 to 1958, the country's 20 largest retail grocery chains acquired retail grocery firms with estimated adjusted sales of $1.8 billion (Table 48); this was 80 per cent greater than the sales of stores acquired by all other grocery retailers.

Because of the prominent role played by the 20 largest grocery retailers in recent merger activity, in the following pages we shall analyze in more detail the impact of their mergers on their individual growth as well as on over-all market structure.

MERGER ACTIVITY OF THE TOP 20 CHAINS

Of the 20 largest chains operating in 1958, and for which sales data were available back to 1940,[8] only A & P, First National, and Fisher Brothers made no mergers according to our data (Table 23). The most active acquirer was National Food which acquired 26 retailers operating 585 stores with estimated retail sales of $349 million (1957 dollars). National Food was followed by Winn Dixie whose acquisitions had sales estimated at $242 million, American Stores with $190 million, and Colonial with $148 million.

The 17 chains making acquisitions acquired 123 retail firms with combined sales of $1,986 million (1957 dollars). This equaled 4.62 per

TABLE 23

Retail Acquisitions from 1941 to 1958 by the 20 Largest Chains of 1958
(Sales in Millions of Dollars)

Acquiring chain*	No. of mergers	No. of stores	Sales of acquired stores (1957 $)	Acquisitions as per cent of 1958 U.S. grocery store sales	Acquisitions as per cent of 1958 U.S. chain sales
National Food†	26	585	$ 349.4	.81	2.14
Winn-Dixie	11	336	242.2	.56	1.31
American	4	356	189.5	.44	1.03
Grand Union	15	155	171.4	.40	.93
ACF-Wrigley	9	142	166.4	.39	.90
Kroger	8	146	166.3	.39	.90
Safeway	6	629	162.5	.38	.88
Food Fair	11	124	148.5	.35	.81
Colonial	10	106	147.2	.34	.80
Lucky	7	72‡	94.7	.22	.51
Jewel Tea	2	43	52.2	.12	.28
Stop and Shop	5	23	26.8	.06	.15
Thriftimart	3	16	20.6	.05	.11
Loblaw‡	2	19	20.1	.05	.11
Weingarten	1	6	14.0	.03	.08
Red Owl	1	12	9.1	.02	.05
Bohack	1	5	5.3	.01	.03
A&P	...	...	...	...	...
First National	...	...	...	...	...
Fisher Brothers	...	...	...	...	...
Total	123	2,775	$1,986.2¶	4.62	11.02

*Penn Fruit was among the top 20 in 1958 but was excluded because
its sales for 1940 were not available.

†National Food and Loblaw are treated as separate firms although
George Weston, Inc., has an interest in each.

‡Number of stores in one merger not reported. This merger was
counted as involving one store.

¶This total is different from that in Table 48 because mergers
occurring in 1940 are not counted in this table.

59

cent of total grocery-store sales and 11.0 per cent of total chain grocery-store sales in 1958. These are significantly large percentages when we consider that between 1940 and 1958 the top 20 chains increased their share of total grocery-store sales by 6.4 percentage points (Tables 41A and 41B). Hence, the aggregate sales of retailers acquired by the top 20 chains were about 70 per cent as great as the increase in their share of total grocery-store sales. Thus, the increase in the share of these chains of national grocery-store sales can be explained largely in terms of their mergers.

IMPORTANCE OF MERGERS ON GROWTH OF ACQUIRING FIRMS

No completely satisfactory method has been developed to measure the contribution of mergers to a firm's growth.[9] The chief measurement problem here is that mergers have *indirect* as well as *direct* effects on growth. And theoretically — depending on the assumptions made — these indirect effects may increase, decrease, or have no effect on a firm's long-run growth.

The customary procedure used to isolate the merger component of growth is to measure only the direct effects.[10] This procedure will be followed here.

We shall estimate the size of the merger component of a chain's growth by dividing its total sales growth from 1940 to 1958 into the estimated sales of firms it acquired during this period. For example, if an acquiring firm grew by $200 million between 1940 and 1958, and if the total sales of all the firms (in the year they were purchased) it acquired totaled $100 million, we shall attribute 50 per cent of this firm's growth to its mergers. But it should be emphasized that we shall be measuring only the *direct* impact of mergers on growth. For example, consider the case of a chain with sales of $50 million in 1940. If it merged with a $50 million chain in 1941, and subsequently grew by $200 million without any additional mergers, we would estimate that only 20 per cent of its growth was due to merger. This, of course, completely ignores the fact that doubling its size in 1941 very likely played a larger part in its subsequent growth than our measure suggests. Consequently, we believe our estimates are more likely to understate the effect of mergers than to overstate them.

When the above method is used to measure the contributions of mergers to growth, mergers appear to have been most important in the growth of Lucky Stores. Sales of the retailers it acquired were 75 per cent as great as its total sales growth between 1940 and 1958 (Table 24). Six other chains made acquisitions with adjusted sales over 40 per cent as great as their adjusted sales growth during this period. Acquisi-

TABLE 24
Growth of the 20 Largest Chains
from 1940 to 1958 and Per Cent of Growth Due to Mergers

Name of chain*	Per cent of growth due to mergers†	Per cent increase in total sales, 1940-58
A&P	0	87.9
First National	0	58.9
Fisher Brothers	0	81.8
Average‡	0	76.2
Bohack	5.6	159.0
Red Owl	7.0	437.8
Loblaw	9.1	414.5
Safeway	13.4	129.3
Weingarten	13.5	336.4
Average	9.7	295.4
Thriftimart	13.9	985.9
Jewel	14.5	525.7
Kroger	15.0	183.4
Stop and Shop	20.2	250.0
Food Fair	23.8	912.0
American	34.4	188.5
Average	20.3	507.6
Winn-Dixie	41.8	2,046.3
Grand Union	42.5	490.9
ACF-Wrigley	45.8	7,063.6
Colonial	47.1	289.2
National Food	56.4	427.8
Lucky	75.4	1,142.6
Average	51.5	1,910.1
Weighted Average	22.6	

*These are the 20 largest chains in 1958.
†Computed by taking sales of acquisitions as shown in Table 23 as a per cent of the acquiring firm's sales growth. from 1940 to 1958. All comparisons are in comparable dollars.
‡All averages are simple averages.

Source: These are the 20 largest chains which were listed in Moody's Industrials in 1940 and were still operating in 1958. Actually Penn Fruit and Mayfair Markets were larger in 1958 than was Fisher Brothers, but they were not listed in the 1940 Moody's.

61

tions of the other 11 top chains had sales of between 6 per cent and 34 per cent as great as the acquirer's sales growth. Sales of retailers acquired by the top 20 chains were equal to 22.6 per cent of the total growth of the top 20 chains between 1940 and 1958.

Table 24 compares the sales growth of the top 20 firms between 1940 and 1958 with the per cent which their mergers contributed to their sales growth. When this method is used to measure the merger component of growth, there is not a very high correlation between the growth of acquiring concerns and the extent of their growth due to mergers.[11] Although the three firms in our group which made no mergers grew at a lower rate than merging firms, there was considerable variation in the growth of merging firms. For example, whereas 56.4 per cent of National Food's growth may be attributed to mergers, seven other chains having a smaller merger component in their growth grew at a more rapid rate than National Food.

Another method of measuring the possible importance of mergers in an acquiring firm's growth is to compare the sales of the firms which it acquired during a particular period with its sales at the beginning of the period. The hypothesis underlying such a comparison is that the relative growth rates of each firm during a period of merger activity is explained largely by the volume of each firm's mergers relative to its initial size. The data presented in Table 25 support this hypothesis. The firms which made acquisitions with sales equal to between 9 per cent and 37.7 per cent of their 1940 sales experienced average sales growth of 264.8 per cent. At the other extreme, those whose mergers exceeded 200 per cent of their 1940 sales experienced average sales growths of 2013.9 per cent. Statistically the correlation between these factors is extremely high,[12] indicating that the difference in relative growth rates of these chains is closely associated with differences in the relative amount of their merger activity.

It should be emphasized that the close statistical association between these factors does not prove that a particular causal relationship exists between them. For example, these data support the hypothesis that merging firms grow most rapidly, but they likewise support the hypothesis that rapidly growing firms use mergers most extensively in their growth. It is possible that the fastest growers might have grown most rapidly even if they had made no mergers, but considering the market problems of breaking into entirely new markets via the internal growth route, it seems very unlikely that they could have grown as rapidly as they did had they depended entirely on internal growth.

One way of untangling at least partially the effect of mergers on the relative growth rates of these firms is to estimate what size they would

TABLE 25
Sales of Acquired Firms and the Increase
in Sales of the 20 Largest Acquiring Chains, 1940-58

Name of chain*	Sales of acquired firms as per cent of 1940 sales of acquiring firm	Per cent increase in sales, 1940-58
A&P	0	87.9
First National	0	58.9
Fisher Brothers	0	81.8
Average†	0	76.2
Bohack	9.0	159.0
Safeway	17.4	129.3
Kroger	27.5	183.4
Red Owl	30.7	437.8
Loblaw	37.7	414.5
Average	24.5	264.8
Weingarten	45.4	336.4
Stop and Shop	50.4	250.0
American	64.9	188.5
Jewel	76.4	525.7
Colonial	136.1	289.2
Thriftimart	137.5	985.9
Average	85.1	429.3
Grand Union	208.5	490.9
Food Fair	217.5	912.0
National Food	241.2	427.8
Lucky	861.7	1,142.6
Winn-Dixie	855.4	2,046.3
ACF-Wrigley	3,231.8	7,063.6
Average	936.0	2,013.9

*These are the 20 largest chains in 1958.
†All averages are simple averages.

Source: <u>Moody's Industrials</u>, 1940. Penn Fruit and Mayfair
Markets were larger in 1958 than was Fisher Brothers, but they
were not listed in <u>Moody's</u> in 1940.

have been in 1958 had all firms relied entirely on internal growth between 1940 and 1958. This calls for a procedure for isolating the merger
component of growth. The method used here is to assume that if these
firms had relied entirely on internal growth, their 1958 size would have
been their actual size less the total sales of their acquired stores in the
year in which they were acquired. (All comparisons are made in com-

parable dollars.) This method is subject to the criticism that it measures only the *direct* effects of mergers. However, it seems the most satisfactory comparison to make under the circumstances, and its use in this case is not subject to the most severe criticism usually made against it (that it measures only direct merger effects) because most retail acquisitions by these firms occurred since 1952 and hence may have had only a minor indirect effect on sales growth.

Table 26 presents the estimated 1958 sales of these concerns if none had had mergers in its growth. It also ranks these 20 firms according to their actual sales in 1940 and 1958 as well as their estimated 1958 sales had they made no mergers.

If mergers were the only factor causing firms to change their relative position in their industry, and if our method of measuring the impact of mergers on growth were perfectly accurate, ranking these firms on the basis of their estimated 1958 sales would have resulted in placing them in the same rank in 1958 as in 1940.

Actually, all but 6 of these 20 firms held a different rank in 1958 than in 1940 (Table 26). For example, whereas First National was the fourth largest chain in 1940, in 1958 it was eighth largest. In the aggregate, the 14 chains changing their rank gained or lost a total of 56 positions in rank, or an average of 4.1 positions each. For example, First National lost 4 positions by slipping from fourth to eighth place and Food Fair gained 4 positions in rank. This suggests a remarkably mobile size structure among all but the 3 largest chains.

Ranking these firms according to their estimated 1958 sales had they made no mergers, provides a basis for determining the extent of the above changes in rank which may be attributed to mergers. These estimates were made by subtracting the sales of firms acquired by each chain from its 1958 sales. On this basis, between 1940 and 1958 these firms would have changed a total of 50 rank positions even if they had made no mergers. This was only 6 less than they actually experienced. Thus, only about 11 per cent of the shifts in the ranks of these firms can be explained by the merger component of their growth. The remainder would have occurred even if all had grown entirely internally.

This conclusion should be qualified in two respects. First, our method of measuring the effects of mergers takes account of only their direct effects on growth. Hence, it is possible that our ranking based on their estimated 1958 sales exaggerates the instability which would have occurred had they grown entirely internally. Second, in 1940 most of the firms were quite small and a number were of approximately the same size; consequently, even slight differences in growth rates from 1940 to 1958 would have resulted in significant changes within their ranks by 1958.

TABLE 26
Estimated Effects of Acquisitions on the Rank of the Largest Chains
(In Millions of Dollars)

Chain*	1940 sales	Rank in group	1958 sales (1940 dollars)	Rank in group	Estimated sales of acquired firms 1941-1958 (1940 dollars)	1958 sales less sales of acquired firms (1940 dollars)	Rank in group
A&P	$ 1,115.7	1	$ 2,096.7	1	. . .	$ 2,096.7	1
Safeway	399.3	2	915.6	2	$ 69.4	846.2	2
Kroger	258.1	3	731.5	3	71.1	660.4	3
First National	142.7	4	226.7	8	. . .	226.7	6
American	124.8	5	360.1	4	81.0	279.1	4
National Food†	61.9	6	326.7	5	149.3	177.4	7
Colonial	46.2	7	179.8	11	62.9	116.9	11
Grand Union	35.1	8	207.4	9	73.2	134.2	10
Jewel	29.2	9	182.7	10	22.3	160.4	8
Food Fair	29.2	10	295.5	6	63.5	232.0	5
Bohack	25.6	11	66.3	17	2.3	64.0	16
Fisher Bros.	23.1	12	42.0	20	. . .	42.0	19
Loblaw†	22.8	13	117.3	13	8.6	108.7	12
Stop & Shop	22.8	14	79.8	14	11.5	68.3	14
Weingarten	13.2	15	57.6	19	6.0	51.6	18
Red Owl ‡	12.7	16	68.3	16	3.9	64.4	15
Winn-Dixie¶	12.1	17	259.7	7	103.5	156.2	9
Thriftimart	6.4	18	69.5	15	8.8	60.7	17
Lucky	4.7	19	58.4	18	40.5	17.9	20
ACF-Wrigley§	$ 2.2	20	$ 157.6	12	$71.1	$ 86.5	13

*These include the 20 largest chains in 1940, as reported in Moody's, which were still operating in 1958.
†We have treated National Food and Loblaw as separate chains, although George Weston, Inc., controls both.
‡Includes retail sales only.
¶1940 sales are for Winn and Lovett.
§1940 sales are for Wrigley Stores.

However, the basic fact remains that there was considerable mobility within the top 20 chain group, and there very likely would have been considerable shifting of relative positions even if none had grown by mergers. The main effect of mergers seems to have been to accelerate the growth of most of these firms and so to result in some additional mobility within this group. Of course, as mentioned earlier, in the aggregate these mergers contributed enough to the growth of these firms to explain 70 per cent of the increase in their share of total grocery-store sales between 1940 and 1958.

EFFECT OF MERGERS ON LOCAL MARKET CONCENTRATION

The preceding analysis has dealt solely with the effects of mergers on the growth of individual acquiring firms and on national market structure. But, as noted earlier, market concentration not only is highest in local markets, but apparently has increased significantly since 1940. To determine the role which mergers may have played in bringing about this increase in local market concentration, we have made estimates of the extent to which acquiring firms were already operating in the market of the acquired firm at the time of their merger. This was

TABLE 27
Geographic Expansion and Increased
Market Concentration of the Largest Chains, 1942-57*

Chains	No. of retail mergers 1942-57	No. of acquisitions in which operating area not disclosed	No. of cities in which acquired firm operated†	No. of same cities acquiring chain operated previous to merger	Net new cities	Per cent of new cities of total cities
Safeway	3	0	3	2	1	33.3
Kroger	5	0	20	4	16	80.0
American	3	1	23	4	19	82.6
National Food	18	2	37	2	35	94.6
Colonial	9	1	24	3	21	87.5
Jewel Tea	1	0	8	0	8	100.0
Grand Union	12	1	9	2	7	77.8
Food Fair	10	3	9	5	4	44.4
Bohack	1	0	1	1	0	0.0
Loblaw	2	0	8	0	8	100.0
Stop & Shop	3	0	9	5	4	44.4
Weingarten	1	0	1	0	1	100.0
Red Owl	1	0	1	1	0	0.0
Winn-Dixie	10	0	54	14	40	74.1
Lucky	6	1	7	3	4	57.1
ACF-Wrigley	8	0	18	4	14	77.8
Fitzsimmons	3	0	3	2	1	33.3
Total	96	9	235	52	183	
Average						77.9

*A&P, First National, and Penn Fruit did not acquire any retail food stores in this period.
†These include only those of approximately 1500 cities reported in Market Guides, in which these chains operated.

Source: Editor and Publisher, Market Guides, various editions.

done for each acquisition made from 1942 to 1957 by checking all the cities reported in *Editor and Publisher, Market Guides* to determine whether both the acquiring chains and acquired retailer were operating in the same city the year previous to the acquisition. This procedure provides a fairly good approximation of the extent to which mergers involved expansion into new areas rather than additional growth in their established markets, although *Market Guides* sometimes does not name small chains and never names one-store independent retailers. However, 94 per cent of the firms acquired by these chains operated in one or more of the cities appearing in *Market Guides* (Table 27).

On the basis of these comparisons, the acquiring chain operated in only 22 per cent of the cities in which its acquired stores operated. In 78 per cent of these cities, the acquisition involved geographic expansion into new markets rather than increased concentration in the acquirer's existing markets. There was considerable variation in this percentage among the different acquiring chains. For example, National Food, the leading acquirer, made acquisitions in only 5.4 per cent of the cities in which it also operated. The comparable figure for Stop and Shop was 55.6 per cent.

Horizontal mergers have contributed somewhat to the increased concentration which occurred in local markets from 1942 to 1957. This is indicated by the fact that mergers did increase market concentration in one out of five cities in which acquired stores operated.

Unfortunately, our data do not permit us to measure more precisely the extent to which this market concentration has occurred. This is an area of work which should receive additional attention.

CHAPTER FIVE

Vertical Integration in Grocery Distribution

The Theory of Vertical Integration

To this point we have explained the horizontal integration or growth of grocery retailers and the effects of such integration on market concentration. Another significant market structural characteristic is the extent and forms of vertical integration of firms. By vertical integration is meant the extension of control over two or more successive processes of production by a single firm or jointly by several firms. Such control may be achieved in a number of ways. The extreme or highest degree of vertical integration involves such extension of control by means of ownership by one firm of different production or marketing processes. An alternative form of vertical integration is the extension of control over successive processes through contractual arrangements or informal agreements. In this case, "certain production and marketing activities of firms, which otherwise would make decisions independently, become integrated under a single or joint decision-making unit."[1]

The essence of vertical integration is the extension of one firm's control or influence over successive phases of the production or marketing process. So viewed, the method used is only incidental to the objectives sought.

The extension of one firm's scope of influence over successive phases of production may affect vitally the scope of influence of other firms. Hence, the actual or potential extent of vertical integration by firms

68

within an industry becomes a potentially significant characteristic of market structure affecting firm conduct and, ultimately, industrial performance.

Before describing the extent of and apparent reasons for vertical integration in food retailing, it is well to review briefly the theory of vertical integration. This will aid in suggesting hypotheses as to the reasons for and significance of vertical integration in this industry.

Fundamentally, firms expand the scope of their operations vertically because doing so influences their profits. Vertical integration may affect profits in the following ways.

TECHNOLOGICAL BASIS

Sometimes there are physical or technical reasons for a firm to combine two stages of production. This is true whenever the production costs of a firm performing two successive functions are lower than the combined costs of performing these functions under two separate managements. The steel industry provides the classic example of integration for technical reasons. If molten iron is allowed to cool, moved to another plant, and then reheated before further processing, costs are higher than if a continuous process under one management is used. Basically, technological economies of vertically integrated operations result from the Marshallian principle of continuous production.[2]

ECONOMIC CHANGE

In a dynamic economy, change is commonplace. But when it is drastic, change itself may act as a catalyst to integration—sometimes seemingly in conflict with basic technological and other factors.

In a new industry[3] or in an industry experiencing rapid technical, demand, or other drastic changes affecting its profits, a firm which otherwise would not be expected to do so may be encouraged to integrate in successive stages. Often it is one of the first to recognize the profit opportunities in the allied industry, or at least is among the first to be able to take advantage of the situation.

It should be emphasized that integration based on the above conditions alone can be reversed. If firms in other industries can take advantage of innovations affecting profit, the integrated firm may have a profit incentive to specialize in fewer stages of production. In this event the integrated firm could be expected to disintegrate from certain stages of production.

SHORTCOMINGS OF THE MARKET IN COORDINATING ECONOMIC ACTIVITY

When different firms specialize in carrying out successive production and marketing activities, the market is the main coordinator or "integrator" of such successive economic activities. But only if firms are operating in a perfectly competitive system of markets does price perform this integrating job perfectly. In such a theoretical system the firm can always buy the kind and amount of products it wants at prevailing market prices.[4] In this event, price integrates perfectly the activities of all the successive buyers and sellers in a marketing channel. With prices as their guides, firms produce the right products at the right time in response to ultimate consumer demand as reflected perfectly through all stages of the marketing channel.

But the real world departs sharply from this theoretical one. Market knowledge often is poor, and buyers and/or sellers are often few, not many. Consequently, firms have an incentive to seek sanctuary from markets characterized by price and product uncertainty and competitive perils. Such sanctuary may be partially achieved by supplanting the indirect processes of the market with the more direct processes of managerial control. Let us consider the two main types of problems inherent in relying on the indirect processes of the market as integrators of economic activities: (1) the shortcomings of market prices in integrating economic activities and (2) the existence of market structures which generate noncompetitive prices.

SHORTCOMINGS OF MARKET PRICES

In unintegrated marketing channels much is expected of market prices. They are supposed to tell buyers and sellers what quantity and quality of products to produce and when they should be offered for sale. Because of this multipurpose function of market price, firms often find it an unsatisfactory guide on which to base decisions. By becoming vertically integrated a firm may achieve the necessary coordination of the successive production processes. This may eliminate certain risks or costs ordinarily borne by the unintegrated firms. For example, a firm faced with uncertainty of supplies may have to carry larger inventories than the integrated firm which can control its supply.

It should be emphasized that the preceding incentive for integration does not dictate that the firms affected become integrated through ownership. Nonownership integration through contracts may eliminate the problems created by market uncertainties. Of course, if other incentives exist for integrated operations, ownership integration might be the most satisfactory solution to the problems.

MARKET STRUCTURE MOTIVES

Economic theory and industrial experience teach and demonstrate that when sellers are few, they are able to develop certain buying or selling policies of their own. The consequence of oligopolistic market structures, more than any other, has led firms to integrate vertically for two reasons:

First, while such markets tend to result in fairly stable prices or margins, firms cannot sell all they might like at the established prices. Because they recognize that vigorous price competition will only lower prices, not increase sales, firms resort to various nonprice strategies to expand their share of the market. Vertical integration is one such strategy. Through it a firm may tie up—at least for a time—part of its market. In the parlance of industry, this kind of integration is referred to as buying up a part of one's market. Vertical integration for this motive can be achieved either through ownership or nonownership forms of integration.

Industrial history is replete with examples of vertical integration motivated by this characteristic of imperfectly competitive market structure: Shoe manufacturers have bought out shoe retailers or made long-term contracts with them; manufacturers of explosives have bought out cartridge makers; oil refiners have entered the filling-station business.

The second way in which oligopolistic market structures generate integration is that if firms in one industry are few and profit margins become large, firms in related industries may use vertical integration as a device to enter such profitable fields. Thus, oligopolistic market structures in one industry entice new entrants, and they especially attract the entry of firms in related industries.

Industrial history again provides many examples of integration for the second reason: Food processors begin making tin cans; auto makers enter the steel-manufacturing field; and farmers—through their cooperatives—go into food processing.

It should be noted that firms integrating for this reason need not have market power themselves, as demonstrated by the fact that farmers have an incentive to enter related industries that are less competitive. The basic motive underlying such integration is that profits of firms in one industry may be enhanced by integrating into an allied industry, thereby, in effect, sharing in the higher profits of the allied industry.[5] This does not imply that the integrator's profits *must* be lower than those of firms in the industry which it enters. For it is conceivable that the integrating firm may enjoy some additional cost advantages of such integration—such as lower advertising and selling expenses—which enable it to operate the integrated operations more profitably than could an unintegrated firm. Of course, if the reverse were true—if the integrator could not operate the integrated operation as efficiently as if it were operated on an unintegrated basis—profits in the industry which the integrator entered would have to be sufficiently higher to offset this diseconomy of vertical integration.

Vertical integration for the above reason usually must involve owner-ship integration. However, one form of integration which assumes the essential characteristics of the preceding, does not necessarily involve complete ownership integration. An example best illustrates this im-portant case.

Suppose firm *A* is one of many food retailers buying from industry *B,* which has an oligopolistic market structure. Under these market conditions the firms in industry *B* would be in a position to charge firm *A* and other food retailers noncompetitive prices. Suppose further that the only significant barrier to entry responsible for the oligopolistic mar-ket structure of industry *B* is successful product differentiation.

Now, if firm *A* develops good consumer acceptance of its own brands, it can then place these brand names on the products also produced by firms in industry *B.* Thus, firm *A* has in effect integrated into industry *B.* And insofar as profits are high in *B,* firm *A* may expect to share in them to the extent that its brands are comparable to those of firms in *B.*

In this case, whether firm *A* also integrates into industry *B* by mak-ing its own products or by simply buying on a "private-label"[6] basis de-pends on the structure and behavior of firms in industry *B.* If firms in *B* refuse to sell their products to *A* on a private-label basis at lower prices than they charge for products sold under their labels, *A* will be forced to manufacture its own products. But if there are several firms in *B* willing to sell to *A* on this basis, *A* will not actually have to integrate into industry *B* to gain the benefits of developing its own brands.[7]

The preceding discussion has suggested a number of alternative hypotheses as to the development of vertical integration. In the real world all of these, plus many other reasons,[8] seem to be responsible for vertical integration. In the succeeding section we shall analyze the ex-tent to which vertical integration exists in food retailing and the main reasons for its development in this industry.

Vertical Integration by Grocery Chains

PRE-1940 INTEGRATION

Vertical integration by food chains is not a recent economic develop-ment. As early as 1904 Kroger acquired a beef-packing plant and by 1911 was operating a hog-packing plant as well. By 1920 Kroger oper-ated 14 manufacturing plants, consisting of 7 bakeries, 2 meat plants, a preserve plant, and 4 other food-processing and packing plants.[9]

A & P was the second most active early integrator. By 1920 it was operating eight plants including three coffee-roasting plants, two bakeries, two food factories, and a cheese warehouse.[10] Three other early integrators were Grand Union, American Stores, and Jewel Tea, which by 1920 operated eight, five, and two plants, respectively.

During the 1920's the original integrators expanded their manufacturing operations, and many additional food chains entered manufacturing. By 1930 A & P was operating 70 plants, Kroger 25 plants, and Safeway 20 plants (Table 49).

In fact, the FTC found that during the 1929–32 period, 13 grocery and meat chains and 12 grocery chains operated manufacturing plants.[11] Although these 25 chains represented only 12 per cent of all grocery and meat chains and specialized grocery chains reporting to the FTC, they accounted for 91.6 per cent of the total sales of the reporting chains.

Chain-manufactured items accounted for 12.1 per cent of total sales of all grocery and meat chains and 5.4 per cent of the sales of chains handling only groceries,[12] or 11.4 per cent of the combined sales of grocery chains and grocery and meat chains.

Between 1930 and 1940, 8 of the 10 chains for which we have comparable data did not increase greatly the number of their manufacturing plants (Table 49). The chief exception was Safeway, which increased its number of plants from 20 to 48; the other main exception was Kroger, which increased its plants from 25 to 34.

EXTENT OF INTEGRATION INTO FOOD MANUFACTURING, 1954 AND 1958

In 1958, 62 of the 165 grocery chains reporting in the FTC's Food Inquiry had entered food manufacturing (Table 28). In 1954, 51 of these chains had begun food manufacturing. In 1958, these chains operated 326 food-manufacturing plants with combined shipments valued at $1.3 billion.

Among the chains, most integration took place in the field of bread baking. In 1958, 45 chains operated a total of 147 bakeries with combined sales of $379.5 million. Coffee roasting was next in importance with 22 chains operating 39 plants with combined sales of $234.4 million. Other leading products were meat packing and dairy products.

To estimate the relative importance of chain manufacturing to total chain sales, we have estimated the total wholesale value of chain sales in 1954 and 1958 for the various commodities shown in Table 28. Several of the product classifications used by the FTC have been combined in Table 29 because they were too ambiguous or overlapping to list separately.

According to our estimates, coffee roasting and baking clearly are

TABLE 28
Food-manufacturing Plants Operated by Food Chains

Kind of establishment	Number of chains reporting		Number of establishments		Total value of shipments (000 omitted)		
	1954	1958	1954	1958	1954	1958 To own stores	To others
Meat-packing plants	5	5	9	9	$ 94,500	$ 98,800	$ 50,200
Prepared meats	9	10	11	13	38,200	54,200	23,900
Poultry-dressing plants	2	4	2	4	3,400	5,200	1,900
Dairy products, except milk	18	19	32	41	34,700	44,200	10,600
Concentrated milks	5	5	12	12	46,800	46,600	10,600
Fluid milk and other products	9	12	22	27	57,500	80,800	15,100
Canning, preserving, and freezing	5	7	11	13	77,000	88,100	11,000
Bread and related products	38	45	126	147	289,500	375,700	3,800
Confectionery and related products	6	7	6	7	31,000	43,000	200
Miscellaneous food preparations and kindred products (except coffee)	11	9	16	14	85,700	84,500	20,800
Coffee, roasted or concentrated	21	22	38	39	316,700	216,300	18,100
Total	51	62	285*	326*	$1,075,000	$1,137,400	$ 166,200

*Some companies reported the same establishment in more than one category.

Source: Federal Trade Commission, Economic Inquiry into Food Marketing, Interim Report, 1959.

74

of the greatest relative importance. In 1958 the value of shipments of chain bakeries was 39.4 per cent as great as the estimated wholesale bakery sales of all chains. The value of coffee manufactured by chain plants was 41.6 per cent as great as estimated total coffee sales of chains. Chains sold to others very small amounts of coffee and bakery goods from their plants. Meat packing was next in importance of products manufactured, although it was relatively much less important than coffee or bakery goods. The total shipments of the chain meat-manufacturing establishments were only 7.9 per cent of total meat sales of chains

TABLE 29
Per Cent of Sales of Chain-produced Products
(Values in Millions of Dollars)

Products	Estimated wholesale value of all chain-store sales*		Value of shipments of food-manufacturing plants of chains†		Per cent of chain-made products as per cent of chain sales		Value of shipments to chains' stores†	Per cent of total chain sales from own plants
	1954	1958	1954	1958	1954	1958	1958	1958
Meats (except poultry and seafoods)	$ 2,097	$ 2,877	$ 132.7	$ 227.1	6.3	7.9	$ 153.0	5.3
Poultry dressing	310	424	3.4	7.1	1.1	1.7	5.2	1.2
Dairy products (except evaporated and condensed milk)	1,020	1,399	92.2	150.7	9.0	10.8	125.0	8.9
Evaporated, condensed, and dry milk	235		46.8	57.2	19.9		46.6	
Canning, preserving, and freezing	947	1,300	77.0	99.1	8.1	7.6	88.1	6.8
Bread and related products	641	963	289.5	379.5	45.2	39.4	375.7	39.0
Coffee	410	563	316.7	234.4	77.2	41.6	216.3	38.4
Confectionery and related products	137	188	31.0	43.2	2.3	2.3	43.0	2.3
Total above	5,797	7,714	989.3	1,198.3	17.1	15.4	1,052.9	13.6
Miscellaneous food preparations and kindred products‡	3,607	4,948	85.7	105.3	2.4	2.1	84.5	1.7
Total food	9,404	12,662	1,075.0	1,303.6	11.4	10.3	1,137.4	9.0
All products (including non-food)	$ 10,842	$ 14,872	1,075.0	$ 1,303.6	9.9	8.8	$ 1,137.4	7.6

*These estimates were computed by estimating total chain retail sales of these products (1) by using the per cent of total sales which various commodities represented as reported in the Super Value Study, and (2) by computing estimated wholesale sales by using the average retail markups for these products as reported in the Super Value Study. This procedure was not used for concentrated milk because the Super Value Study understates significantly the average chain's sales of this product. The wholesale value of chain sales of concentrated milk in 1954 was estimated by assuming that chains sold the same percentage of this product as they did of all food products. This percentage was then applied to the total value of shipments of concentrated-milk plants in 1954 as reported in the Census of Manufacturing, Bureau of Census, U.S. Department of Commerce.
†Federal Trade Commission, Economic Inquiry into Food Marketing, 1959, Chains, Table 7.
‡Excludes non-food products.

in 1958. However, only 5.3 per cent of the chains' meat products were from their own plants. The difference between the preceding two percentages represents meat shipments to other than chains.

The other leading category of chain-manufactured products is dairy products. In 1958 the total value of shipments from chain dairy plants of all kinds amounted to $207.9 million. Evaporated and condensed milk were of greatest relative importance. According to our estimates, in 1954 fully 19.9 per cent of total chain sales of concentrated milk was manufactured in chain plants. This is an especially large percentage in view of the fact that only five chains have concentrated-milk plants. These five chains[13] accounted for 60 per cent of total grocery-chain sales in 1954. Thus, these chains apparently produced about one-third of the concentrated milk sold through their stores. Although we have not made estimates for 1958, apparently these chains produced at least the same relative amounts in 1958 as in 1954.

Other dairy products produced by chain plants accounted for 10.8 per cent of total chain sales of these products. The chains owning these plants did not sell all of this output through their own stores. In 1958, shipments from chain plants through the owners' stores accounted for 8.9 per cent of chain sales.

Other leading food products produced in chain plants were canned goods and confectionery and miscellaneous products.

Between 1954 and 1958 the value of shipments from chain plants increased in all categories except coffee. The latter decrease is due primarily to lower coffee prices in 1958 than in 1954. However, in relative terms, our comparisons suggest that a smaller percentage of chain sales of canned and frozen products, bread, and miscellaneous food products were shipped from chain plants in 1958 than in 1954. Thus, on balance, it appears that no great change occurred in the relative importance of total chain manufacturing between 1954 and 1958.

The most significant change in chain integration during this period was the entry of 11 more chains into food manufacturing. For while their entry did not affect significantly the aggregate value of shipments from chain plants, their entry portends the growing importance of chain integration into food manufacturing. This increase in the number of chains entering food manufacturing reflects the fact that as additional chains grow larger they become potential integrators into more and more industries. Estimates are made below of the number of the top 40 chains which could have integrated into 17 different fields of production in 1957.

Although the number of grocery chains entering manufacturing increased from 25 between 1929 and 1932 to 62 by 1958, apparently the percentage of total grocery products manufactured by chains did not increase significantly over this 30-year period. The 1933 FTC chain-store study reported that chain-manufactured products represented 11.4 per cent of sales of grocery chains and grocery and meat chains. This is not greatly different from the percentages estimated above for 1958 (Table 29). This suggests that during the past 30 years no drastic change has occurred in the relative volume of grocery-chain manufacturing. Whereas additional chains have integrated into manufacturing and the original integrators have entered new fields, the leading integrators in 1929— A & P and Kroger—have declined sufficiently in relative importance[14] to offset the other factors tending to increase the relative importance of chain manufacturing. Moreover, it is possible that today leading chains are manufacturing a lower percentage of some of the leading products they manufactured from 1929 to 1931. For example, of the six chains supplying information on the proportion of their bread sales originating in their own plants in 1931, four reported 100 per cent, one reported 92 per cent, and one reported 90 per cent.[15] Although comparable data are not available, we believe this to be a higher percentage than the leading chains manufacture today.

Another factor tending to reduce the relative importance of chain manufacturing relative to total chain sales is that today chains account for a larger percentage of total grocery-store sales than they did from 1929 to 1931. At that time chains with over three stores accounted for about 37 per cent of total grocery-store sales whereas in 1958 they accounted for about 43 per cent. But even after adjusting for this expansion in the relative volume of chain stores, available data suggest that no drastic change has occurred in the relative volume of chain-store manufacturing over the past three decades.

The most significant change in chain integration into manufacturing between 1929 and 1958 is the number of chains so integrated. Whereas only 25 of the 186 grocery chains reporting in the 1933 FTC study were in manufacturing, 62 of the 165 chains in the FTC's 1959 study were in manufacturing. This represents a significant change in market structure with implications for competitive behavior among grocery chains and between chains and their suppliers.

VERTICAL INTEGRATION OF THE 20 LARGEST CHAINS, 1940–57

Since the 20 largest chains account for most of the food manufacturing carried on by grocery chains, we shall analyze in detail the extent and nature of their operations in this respect.

Since 1940, past integration trends have continued. Most of the early integrators have continued to expand their manufacturing operations and many of the smaller chains have entered various fields of manufacturing. Although our sources often do not give the number of food plants owned by all chains, it is apparent that between 1940 and 1957 a gradual upward trend occurred in the number of plants owned by the 20 largest chains. A rapid increase occurred during World War II. Between 1940 and 1946 the number of plants operated by the 20 largest chains increased from 192 to 237 (Table 50). In the post-war years the number of chain plants apparently declined. Our data show a decline of 13 plants between 1946 and 1948. Since 1951 there has been a substantial increase, from 225 to 306. However, nearly one-third of this increase is due to Safeway's addition of 27 egg-candling plants in 1953.

Unfortunately, it is not possible to know the exact nature of the products produced in different manufacturing plants. Secondary sources often do not define precisely the product made or the manufacturing or packing function performed at chain-operated plants. Moreover, sometimes when chains operate multipurpose plants, the different products produced are not specified. In spite of these shortcomings of published data, it is possible to get a fairly good picture of the leading products manufactured by the top 20 chains.

The following three products were produced by the largest number of the top 20 chains in 1957. Bakery products were manufactured by 15 chains; coffee roasting was carried on by 10 chains; and meat packing and processing were done by 7 chains. The number of chains manufacturing selected items are listed in Table 50. These data indicate that one or more of the top chains have entered the manufacture of all of the leading food products as well as many minor ones. Moreover, it should be noted that in 1957 chains operated 14 plants for which the products were not classified; thus the number of products actually manufactured exceeds those listed in Table 50.

Another important point to note is that while the total number of manufacturing plants operated by these chains increased between 1940 and 1957, there were exceptions to this over-all trend in some commodities. The leading example is meat packing, where the number of plants operated declined from a high of 39 in 1946 to 17 in 1957. Although our data on meat-packing operations are unsatisfactory in that they do not always indicate the nature of operations carried on in these plants, it appears that the chains cut back on their meat-packing operations after World War II.

RELATIONSHIP BETWEEN SIZE OF CHAINS AND VERTICAL INTEGRATION

There is a positive relationship between the size of chains and the extent of their integration into manufacturing. By 1957 the four largest chains on the average had entered 10.5 of 17 important grocery-manufacturing industries, whereas the 5th to 8th largest had entered 4.6 of these industries and the 9th to 20th largest had entered only 1.9 (Table 30). Significantly, the smallest chains experienced the greatest relative increase in integration into these industries between 1942 and 1957.

Especially relevant from the point of view of potential market structure is the question of how large chains must be to integrate into food manufacturing. On the basis of economic theory and industrial experience we would expect the answer to this question to vary considerably depending upon the industry involved; that is, the barriers confronting chains desiring to enter manufacturing industries may be considerably higher in some industries than in others. One means of estimating the number of chains which are potential entrants into food manufacturing is to compare the size of firms which actually enter various industries with the current sales of other chains. Thus, if the smallest chain which integrated into the coffee roasting field had retail sales of $53 million (adjusted to 1957 price levels) in the year it integrated, we might assume that all chains with sales in excess of $53 million in 1957 were potential integrators into this field.[16] On this basis, all 20 of the largest chains were large enough in 1957 to enter the fields of poultry dressing, baking, butter making, ice-cream making, coffee roasting, and meat packing (Table 31). All but 2 of the top 20 chains were large enough

TABLE 30
Integration by the Largest Chains of 1957

Size grouping of chains	Average number of 17 industries* into which chains integrated	
	1940	1957
Four largest	6.5	10.5
Fifth to eighth largest	4.0	4.6
Ninth to 20th largest	.8	1.9
Average of 20 chains	2.6	4.2

*These are the industries listed in Table 31 plus the fluid-milk industry. Because the operations of some plants are not disclosed, this understates the actual extent of integration for chains of all size classifications. This table is based on Moody's whereas Table 31 includes information from other sources.

TABLE 31

Actual and Potential Integrators among the Largest Food Chains
(Sales in Millions of Dollars)

Industry*	Sales of smallest integrator† (1957 dollars)	Actual integrators among top 20		Potential integrators among top 20 of 1957‡		Potential integrators among 21 to 40 largest	
		1940	1957	1940	1957	1940	1957
Poultry dressing¶	$ 30.9	1	2	14	20	0	20
Baking¶	34.9	11	19	14	20	0	20
Butter	50.1	1	4	14	20	0	14
Coffee roasting¶	53.3	8	15	14	20	0	12
Ice cream¶	58.7	1	4	10	20	0	12
Meat packing	68.9	3	7	8	20	0	11
Jams and jellies	137.1	3	6	6	18	0	0
Fruit and vegetable canning¶	139.5	4	4	6	18	0	0
Peanut butter¶	226.3	3	5	5	13	0	0
Cheese	280.3	2	2	5	12	0	0
Salad dressing¶	291.8	4	6	5	12	0	0
Evaporated milk	306.5	3	5	4	12	0	0
Biscuits and crackers¶	736.1	0	3	1	5	0	0
Gelatin desserts¶	817.6	1	3	1	4	0	0
Margarine	1,083.3	0	1	1	3	0	0
Cereal preparation¶	$ 1,989.3	1	2	1	2	0	0

*Comparison was restricted to this group of industries because these were the leading industries into which these chains integrated and for which market concentration data could be obtained which is used in the comparisons in Table 32.

†These are the sales of the smallest chain to have integrated into a particular industry in the year it integrated.

‡Computed by assuming that all chains which had 1940 or 1957 sales (in adjusted prices) greater than the smallest chain entering an industry were also large enough to have integrated.

¶The number of chains integrating into this industry is greater than the number reported in Table 50 because this table is based on information reported in Moody's plus information received from industry and other sources.

Source: Computed from Moody's Industrials, various editions, except as noted in ¶ above.

80

in 1957 to enter fruit and vegetable canning and jam and jelly processing. The two products which fewest firms were capable of producing in 1957 were cereals and margarine.

It is significant that 12 or more of the second 20 largest firms were large enough in 1957 to begin production of 12 products (Table 31). This suggests the large number of chains which were large enough in 1957 to have integrated into the manufacture of various products.

One can appreciate the change which has occurred in the vertical integration structural variable since 1940 by comparing the number of chains which were large enough to have integrated into these industries in 1940 and 1957. The method used to arrive at this figure was to compare the 1940 sales (expressed in 1957 dollars) of these 20 chains with the sales of the smallest integrator into various industries as explained above. This comparison reveals that whereas all of the top 40 chains in 1957 were large enough in 1957 to enter the fields of baking and poultry dressing, in 1940 only 14 of the 40 largest chains of 1957 were large enough to do so. For all other products the number of potential integrators in 1940 was substantially less than in 1957. For example, in 1940, only one chain was large enough to integrate into the manufacture of biscuits and crackers, but by 1957, four other chains were large enough to do so.

Admittedly, this procedure gives only a rough approximation of the increase in the number of potential integrators since 1940. However, these comparisons strongly suggest that the rapid horizontal integration of the smaller chains—especially among the 9th to 20th largest group— has resulted in a very substantial increase in the number of potential integrators into food manufacturing. This might well be one of the most significant structural changes occurring in food retailing since 1940. Although most of these chains are still of quite modest size relative to the nation's traditional leaders, they have assumed sufficient size to do many of the things which hitherto were restricted to only the largest chains.

MOTIVES FOR CHAIN INTEGRATION INTO FOOD MANUFACTURING

As shown above, economic theory suggests a number of alternative reasons for integrating successive production and marketing stages under a single management. Study of a number of the leading industries into which chains have integrated seems to provide illustrations of most of the motives mentioned above.

Chains, by operating their own coffee plants, bakeries, meat-packing plants, and other facilities, conceivably are able to control product quality of all these important items. Hence, the alleged quality-control motive for integration is suggested.

Integration also could conceivably result in some special cost advantages resulting from closer coordination of manufacturing and distribution. For example, packing materials account for a large proportion of coffee-packing costs, ranging from 40 per cent to 75 per cent of these costs.[17] The higher costs are associated with those firms packing larger proportions of their output in vacuum tins. Chain stores, through more direct control of retail store inventories, are in a favorable position to synchronize roasting operations and sales, thereby permitting the use of the lower-price paper bags.

There are many other examples where closer coordination of manufacturing, wholesaling, and retailing may reduce manufacturing costs, result in products more acceptable to chains, and permit better inventory control. However, it should be noted that these kinds of motives for integration are not sufficient reasons for entrance by chains into manufacturing. These economies can often be achieved through nonownership integration between chains and their suppliers, often referred to as specification or contract buying. (Such nonownership integration is discussed below.) Hence, we must look to other motives for ownership integration by chains into manufacturing.

It is the hypothesis of this study that grocery-retailer integration into manufacturing is explained largely by the market structure of the industries supplying grocery retailers. Specifically, grocery retailers have the greatest incentive to integrate into those manufacturing industries in which firms have the greatest amount of market power in selling. The relatively high profits of such industries act as a strong motive for entry by retailers. Moreover, insofar as the main source of market power in such industries results from successful product differentiation due to large advertising expenditures, not only may chains anticipate sharing in the high profits of such industries, but they may enjoy the added benefit of savings on advertising. Several examples will illustrate this hypothesis.

The dairy industry actually is composed of a number of several different industries, each with markedly different market structures. The most competitive is butter manufacturing which in 1954 had 1,172 firms, the 20 largest of which accounted for only 28 per cent of total sales. The evaporated-milk industry, on the other hand, had relatively few firms, and the 20 largest accounted for 97 per cent of industry sales.[18] Moreover, large evaporated-milk concerns sold successfully differentiated products,[19] whereas butter brands enjoy only slight differentiation.

These important differences in market structure are reflected in the differences in the profits in these industries. For example, in 1940, the base year of the present study, the Federal Trade Commission reported an average rate of earnings on investment of 20.95 per cent (before corporate taxes) for a sample of 20 evaporated-milk concerns compared to only 9.93 per cent for a sample of 12 butter concerns.[20] In the same year, the three largest grocery chains averaged 13.4 per cent (before corporate taxes) on their equity capital.[21] Thus, these chains had a definite incentive to enter evaporated-milk manufacturing, whereas it would appear that they would be better off buying butter rather than manufacturing their own.

In addition to this incentive for integration, chains could hope to gain further by saving considerable amounts of the advertising expenses incurred by other evaporated-milk manufacturing firms. In 1940, the above-mentioned evaporated-milk firms spent 2.9 cents of each sales dollar for advertising. This was 51 per cent as great as their net profit.[22] Butter-manufacturing firms spent only .6 per cent of their sales dollar on advertising, which was only 22 per cent as great as their net profits.

Thus, in 1940 grocery chains had a much stronger incentive on both of the above counts to integrate into evaporated-milk manufacturing than into butter manufacturing.

There are many other illustrations of these two incentives for chain integration into manufacturing. For example, for bread and other bakery products a relatively few firms typically supply all the requirements in even large local and regional markets. Moreover, in 1940, firms making bread and bakery products spent 24.24 cents of each sales dollar on selling effort and 2.63 cents on advertising. This compared with net profits of 5.3 cents per dollar of sales.[23]

Similarly, in 1939, 24 coffee processors selling to all classes of customers spent 6.1 cents per dollar of sales on advertising and sales promotion.

The above examples are intended to illustrate, not prove, the hypothesis that chains have a strong profit incentive to integrate into industries in which firms have market power and spend large amounts on advertising and other selling efforts to attain and maintain such power. We shall attempt to test this hypothesis by analyzing the relative extent of integration by chains into 16 industries which chains had entered by 1957.

In our analysis we assumed that there is a perfect correlation between market concentration and market power, and consequently, profit rates.[24]

There obviously are a number of objections to these assumptions. First, market concentration is only one structural variable affecting market performance. However, it does reflect the other main variables —product differentiation and ease of entry. If, as seems realistic to us, one of the main sources of high market concentration in food manufacturing is successful product differentiation, then high concentration reflects successful product differentiation, and the latter in turn constitutes the main barrier to entry.[25]

Some readers may object to the above use of market concentration because of their belief that market conduct is determined largely by factors not related to market structure.[26] We believe, however, that while competitive conduct is determined by a great variety of factors, market structural relationships are the most important such determinants. Therefore, we shall assume that concentration ratios reflect the relative market power of various grocery-manufacturing industries and that consequently, other things being equal, grocery retailers will enter to a larger extent industries with high concentration than those with low concentration. It is more difficult for chains to enter some industries than others; therefore, our analysis must take into account differences in barriers to entry.

The main barriers to entering an industry are the following: (1) economies of scale in manufacturing which require large initial capital outlays by prospective entrants, (2) successful product differentiation by existing firms which new entrants have difficulty duplicating, and (3) unique technical or management know-how and strategic patents.

The generally profitable nature of large chains permits most of them to obtain the necessary funds to buy or build a manufacturing plant of efficient size. They are able to hurdle the last-mentioned barrier to entry by acquiring a going concern. They may overcome, at least partially, the product differentiation barrier once they have established their own brands in which consumers have faith. However, to overcome completely this barrier to entry a chain must be large enough to sell all the output of an efficient-sized plant through its retail stores. Otherwise the chain must either operate a plant smaller than optimum size or else sell some of its products to other retailers on essentially a private-label basis. We may expect considerable variation in the minimum size necessary for a chain to operate an efficient manufacturing plant. For example, in baking, where plants of efficient size are relatively small, we may expect that many chains are large enough to operate their own bakeries; but in evaporated-milk manufacturing we may expect that relatively few are large enough to do so. Consequently, the barrier confronting chains wishing to enter the baking field is lower than it is for chains entering the manufacture of evaporated milk.

Any measure of the relative extent to which chains have entered various industries must take account of the fact that the height of the barriers to entering various food industries varies greatly. In our analysis we shall express the height of these barriers in terms of the size which a chain must be in order to overcome them. To arrive at an estimate of the minimum size necessary for a chain to enter a given industry, we used the actual size of the smallest chain entering that industry. These minimum sizes, expressed in 1957 dollars, are shown in Table 31 for 16 industries. Using these minimum-size figures, we then estimated the number of the top 20 chains which were potentially large enough by 1957 to have integrated into 16 food industries.[27] We then computed a relative integration index for each of these industries. This index is the ratio of integrators to potential integrators and is shown in Table 32.

TABLE 32
Extent of Integration by the Top 20 Chains by 1957

Industry*	Index of relative extent of vertical integration by top 20†	1954 concentration ratios †		
		4 largest firms	8 largest firms	20 largest firms
Poultry dressing	10	17	23	33
Cheese	17	23	28	35
Ice cream	20	33	41	52
Butter	20	14	19	28
Fruit and vegetable	22	28	38	50
Jams and jellies	33	26	36	53
Margarine	33	39	64	93
Meat packing	35	39	48	56
Peanut butter¶	38	54	65	79
Evaporated milk	42	79	86	97
Salad dressing	50	60	70	81
Biscuits and crackers	60	66	73	81
Gelatin desserts	75	80	89	95
Coffee roasting	75	54	68	82§
Baking	95.	80	90	100**
Cereal preparation	100	78	89	98

*These industries are those into which the 20 largest chains had integrated and for which estimates of of market concentration ratios were available.

†This index was computed by dividing the number of the top 20 chains which actually had integrated into these industries by the number of potential integrators as shown in Table 32.

‡These concentration ratios measure the per cent of industry sales accounted for by the 4, 8, and 20 largest firms. Except as noted, concentration ratios are for product and industry classifications for these industries as reported in <u>Concentration in American Industry</u>, Report of Subcommittee on Antitrust and Monopoly, 85th Cong., 1st sess. (1957), Tables 38 and 42. Product classes were used when given.

¶Estimates for 1958 were supplied to us by Market Research Corporation of America, Chicago, Illinois.

§The concentration ratios were obtained by dividing the estimated value of shipments of the top 4, 8, and 20 largest nonchain producers respectively by total value of shipments of the industry minus the value of shipments to chain stores from chain-operated roasting plants and the value of shipments of roasting plants owned by voluntary and cooperative wholesalers.

**Our estimate of top nonchain wholesale bakeries in regional markets. The estimates were made by taking a weighted (by city size) average of the concentration ratios in 19 markets as reported in various newspaper market surveys. Slater reports that even in a market as large as Chicago, 77.2 per cent of <u>all</u> bread sales are accounted for by 10 bakeries (including three chains) and the remaining 22.8 per cent is sold by <u>retail</u> bake shops. Packaged cakes are made by only seven bakeries in this market. Slater reports that in smaller markets practically all bread sales are accounted for by less than 10 bakeries. Charles C. Slater, <u>Baking in America</u>, Vol. II (Evanston: Northwestern University Press, 1956), pp. 130-34.

For example, by 1957 all 20 of the largest chains were large enough to have entered the fields of poultry dressing and baking. However, only two reportedly were still engaged in poultry dressing, whereas 19 had entered the baking field; thus the relative integration index for these two industries was 10 and 95 respectively, indicating the greater relative integration into the manufacture of baked goods.

When this index is correlated with the 1954[28] concentration ratios of the four largest firms in their corresponding industries, the correlation coefficient is .85. When the concentration ratios of the eight largest firms in each industry are correlated with the integration index, the resulting correlation coefficient is .85. When the concentration ratios of the four largest firms are used, the correlation coefficient is .80.[29] A correlation coefficient of .85 means that about 72 per cent of the variation in the degree of chain integration into various industries is explained statistically by differences in the degree of market concentration in these industries.

But just what does this close correlation suggest? Can we use it to project the extent to which the 20 largest chains will integrate into various lines in the future? Unfortunately we cannot, since we have measured only the relationship between the *relative* extent of integration and market concentration at one point in time;[30] we have not demonstrated exactly how much integration is likely to occur in the future. Presumably, however, if other things do not change, that is, if chains simply are given time to adjust to existing market structure conditions, we may expect more of them to enter the heavily concentrated industries; theoretically, as long as market structure conditions do not change, all the potential integrators may eventually enter the most highly concentrated industries.

Integration patterns of the past five years clearly bear out the tendency in this direction. Whereas three of the industries in Table 32 had concentration ratios of less than 50 for the 20 largest firms, not one chain integrated into any of these industries since 1952. On the other hand, one chain actually discontinued its poultry-dressing operations since 1952. Significantly, the concentration ratios of the 20 largest poultry-dressing firms dropped from 58 in 1947 to 33 by 1954. Also, another chain discontinued its cheese operations. Cheese manufacturing too was not very concentrated in 1954, with the share of the top 4 firms declining slightly between 1947 and 1954—from 27 per cent to 25 per cent. The post-1952 integration of the top 20 chains was quite different in the more concentrated industries. Four chains entered the 5 industries with 1954 concentration ratios of between 50 and 79 for the top 20 firms, and 9 entered the 8 industries with concentration ratios exceeding 80.

Of course, the fact that market conditions are continually changing makes prediction of future integration trends hazardous. First, as they become more horizontally integrated, additional chains will become potential integrators, thus increasing the number of chains which have the ability as well as the incentive to enter various industries. This tendency encourages additional integration by chains.

Second, market structures and demand conditions change over time, and as these conditions change, the incentive for chains to enter manufacturing may diminish or increase. For example, although the manufacture of evaporated milk is one of the most concentrated industries included in Table 32, the relative extent of chain integration in this field has declined in recent years. This decline may be traced to the fact that as consumption of evaporated milk fell after 1948, excess capacity developed, causing this industry to become less profitable than it was at the time chains originally started to integrate (all chain integration occurred prior to 1948). Consequently, today chains may be able to buy private-label evaporated milk as cheaply as they can manufacture it themselves. Hence, they do not have as great an incentive to integrate into this field as they originally did, although, on the basis of concentration ratios alone, we would expect them to have a strong incentive.

Third, even if market structures, and consequently profit rates in food manufacturing, remain unchanged, changes in the market structure of food retailing may change. Insofar as such changes influence competitive behavior and profits in food retailing, they may affect earnings in grocery retailing vis-à-vis grocery manufacturers, and hence the relative incentive to integrate into manufacturing.

Finally, although market structure considerations may well be a dominant motive for chain integration into manufacturing, chains doubtless have other motives for owner integration. Especially important may be the fact that existing marketing institutions are not organized to supply chains with the proper quality products or services. This motive may be most common in nonprocessed products. However, even in these products chain integration may be only temporary. (We are inclined to the view that customarily chains are able to get manufactured products of adequate quality.) For example, some western chains allegedly went into livestock feeding after World War II in order to assure themselves of good quality beef. However, as others began providing them with adequate products, they "disintegrated." Similarly, following World War II, several chains integrated into egg candling and farm procurement. But in recent years some chains have encouraged others to perform these functions.[31]

Meat packing provides another example. Apparently various factors motivated the original integration of chains into packing. High market concentration[32] may have been a factor in the period before World War II, and uncertain supplies apparently played a leading role in the wartime integration.[33] But while our data are incomplete on the extent and precise nature of meat-packing operations of chains, apparently in recent years chains have disintegrated from the most competitive sector, meat slaughtering,[34] and expanded in the less competitive and more profitable sector of meat processing such as sausage making.[35]

Although we have not been able to test this hypothesis adequately, we believe that much ownership integration initiated by chains primarily for nonmarket structure reasons will not endure, or at least will decline in relative importance. Chains may be expected to disintegrate from these lines if other firms—operating at essentially competitive returns or at least significantly lower than those of chains—are willing and able to provide them with the services and products they want. Of course, chains may maintain some operations in these fields as a yardstick of the potential profits others may earn. But as a rule, we would expect chains to rely on nonownership forms of integration to achieve most of the advantages of integrated operations, except when market structure considerations are involved.

Vertical Mergers by Grocery Chains, 1940–57

Vertical mergers differ in two important respects from horizontal mergers. First, rather than expand the volume of the existing production or marketing functions of a firm, as is the case with horizontal mergers, vertical mergers involve the extension of a firm into new stages of production or marketing. Second, whereas horizontal mergers result in an increase in the acquiring firm's share of its industry sales—either locally or nationally—vertical mergers do not do so since they involve entry into a new industry.

MOTIVES FOR VERTICAL MERGERS

As with horizontal mergers, there are two levels of motives for vertical mergers. First, firms have an incentive to integrate vertically, and second, they have special incentives to prefer to achieve such vertical growth via merger rather than by internal growth. Since the preceding section deals specifically with motives for vertical growth, here we shall discuss only the motives grocery chains have for growing by merger once they decide that an economic reason exists for their integration into grocery manufacturing.

First, no matter how competent the management of a firm is in performing the functions associated with grocery retailing, it does not necessarily have the technical and other know-how necessary to run a grocery-manufacturing concern. Consequently, it may find that it is preferable to take its first step into manufacturing by the merger route, thereby gaining all the specialized management know-how possessed by a going concern.

Second, sometimes existing firms in an industry have control of special patent or process know-how which would make it extremely difficult for a new firm to enter an industry. Then, the most effective way for a new firm to make its initial entry into such an industry is by acquiring a going concern.

Third, a potential entrant must consider postentry price factors which result from growing internally. There may be a problem of raw-product procurement for a new firm in products such as dairy products or processing vegetables. It may have to offer producers better prices or other payment in order to win the market from existing processors. Purchasing an existing firm would not change raw-product prices.

Fourth, sometimes entry into an industry by internal growth is made extremely difficult because existing firms have succeeded in differentiating their products through extensive advertising. Bain has found that in most of the industries he studied, such differentiation was the greatest barrier confronting new firms wishing to enter an industry.[36] A chain could overcome this barrier were it to enter by acquiring an established firm. But since chains usually sell their manufactured products under their own labels or brands, this is not a serious barrier to entry confronting chains desiring to integrate into many fields of grocery products.

Fifth, sometimes manufacturing facilities can be purchased much more cheaply than they could be built. This is especially likely to be true in industries with excess capacity.

Sixth, the special economic conditions associated with wartime often make merger the only way in which a firm may obtain necessary facilities.

Seventh, sometimes mergers may be more easily financed than internal growth. A firm may be bought through stock exchanges which may be preferable to placing new stock on the market to finance building new facilities.

Often it is impossible to isolate the factor most responsible for a merger. More often than not several of the above considerations, and perhaps others as well, may be involved.

EXTENT AND TYPES OF MERGERS[37]

Since 1940, retail grocery chains made at least 81 vertical acquisitions (Table 51). Sixty-eight of the 81 mergers recorded here were made by the 20 largest retail grocery chains of 1958 (Table 52). The remaining acquisitions involved single vertical acquisitions by eight smaller food chains.

While grocery chains made vertical mergers in all but two years from 1940 to 1958, the greatest amount of merger activity occurred during World War II, when 34 mergers occurred in three years, 1943–45 (Table 51). This represented over 40 per cent of all recorded vertical mergers.

Significantly, this high degree of merger activity corresponded with the high degree of merger activity in manufacturing generally during World War II, which suggests that common causes were present.

Safeway was the most active acquirer; it made 31 vertical mergers during this period. National Food was second with 10 mergers (Table 52).

Vertical merger activity increased from 1954 to 1958. This increase in vertical-merger activity corresponds with the increase in horizontal-merger activity during this period (Table 19). This suggests that the rapid increase in size of a number of chains—due to horizontal mergers —during these years increased their ability and incentive to integrate vertically. Thus, there may be a causal relationship between the rate of horizontal and vertical mergers by grocery chains.

Eighteen of the vertical mergers involved meat packing, slaughtering, and processing plants (Table 52). It is not possible to classify these plants more precisely than this, but most were listed as packing plants. Safeway accounted for 12 of these acquisitions, National Food for 4, and American Stores for 2.

In addition to meat packing, chains acquired 8 bakeries, 7 butter concerns, 6 other dairy firms, 3 canners, 12 wholesale concerns, and 24 miscellaneous concerns.

In addition to the above chain acquisitions, voluntary and cooperative chains made a number of vertical acquisitions from 1948 to 1958. Voluntary chains acquired eight manufacturing plants and four miscellaneous units, and cooperative chains acquired one coffee plant and one dairy plant.[38]

ENTRY OF NEW INDUSTRIES VIA VERTICAL MERGERS

By relating our data on vertical mergers to data presented earlier on the extent of vertical integration by chains, it is possible to estimate the extent to which these chains used mergers to enter new industries.

Between 1940 and 1957, the 20 largest chains added 114 manufacturing plants (Table 50). Since these chains made at least 70 vertical mergers since 1940, this suggests that a high percentage of their additional manufacturing plants were acquired. Of course, it may not be as high as the above comparison suggests since some of the functions of these plants were probably consolidated with other plants or subsequently sold. On the other hand, it may be higher than this if many of these acquisitions involved multiplant firms.

Of special significance is the extent to which these acquisitions involved entry by these chains into new lines. Examples of this are numerous: National Food, American, and Safeway all first integrated into meat packing via mergers. Red Owl entered baking in 1942 by acquiring two bakeries. Similarly, ACF-Wrigley entered baking in 1955 by buying Dutch Oven Baking Co.

In 1950 National Food bought Everywoman's Magazine, Inc. In 1956 Food Fair bought interest in two stamp companies. In 1955 ACF-Wrigley entered frozen-food production by buying the Oklahoma Frozen Food Corporation.

Safeway provides the leading example of using mergers to enter new industries. In 1943 Safeway bought the Guthrie Biscuit Co. and expanded into the Midwest in 1952 by buying the Junge Biscuit Co., Joplin, Missouri. In 1943 Safeway entered the field of gelatin desserts by buying the Jell Well Dessert Co., Los Angeles. In 1948 Safeway entered soap manufacturing by buying the Par Soap Co., Oakland, California. In 1945 Safeway entered butter manufacturing by buying six creameries in Wisconsin, Colorado, and Oklahoma. In 1951 Safeway entered ice-cream manufacturing by buying the Welcome Ice Cream Co., Seattle.

Significantly, even a few relatively small chains entered manufacturing through mergers. In 1954 Schaffer Stores, New York, which had sales under $40 million, acquired the Levering Coffee Co. In 1957 Alpha Beta Stores, which had sales under $60 million, acquired the Olsen Bakery Co. In 1954 Fred Meyer Stores, Portland, Oregon, acquired the Hazelwood Dairy.

Of course, other small as well as large chains made vertical acquisitions which were not reported in the sources used in this study. But while our data on vertical mergers are not complete, it is apparent that food chains have used mergers to enter many fields of manufacturing. In truth, they suggest that this is the usual means used by chains to enter new fields. However, once they have entered a new field via merger, thereafter they grow mainly by internal means.[39]

NONOWNERSHIP FORMS OF VERTICAL INTEGRATION BY RETAILERS

Vertical integration through ownership of manufacturing, wholesaling, and retailing facilities illustrates the ultimate degree of potential control over these stages of production and marketing. Actually, however, there are varying degrees and forms of vertical integration in food distribution besides this extreme case. Some of the objectives and effects of these less complete forms of integration are similar to those achieved when actual ownership of successive stages exists. The unifying economic result of these various integration forms is that certain decisions are made jointly rather than individually; that is, firms in different stages of the marketing system coordinate certain of their operations through formal or informal agreements rather than rely upon open markets—and the prices generated therein—to coordinate their operations.

Mass merchandising encourages retailers to develop some control over their sources of supply in order to get the proper quality and quantity of products necessary to best satisfy their retail demand. This may require close coordination of their retail sales and wholesale procurement policies.

Theoretically they could obtain the necessary products through their price offerings to sellers. But as Collins and Jamison have pointed out, "The complexity of the demand function plus uncertainties surrounding interfirm relationships in general make it difficult, if not impossible, for the producer to translate a price quotation . . . first into the set of product characteristics that is implied and then in turn into a set of production operations to achieve this result."[40] Although they are referring to farm producers in their discussion, their reasoning is also applicable to many other suppliers of food retailers. Hence, retailers often have an incentive to become integrated with their suppliers in some manner.

Data on the extent and nature of nonownership integration by chains are quite sparse. We shall discuss only two aspects of it: specification buying by retailers and so-called private labels. These two are intricately interrelated. In fact, it is our hypothesis that specification buying is largely an outgrowth of retailers' decisions to increase their control over their selling policies, which in many products is intricately related with their policy of developing their own brands and labels. Consequently, we shall begin our treatment of nonownership integration with the origins and bases of private-label selling by food retailers.

RETAILER'S AND MANUFACTURER'S LABELS

Most frequently, private labels or brands are considered to be those labels owned by retailers and sold exclusively in their own stores, as contrasted to so-called nationally advertised brands of manufacturers or distributors. Another distinction sometimes made is that private-label products are those manufactured by food processors under a retailer's label. These distinctions lack precision, however, since sometimes private brands are also virtually nationally advertised by retailers and because retailers may either manufacture or buy from others the products sold under their labels. Thus, for greater distinction, we shall henceforth refer to retailer labels and to manufacturer—including wholesale distributors—labels.

HISTORIC DEVELOPMENT OF RETAILER LABELS

Probably no more controversial aspect exists in food distribution than the so-called battle between retailer labels and manufacturer labels.[41] But the issue really is new only in intensity. As early as 1930, 45.1 per cent of the grocery and meat chains reporting to the Federal Trade Commission inquiry had their own labeled merchandise. These accounted for 96.1 per cent of the stores and 95.8 per cent of the sales for the total reporting food chains.[42]

Kroger Baking Company and A & P accounted for about one-third of the sales of retailer labels for all types of chains with retailer labels in 1930. Kroger had 92 products under their own labels, followed by A & P with 69. Grand Union, National Food, First National Stores, H. C. Bohack, and American Stores each had more than 40 commodities under their own labels.[43]

Early use of retailer labels appears to have been related to commodities manufactured by food chains in their own plants. The use of retailer labels developed at about the same period that food-chain manufacturing was becoming established, and thus may be considered initially as an outgrowth of ownership forms of vertical integration. The commodities most frequently sold by food chains from 1929 to 1932 under their own labels were coffee, bakery products, mayonnaise, tea, dry and smoked meats, and packaged dry groceries;[44] these were also most commonly manufactured by food chains in their own plants.

Retailer labels, as with vertical integration, were related to the degree of horizontal expansion by food chains. Of the chains in 1930 which had retailer labels, the average number of stores per chain was 156, compared to 14 stores for chains which reported having no labels.[45]

In 1958, a sizable percentage of small chains, and even small independent supermarkets, sold groceries under their own labels. According to a *Super Market Merchandising* study, only 16.7 per cent of a sample of 24 independent retailers operating from 1 to 3 supermarkets sold no dry groceries under their own labels (Table 33). About 3 out of 4 chains with from 11 to 99 stores had their own brands on a sizable number of products and only about 17 per cent did not handle any private-label products.

The increasing volume of private-label sales by even small independent supermarkets is indicated by the fact that whereas retailers with from 1 to 3 supermarkets sold only 1 per cent of their dry groceries under their own labels in 1953, by 1958 4.8 per cent of such sales were under their own brands (Table 34). Chains with from 11 to 99 stores increased their private-label sales of dry groceries from about 5.6 per cent in 1953 to about 11.5 per cent in 1958.

TABLE 33
Per Cent of Grocery Retailers
Selling Dry Groceries under Retailer Brands, 1958

Company size	Number of companies	Per cent of companies			Per cent of stores		
		With brands	Limited brands	No brands	With brands	Limited brands	No brands
1-3 stores	24	45.8	37.5	16.7	41.1	43.2	15.7
4-10 "	55	56.3	16.4	27.3	57.4	15.7	26.9
11-25 "	26	76.9	7.7	15.4	78.1	9.0	12.9
26-99 "	22	72.7	9.1	18.2	76.3	11.1	12.6
All companies	127	61.4	17.3	21.3	71.5	12.6	15.9

Source: Super Market Merchandising, Research Report, August 20, 1958

The item most commonly sold under retailer labels is coffee; 87 per cent of the stores with private labels had their own brands of coffee (Table 35). Other leading private-label items are salad dressing, 72 per cent; margarine, 70 per cent; and canned milk, 65 per cent.

Not only is private-label selling commonplace, but most retailers with under 100 supermarkets contemplate adding new items. According to the above cited *Super Market Merchandising* study, companies operating 59.4 per cent of the stores intend to add new private-label products in the future, contrasted to only 2.6 per cent which plan to cut down on their own labels.[46]

The largest chains generally sell a substantial percentage of their grocery products under their own labels, although there is considerable variation among large chains in this respect. The country's largest chain,

TABLE 34
Per Cent of Total Dry-Grocery Sales
of Retailer Brands

Company size	Number of companies	Per cent of grocery sales by chain brands		
		1958	1956	1953
1-3 stores	24	4.8	2.8	1.0
4-10 "	55	7.4	4.5	1.9
11-25 "	26	11.8	6.3	5.2
26-99 "	22	11.3	8.2	5.9
All companies	127	10.7	7.0	5.0

Source: Super Market Merchandising, Research Report, August 20, 1958.

A & P, in 1958 sold an estimated 20 per cent of its groceries under its own brands; on the other hand, the third largest chain, Kroger, sold only 9 per cent of its groceries under its own brands.[47] Other leading chains did the following percentage of their business under their own brands: Safeway, 10 per cent; American, 10 per cent; and Colonial, 25 per cent.[48] Chain-label sales constituted about 15 per cent of the sales of these five large chains.

The above estimates apparently are based only on the importance of chain brands in grocery-department sales. Reliable estimates of the importance of chain brands in total food sales of large chains are not available. It is our judgment, however, that often chain-labeled products constitute over 50 per cent of the food sales of some of the largest chains. We arrive at these estimates as follows: The largest chains often sell the greater part of their meat,[49] eggs, and baked goods under their own labels. These three items alone account for over one-third of the food sales of a typical supermarket. We estimate that about 15 per cent of the other grocery products (excluding produce) of large chains are sold under their own labels.[50]

Finally, we believe that all fresh produce which does not bear a

TABLE 35
Per Cent of Stores Carrying
Their Own Brands of Various Products, 1958*

Product	Per cent of stores	Product	Per cent of stores
Coffee	87	Household	
Salad dressing	72	cleaning supplies	37
Margarine	70	Tea	37
Canned milk	65	Cheese	34
Canned vegetables		Frozen fruits and	
and juices	60	vegetables	34
Ice cream	57	Condiments	33
Canned fruits and		Olives and pickles	32
juices	54	Soft drinks	25
Baked goods	49	Paper goods	25
Peanut butter	48	Beer	22
Jams and jellies	46	Frozen specialties	19
Shortenings	43	Crackers	15
Frozen juices	39	Baking supplies	14
		Gelatin powders	1

*Based on replies from 100 of the companies in Table 34 carrying limited or extensive private labels.

Source: Super Market Merchandising, Research Report. August 20, 1958.

supplier's label should most appropriately be classified as being sold under the chain's brand, since customers generally identify the quality of such products with the chain selling them. Because most produce of large chains bears a chain label or is unlabeled, much of the approximately 10 per cent of produce sales should be classified as chain labeled.

Chain labeling of nonfoods has not proceeded as far as in foods. However, in recent years chains have placed their labels on nonfoods as well. Detergents are probably the leading chain-labeled nonfood.

ECONOMIC BASIS OF RETAILER LABELS

The basic economic motive underlying the development of retailer labels is that they increase the retailers' profit margins. The limited evidence available on this score supports this assertion. In 1930, retailers realized gross profits of 20 per cent or more on 73.9 per cent of their own brands, whereas they realized similar margins on only 48.2 per cent of their national brands.[51] Of course, there was considerable variation on this score among different commodities. For example, a chain enjoyed a 30.5 per cent margin on its brands of ketchup compared to between −3.3 per cent and 12.7 per cent for standard brands; in canned milk, however, chain brands averaged a 16.7 per cent markup compared to 20.3 per cent on standard brands.[52]

Apparently this situation has continued up to the present time. Mr. Norman S. Rabb, Vice President of Stop and Shop, Inc., the country's 14th largest chain in 1958, recently explained some of his company's experiences with its own brands. Whereas Stop & Shop had markups of only 12 per cent and 13 per cent on manufacturers' brands of liquid detergents, it enjoyed markups of 34 per cent, 38 per cent, and 39 per cent on its own brands.[53] Similarly, whereas Stop & Shop had a markup of only 15.9 per cent on manufacturers' brands of bread, it enjoyed markups of 23 per cent on its brands. In this case the absolute markup on its brand was 3.91 cents per loaf compared to only 3.5 cents for manufacturers' brands.[54]

Just why is it that chains are able to enjoy greater profits by developing their own brands? To answer this question we must analyze exactly what is involved when a retail firm develops and sells its own brands rather than selling only the brands of others.

Firms develop brands in order to sell their products at a competitive advantage relative to similar products of other firms. Brands are one form of product differentiation; and when such product differentiation is pronounced, firms are able to develop selling policies which are independent, at least partially, of those of other firms. In other words, this gives firms some market power in selling their products.

Retailers buying from firms with market power built on successful product differentiation have an incentive to develop their own brands for such products in order to enjoy greater freedom in their retail merchandising policies and to enjoy profits similar to those of the profitable manufacturers. As pointed out above, the first retailer brands were developed for chain-manufactured products. And as pointed out in our discussion of ownership integration, when chains buy from industries with highly concentrated market structures, many chains integrate by manufacturing their own brand products.

But chains have an incentive to develop their own brands even if they do not buy from manufacturers with market power. Even where they buy a product from a purely competitive industry like the produce industry, a chain may decide that it can enhance the demand for a particular product such as potatoes—or perhaps its entire produce department—by commanding consumer respect for potatoes sold under its brand. In such a case, retailer branding is not motivated by a desire to share in the profits of product differentiation enjoyed by others, but to develop original power—or competitive advantage—of its own based on brands.

There is an important distinction between retailer branding of products manufactured by firms selling in an oligopolistic market structure and those selling in a competitive one. In the former, retailers may have to produce their own products whereas in the latter they can, and usually will, prefer to buy them from others rather than manufacture their own products. The logic underlying this hypothesis is that firms operating in a competitive structure will likely earn lower returns from producing the product than chains expect on their investments. Consequently, chains may enjoy the advantages of selling a differentiated product bought from firms which do not enjoy market power based on product differentiation.

Once chains have developed a line of differentiated products, they are in a position to place their brand on practically any additional products with no additional advertising expenses. This places them in an extremely favorable position vis-à-vis their suppliers. They are in the unique position of being able to integrate into many lines of manufacturing because they can overcome the product differentiation barrier to entry, probably the most formidable barrier to entry confronting other prospective entrants.[55] But chains need not actually manufacture their own products to take advantage of their product differentiation. In fact, as our preceding treatment of ownership integration by chains suggests, they are most likely to integrate through ownership of manufacturing facilities into the most concentrated industries, or those with the most market power. In industries with a fringe of "independent" firms willing to sell undifferentiated products, chains might ordinarily be expected to buy their products on specification from some of these independents. Independents are willing to do so because chains can pay them as much as or more than they can receive from selling under their own brand. Chains can do so because they need spend considerably less for advertising and promotion than would a food manufacturer. Moreover, by coordinating closely the manufacturer's and the chain's operations through a form of nonownership integration, other manufacturing and marketing economies may be achieved which permit the chain to pay the supplier a better price than he could obtain elsewhere.

Of course, it is possible that chains may be able to buy some requirements even from firms which have developed their own brands. First, big suppliers may be willing to sell some of their output under retailer labels at prices below that sold under their own brands in order to forestall entry by chains into manufacturing. This is allegedly the reason Ralston-Purina gave A & P special discounts on private-labeled corn flakes during the 1930's. A & P told Ralston-Purina that it could save 21 cents per case on the price it was paying Ralston by manufacturing its own flakes. Ralston finally offered A & P an additional allowance of 10 cents per case, for a total of 17.5 cents a case. A & P did not build its own plant.[56]

Another reason why large firms may sell under retailer labels is the recognition that if they do not, other firms will; and if the other firms expand their capacity it may create excess capacity in the manufacturing industry, especially if retail-label sales are expanding at the expense of manufacturers' labels. Such excess capacity may in turn lower profit margins for all manufacturers as each firm strives to maintain capacity. Under these threatened circumstances large manufacturers may enter the retailer-label business on a large scale, while at the same time maintaining and even attempting to expand sales under their own brands.

Specification Buying and Retailer-Supplier Integration

It is important to recognize the role that specification buying plays when retailers purchase for sale under their brands. At the outset it should be recognized that as soon as one buys an unbranded product, one must buy on some physical specification basis. In other words, whereas a chain simply may order a certain number of cases of Del Monte peas of a certain can size, if it buys peas for its own labels it must use some physical specifications to describe the product purchased. Thus, specification buying is an almost inevitable by-product of buying unbranded merchandise. Of course, chains may decide that they want products of a certain variety and quality in which case they may compel suppliers to meet these specifications in order to sell to chains. This reason is presumably based on the fact that existing manufacturers are not supplying retailers with merchandise of adequate quality.

It is not yet clear how much chain specification buying from food manufacturers is motivated by the latter reason. This point needs more study.

Specification buying of fresh fruits and vegetables has important implications for producers, shippers, and wholesalers. Specification buying in fresh products apparently developed at about the time retailers began buying some of these requirements directly from producers and shippers rather than from the more traditional wholesale markets.

Direct buying resulted when retailers found that they could perform the wholesaling function for these products more efficiently than could existing wholesale agencies. Moreover, by prescribing the specifications of the products they purchased, they were able to improve product quality as well.

This development is not new in food retailing. Hoffman and Bevan described and appraised this practice as it existed in the mid-1930's.[57] They reported that direct buying from producers by chains was, in part, an effort to obtain fresh products of uniform quality in standardized packages. They concluded that chains enjoyed significant economies from integrating the functions of wholesaling and jobbing with that of retailing.

Folz recently completed an interesting study of the current procurement practices by large chains.[58] Folz attributes many of the procurement policies of grocery retailers to the rise of the modern supermarkets. He finds that while buying practices of chains differ in many details, "there is a strong and persistent tendency to buy direct."[59]

Although supermarkets may place special emphasis on direct buying and specification buying of fresh fruits and vegetables, we believe the primary bases for these practices in the produce field, as with manufactured products, are to be found in the organizational characteristics of large-scale retailing firms rather than large-scale stores (supermarkets). Hoffman and Bevan's description of the manner in which large chains had integrated retailing and wholesaling in the mid-1930's sounds very similar to what Folz found over 20 years later. And since supermarkets were relatively unimportant in the early 1930's, even among large chains,[60] apparently direct buying was an outgrowth of large-scale operations of retail firms rather than supermarkets per se.

Thus, we believe the increasing importance of direct buying and specification purchasing, and the generally increased vertical integration of activities from farmers to retailers, are to be explained, in the first instance, by the changing degree of horizontal integration of grocery firms. As with chain-ownership integration into manufacturing, the most significant changes of recent years are attributable largely to the growing number of chains—as well as affiliated independents—which are becoming sufficiently horizontally integrated to take advantage of various forms of the vertical integration.[61]

It is important to note the parallels between specification buying of fresh products, and manufactured products sold under retailer labels. Whenever chains buy directly from producers rather than take what is offered in wholesale markets, they must use physical specifications to describe the products they intend to purchase. Moreover, when they become integrated with suppliers on some kind of nonownership basis, they almost certainly will attempt to get a supply of products which best suits their demand at retail. Thus, while specification buying of some variety is an almost inevitable concomitant of direct buying, it usually assumes special importance as retailers and producers integrate their operations in some manner. Then chains are likely to encourage producers to control certain of their production and marketing operations so as to satisfy certain product attributes which retailers think are especially important.

Entry of Grocery Wholesalers and Manufacturers into Grocery Retailing

Although grocery retailers have integrated into grocery wholesaling and manufacturing for over 50 years, it is only in recent years that manufacturers have begun integrating into grocery retailing. Apparently they have achieved this integration largely by acquiring existing chains. No reported acquisitions of this type occurred between 1940 and 1948. Since then, however, at least 5 grocery manufacturers acquired complete or partial control of at least 40 grocery retailers. At the time these firms were acquired they operated 1,420 stores and had combined sales of $1,110 million. Moreover, at least 9 grocery wholesalers also made acquisitions from 1948 to 1958; they acquired 131 retail stores with combined sales of $63.2 million (Table 36).

The most notable such acquisition was the purchase by George Weston, Ltd., of a 37 per cent stock interest in National Food in 1955. George Weston, Ltd., controls a large number of food-manufacturing concerns in Canada and the United States and is especially prominent in baking. National Food was the country's 5th largest chain in 1955 and had sales of $576 million in that year. In 1953 George Weston, Ltd., also bought a controlling interest in Loblaw, Inc. Loblaw was the country's 13th largest chain and had sales of $166 million. By 1958 National Food and Loblaw had combined sales of over $1 billion, which were greater than those of all but the 3 largest chains. National Food and Loblaw made at least 14 retail acquisitions since being acquired by George Weston, Ltd.

Consolidated Foods apparently is the next most important integrator into food retailing. Beginning in 1956 it acquired Piggly Wiggly Midwest Company with 34 stores and Klein Supermarkets with 23 stores. In 1958 it acquired the Lawson Milk Company which had previously integrated into food retailing and was operating 175 retail stores in Ohio. In 1959 Consolidated acquired Quality Food Stores which operated 12 super-markets in Minnesota. These acquisitions have so transformed Consolidated's operations that by 1959 retail sales accounted for over one-third of its annual sales of about $360 million.[62]

Arden Farms, the country's 7th largest dairy processing firm in 1958, began integrating into food retailing in 1948 through the purchase

TABLE 36
Grocery Retailers Acquired by Grocery Manufacturers,
  Grocery Wholesalers, and Nongrocery Firms, 1948-58
  (Sales in Millions of Dollars)

Nature of acquiring firms	Number of acquiring firms	Number of acquired retail firms*	Number of retail stores acquired	Sales of acquired retailers in year of acquisition
Grocery manufacturers	5†	40	1,420	$ 1,109.6
Grocery wholesalers‡	9	.. ‡	131	63.2
Nongrocery firms	5	16	308	445.6
Total	19	56	1,859	$ 1,617.2

*This table includes stores acquired by chains subsequent to the latter's acquisition by grocery manufacturers and nongrocery firms. Ten acquisitions with combined sales of $886 million shown in this table do not appear in Table 19.

†Consolidated Foods, which acquired three chains from 1948 to 1958, is listed as a manufacturer although its wholesale and man-ufacturing operations are of about the same magnitude.

‡These data are based on the Federal Trade Commission, Ec-onomic Inquiry into Food Marketing, Interim Report. This source did not report the number of acquired firms.

Sources: Supermarket News, Moody's Industrials, Progressive Grocer.

of Mayfair Markets. Mayfair subsequently purchased at least 17 grocery retailers and by 1958 had sales of $118 million. By 1958 it had become the country's 21st largest chain.[63]

An interesting example of food processors integrating into food retailing is the creation of P & C Food Markets, Inc., Syracuse, New York, by several farmer cooperatives. Three farmer cooperatives—Co-op G.L.F. Exchange, Inc., Ithaca, New York; Producers Livestock Association, Inc., Columbus, Ohio; and Dairymen's League Cooperative Association, Inc., New York—currently own about 90 per cent of the voting stock of P & C.[64] P & C stock was originally held by over 20 different farmer cooperatives.[65] In 1958, P & C was operating 39 supermarkets.

This development of group integration into food retailing is comparable to the action followed by groups of chains and independents which join in integrating into food wholesaling and manufacturing. And the basic motive is the same—to achieve larger size; unless a processor is diversified, it must buy an extremely large chain in order to sell significant quantities of its products through chains.

In addition to the above retail acquisitions by grocery manufacturers, at least nine grocery wholesalers made retail acquisitions from 1948 to 1958. These acquisitions were made by wholesalers which sponsored voluntary chains. We have discussed this development previously.

We estimate that the retail chains controlled or completely owned by grocery wholesalers and manufacturers had sales of about $1.5 billion in 1958, or about 8 per cent of total sales of chains with 11 or more stores.

MOTIVES FOR INTEGRATION BY MANUFACTURERS AND WHOLESALERS

Changes in the structure of food retailing apparently underlie the recent integration into retailing by manufacturers and wholesalers. As discussed below, one of the apparent effects of these changes is to increase competitive behavior in manufacturing, which in turn decreases manufacturing profits relative to food retailing. Consequently, manufacturers may view integration into retailing as a partial escape from the struggle for shelf space. They, in effect, buy their own market when they integrate into retailing.

The motive in wholesaling is somewhat comparable, although the wholesaler often is in an even worse competitive position than the manufacturer. As chains become large and perform their own wholesaling function, many existing wholesalers must either integrate into retailing or perish. As discussed below, many wholesalers have met this challenge through nonownership vertical integration by establishing voluntary chains. But apparently some feel that this is not the final solution to their problem and have therefore actually integrated into retailing through ownership means. The extent of this development is not yet clear.

Conglomerate Relations in Grocery Retailing

A number of nonfood firms have entered food retailing in recent years by acquiring food chains. Such acquisitions involved neither horizontal nor vertical integration. They are most appropriately classified as "conglomerate" mergers. Edwards has defined the conglomerate firm as "one whose various activities are not bound together by the appropriate intermediate activities that would give coherence."[66]

The leading example of conglomerate mergers in grocery retailing is the purchase by ACF-Brill Motors in 1955 of the 60-unit Wrigley chain with sales of about $100 million. ACF-Wrigley subsequently merged with at least six other retailers with combined sales of over $150 million. Other firms making conglomerate acquisitions are Magic Chef, Inc., a range manufacturer which in 1957 purchased a 6-unit chain; Williams-McWilliams Industries, Inc., a harbor-dredging firm which in 1957 acquired a 52-unit chain with sales of $30 million; and Chicasha Cotton Oil Co., which in 1957 acquired two chains.

Since 1940, there have been at least 16 conglomerate mergers involving grocery firms with combined sales of about $450 million when acquired (Table 36). Significantly, none of these acquisitions occurred before 1955.

Apparently the basic reason nonfood firms enter food retailing is because of its relatively high earnings. For example, Magic Chef cited as its reason for entering food retailing the desire to offset losses which it had incurred in range manufacturing. In 1956, Magic Chef's losses amounted to $1,173,733.[67] Chicasha Cotton Oil Co., which in 1957 acquired two chains, earned only 4.78 per cent (after taxes) on its equity capital in 1956. Similarly, Williams-McWilliams enjoyed net earnings of 9.58 per cent. These earnings compare with average net earnings of 35 chains in 1956 of 15.5 per cent,[68] certainly a significantly more promising area for investment.

The effects on market structure of conglomerate mergers are difficult to evaluate. In some cases they would seem to have little effect, as for example, when the acquiring firm later divests itself of the activities it originally engaged in. This has happened in the case of both ACF-Brill and Magic Chef, both of which recently disposed of the nongrocery portions of their operations.

Perhaps the main effect of conglomerate mergers to date has been to bring about changes in the management of acquired chains and make available greater funds for expansion. For example, since acquiring

Wrigley in 1955, ACF-Wrigley has acquired at least six other chains, and by 1958 had sales of $383 million; this made it the country's 12th largest chain.

Since all recorded conglomerate acquisitions occurred after 1955, it is too early to determine their effects on the growth of the individual retailers involved, much less on market structure in general. We must, therefore, conclude that, up to the present, conglomerate mergers have had little effect on the structure of grocery retailing.

CHAPTER SIX

Vertical Integration
By Affiliated
Independents

By 1958 affiliated independent retailers accounted for 73 per cent of total sales of independents (Table 45). These affiliations take two forms: (1) voluntary groups or chains, wherein a grocery wholesaler provides a variety of services for a group of affiliated independent retailers, and (2) cooperative groups or chains, wherein a group of independent retailers affiliate with one another to achieve some advantages of large-scale buying, advertising, and merchandising through ownership of a wholesale unit.

Both forms of affiliation represent attempts of independents to achieve some of the advantages of integrated operations achieved by corporate chains. These affiliations involve both horizontal and vertical integration—horizontal integration insofar as retailers affiliate in performing certain of their retail merchandising functions, and vertical integration in that they integrate the retailing and wholesaling functions and, to a minor extent, even the manufacturing function.

An important difference between voluntary and cooperative affiliations is that in the former, wholesalers are the integrators; that is, they take the initiative in setting up their groups. In cooperative groups the retailers are the integrators; that is, they own jointly wholesaling and manufacturing facilities and operate them for their benefits. Moreover, voluntary chains represent a form of nonownership integration in that they are bound together through contracts and other nonownership means, whereas cooperative chains involve a form of partial ownership integration in that affiliated retailers actually own jointly their wholesale operations while integrating some of their retail operations on a nonownership basis.

In this chapter we shall analyze briefly the extent of vertical integration of voluntary and cooperative chains. This is important because of the current market structure of grocery retailing. Also, the success of independents in achieving the advantages of vertical integration will determine in part their future success in competing with corporate chains, which in turn will affect the future market structure of grocery retailing.

Services of National Organizations of Affiliated Independents[1]

The affiliated-independent class of food retailers has three structural levels of organization. At the top are national organizations which sponsor wholesalers and which solicit new groups. At the intermediate level are the local wholesale units, the core of the affiliated independent groups. The third level is comprised of the independent retailer members. In the cooperative groups the wholesaling function is not distinct in ownership as with the voluntary groups, since retailers own the wholesale warehousing organization and operate their stores in a partially coordinated manner with the wholesale unit.

There exists as much difference in services and in operating procedures within each type of organization as exists between voluntary and cooperative chains. Therefore, in examining the functions of national organizations, it serves little purpose to distinguish between them by form of organization except in order to distinguish the ownership of the two types of organizations. Some would consider this to be a primary and major difference between the two.

Basically, both types of overhead organization are types of national trade associations to which individual retailers are only indirectly affiliated.[2] Direct affiliation exists between wholesalers and the overhead national organizations, and retailers are affiliated directly with the local wholesaler. The tie between superior levels and lower levels is derived from contractual arrangements which specify obligations of each, services to be provided, and fees to be paid.

As national "trade associations," the overhead organizations take part in diverse activities which are designed to further the interests of retailers affiliated with wholesaler-members of the national organizations.

Activities which are carried on by national associations which correspond to those of trade associations are "obtaining and furnishing information with respect to pending and proposed legislation, and developing promotional and educational activities for the mutual advancement of members."[3] Nearly all conduct retailer-education programs through which members are informed on current developments and trends in retailing. Retailer education is conducted largely through workshops held in conjunction with wholesalers and through house organs. Objectives of educational workshops are to bring to the attention of retailers new methods and ideas of operation and means by which efficiency and sales can be improved. Attention is given to methods of displaying merchandise, check-out procedures, and financial accounting.

Many offer engineering assistance to wholesalers and retailers, ranging from remodeling of existing retail units, to planned store layouts for modern supermarkets. Through such architectural services, uniformly designed structures are built by retailers, with efficiency in operation and group identity in mind.

Other services provided by national headquarters often include local advertising layouts, control of brands, group insurance, accounting services, and special promotion campaigns.

Retailers pay fees to the national organizations for services performed. Retailers who are affiliated with the Independent Grocers Alliance pay directly to the national organization a charge of one dollar a week. In addition, wholesaler-affiliates of IGA pay for services of central IGA personnel on a per diem basis whenever these services are used. It appears, however, that a major source of IGA revenues results from ownership of IGA labels by the central organization for which a fixed charge is made. This charge becomes a part of the cost of merchandise purchased by retailers under the IGA labels from wholesalers.

No initial membership fee is required of retailers for joining Cooperative Food Distributors of America. Wholesalers, however, are assessed an annual fee based on their wholesale dollar volume. This ranges from $125 to $1,000 depending on sales.[4] Since CFDA wholesale houses are retailer-owned, the fee is in essence paid by retailers.

Some national overhead groups appear to go beyond the common run of trade associations, however. National overhead groups sponsoring wholesalers with which retailers form voluntary associations for procuring supplies and receiving services have a deeper vested interest in retailer members than do most of the trade associations.

The exact nature of current buying activities of national associations is difficult to determine. Not one states that brokerage activities or services are performed, and most state that no buying of merchandise is carried on for resale to wholesalers.

Brokerage activities of national associations came under scrutiny of the Robinson-Patman Act by the Federal Trade Commission in 1953. As a result IGA reportedly ceased brokerage operations on July 23, 1953.[5] Evidently this action was a curtailment of activities rather than complete elimination of buying operations, since IGA headquarters employs four meat selectors who buy meat for all wholesalers who desire this service.[6] Furthermore, IGA claims to have "a combined buying power second only to the largest national chain . . . ,"[7] a claim difficult to accept in view of assertions by IGA headquarters that they do not buy for wholesaler affiliates.

A Red and White Corporation booklet states that the corporation "handles all quantity and net buying arrangements which are available to wholesalers on a national basis. There are a number of products which come under quantity discounts which are handled. The Corporation takes title to the merchandise and rebills it to the wholesalers."[8]

Thus, while some national organizations may not procure merchandise for their wholesaler affiliates, the examples cited suggest that at least for some products, certain organizations may be so engaged. Precise information on this aspect of national organization activities would be best obtained through official government inquiry.

Local Voluntary and Cooperative Chains

The preceding discussion dealt mainly with the national overhead organizations of affiliated groups. Although these units perform some important functions for their affiliates, most wholesale functions are performed by the local or regional sponsors of retailer groups. For example, in 1956 Cooperative Food Distributors of America had 91 local cooperative groups affiliated with it, and these local units were comprised of about 22,000 independent retailers.

It is with the operations of these local voluntary and cooperative groups that we shall be most concerned here.

TYPES OF MERCHANDISE AND SERVICES SUPPLIED

One indication of the effectiveness of affiliated groups is the extensiveness of the functions they provide and the extent to which affiliated retailers take advantage of them. The recent FTC food inquiry provides some revealing information along these lines. According to its findings, there are relatively few functions which are provided by the majority of voluntary and cooperative groups (Table 53).

Purchasing of dry groceries and advertising services seem to be the main services provided: 98.6 per cent of all cooperative and 90.3 per cent of all voluntary sponsors purchase dry groceries, and 84.7 per cent of the cooperatives and 90.3 per cent of the voluntary sponsors provide advertising services. Other functions provided by over 50 per cent of the voluntaries are warehousing, purchasing nonfoods, and purchasing frozen foods. Over 50 per cent of the cooperatives provide services for the following other items: warehousing, purchasing nonfoods, providing managerial advice, free delivery, and store engineering.

Perhaps even more important than the services offered by wholesalers is the number of retail stores which actually receive various services. Purchasing of dry groceries is the most important function utilized by retailers affiliated in both voluntary and cooperative groups. Next in importance for both types is advertising services. Relatively few retailers take advantage of most other services. For example, dairy products are purchased for only 40.4 per cent of the cooperative affiliates and 30.6 per cent of the voluntary affiliates; the comparable percentages for meat procurement are 18.3 per cent and 17.6 per cent, and for produce procurement 27.2 per cent and 23 per cent. Products in these three product classes constitute about 40 per cent of total sales in modern supermarkets.

There do not seem to be large differences between voluntary and cooperative members in terms of the percentages of retailers purchasing various types of products. However, more voluntary retailers seem to be receiving management assistance of various types. For example, whereas 27.2 per cent of the cooperative retailers receive assistance in store engineering, 42.4 per cent of the voluntary retailers get such assistance. The respective percentages for other services are as follows: management advice, 36.7 per cent and 55.5 per cent; floor display aids, 21.2 per cent and 32.8 per cent; accounting system, 10.1 per cent and 13.5 per cent; and record-keeping aids, 15.2 per cent and 20.8 per cent.

Data from another source suggest that a higher percentage of voluntary and cooperative groups supplies affiliates with products than the FTC study indicates (Table 54). For example, whereas the FTC found that only 19.4 per cent of the cooperative groups and 24.4 per cent of the voluntary groups purchased meat for members, the *Index of Voluntary Chains and Retailer Cooperatives* reported that in 1956, 60.3 per cent of the voluntaries and 39 per cent of the cooperatives supplied this service (Table 54). This source also reports higher percentages for frozen foods, produce, dairy products, and bakery products. We have not been able to reconcile these differences, but it is our judgment that the FTC's compilation represents the most accurate indication of the functions provided by these groups.

EXTENT OF PRIVATE-LABEL MERCHANDISING

As indicated previously, all large and most other corporate chains have developed their own brands or labels for some of their products. Development of a successful retailer label is generally recognized as an important basis of chain success. Consequently, the extent to which affiliated independents have developed such labels is an important indicator of their relative success.

About 50 per cent of the voluntaries and 40 per cent of the cooperatives reportedly carried a full line of private-label merchandise (Table 55). All but about 17 per cent of the remainder carried a limited line of private-label merchandise. However, these references must be to a full line of *dry-grocery* products, since relatively few handled a full line of products. As shown in Table 56, only 4.5 per cent of all voluntaries carried all six of the product lines listed in Table 54. Cooperatives were not significantly different in this respect. Fully 64 per cent of the voluntaries and 70 per cent of the cooperatives carried only three or fewer of these product lines.

An indication of the *degree* of integration in an affiliated group is the extent of centralized control of certain important merchandising decisions. The items listed in Table 57 suggest that such control often is less complete among affiliated independents than in chain organizations. For example, 72 per cent of those affiliated in voluntary chains and 63 per cent of those in cooperative chains must stock brands promoted by the central group. On these and other related decisions many groups apparently have no control over decisions of individual retailers. This suggests that such groups do not operate in as integrated a manner as corporate chains. Moreover, on the basis of this limited evidence, it appears that cooperative chains are somewhat less closely integrated than are voluntary chains.

ASSISTANCE FOR EXPANSION

Corporate chain stores often have separate divisions or subsidiaries specialized in site selection and financing of new stores. Often chains sell their new stores upon completion to investment firms from whom the chains in turn secure a long-term lease. This procedure permits chains to expand rapidly because they need not tie up their funds in real estate and store buildings.

Unless voluntary and cooperative chains develop comparable services for their members, independent retailers wishing to expand may be at a serious disadvantage compared to chains. Consequently, a number of affiliated groups have attempted to provide these services.

By 1958 many sponsors of voluntary chains and cooperative chains helped select sites, obtain credit for new stores, and obtain leases (Table

58). A much smaller percentage of unaffiliated wholesalers provided such services.

Some independent retailers not only have become integrated with the wholesaling function, but through their voluntary or cooperative wholesalers have integrated back into manufacturing. By 1958, 29 voluntary wholesalers owned a total of 44 plants with sales of $42.8 million, and 7 cooperative wholesalers owned 9 plants with total sales of $12.9 million (Table 59). Thus in 1958 the total shipments of manufacturing establishments owned by sponsors of voluntary and cooperative chains amounted to $55.7 million. Significantly, this was only about 4.3 per cent as great as total shipments from manufacturing plants owned by 62 corporate chains (Table 29).

Twenty of the 44 voluntary plants and 5 of the 9 cooperative plants were coffee-roasting plants. The cooperatives' other 4 plants and 10 of the remaining voluntary plants made dairy products. Voluntaries also had 4 bread, 6 canning, and 4 miscellaneous plants.

The motive for this backward integration by these groups is the same as that of corporate chains. Simply put, they can improve their profit position by manufacturing these products rather than by buying them from others.

It is significant that voluntary and cooperative chains integrated into those industries which are relatively easy to enter for retailers with their own labels. As estimated earlier, bread baking, coffee roasting, most dairy products, and canning are industries which are relatively easy to enter. But voluntaries and cooperatives have not entered any of the most difficult industries to enter, for example, the fields of biscuits and crackers, salad dressing, gelatin desserts, and cereals. Thus, not only are affiliated independents integrated into manufacturing on only about one-twentieth the scale of corporate chains, but they are not at all integrated into what probably are the most profitable areas of grocery manufacturing. This may place them at a distinct disadvantage in competing with large corporate chains which are able to enter such industries.

Apparently voluntary and cooperative chains, like corporate chains, have used mergers extensively when integrating into manufacturing. According to the FTC study, sponsors of voluntaries acquired eight manufacturing firms and cooperative chains two manufacturing firms.[9] Thus they apparently obtained most of their increased manufacturing facilities from 1954 to 1958 via the merger route.

RELATIVE EFFICIENCY OF VOLUNTARY AND COOPERATIVE CHAINS

Several criteria can be used to measure the effectiveness of voluntary groups and cooperative groups. One criterion which may be useful for some purposes is the comparison of wholesaler margins of affiliated groups with those of nonaffiliated general-line wholesalers. This indicates to some extent whether affiliated groups have achieved some advantage by integrating into wholesaling. In view of the objectives which spurred independent retailers to affiliate horizontally, however, this measure is only partially satisfactory.

A more effective criterion would be to compare the efficiency of affiliated groups with regional and national corporate chains at both the wholesale and retail levels in order to determine the success of the affiliated groups. In this context, success refers to the degree to which these groups have equaled operating ratios or margins of corporate chains at the wholesale level, and the extent to which these are reflected in competitive retail prices. Consequently, comparisons of retail prices provide an indirect, yet plausible, criterion in view of the objectives of affiliated independents to match corporate chain operations which would reflect in competitive retail prices.

Below we shall compare (1) operating margins of voluntary, cooperative, and full-service wholesalers, and (2) retail food prices of independents and chains.

COMPARATIVE WHOLESALING EFFICIENCY

Historically, retailer-cooperative wholesale operations have been conducted at lower cost than has voluntary-chain wholesaling. In fact, the Chain Store Inquiry of the 1930's concluded on this point as follows:

> Higher wholesaler-retailer (voluntary chain) operating expense characterizes not only the figures of the total operating expense, but nearly every item, regardless of whether the figures are compared directly or on the basis of percentage of sales.

> Depending upon the year, group, and item, these detailed expenses range up to in excess of seven times the corresponding cooperative-retailer costs and quite commonly exceed them from one to three times.[10]

According to the U.S. Census of Business, in 1935 operating expenses of cooperative wholesalers averaged only about half those of voluntaries. In recent years, the differences between voluntaries and cooperatives have narrowed (Table 60).

According to these data, voluntary-chain wholesale operations in 1954 showed some advantage over independent full-service wholesalers, a position achieved only in recent years.

Direct comparisons of wholesaling costs of affiliated groups with corporate chains cannot be made, since data on corporate chains do not distinguish wholesaling costs from other costs of their operations; but generally it is conceded that corporate-chain costs, on the average, are lower than for averages of affiliated groups.

COMPARISON OF RETAIL FOOD PRICES BY TYPE OF STORE OWNERSHIP

Several studies of grocery-store prices have indicated that chain prices are generally lower than those of unaffiliated, affiliated, and independent stores.

Converse found that in the Champaign-Urbana area, corporate-chain food prices in 1937 were lower in nine commodity groups (excluding meats) than in independent stores.[11]

A second study in 1953 in Champaign-Urbana came essentially to the same conclusion, except that chain-store prices were not consistently lower for all nine commodity groups. Corporate chains were found to have lowest price for poultry, fruits, and vegetables. Voluntary-chain and independent stores were found to have lowest prices on meats.[12] It was not specified, however, whether there was a quality difference in meats, a factor which could reflect the price differences.

From 1953 to 1954 a similar study was conducted by Hirsch in the St. Louis market.[13] Differences in costs of a "basket" of food purchased in five types of food stores were determined for typical purchases of urban wage earners and clerical workers.

A given dollar expended for the market basket purchased 19 per cent more in the national chain, 12 per cent more in the local chain, 11 per cent more in the sectional chain, and 10 per cent more in the voluntary chains as compared with prices in the independent store.[14]

Research cited suggests that voluntary chains have not succeeded in achieving their objective of retail prices equal to corporate chains. It does indicate, however, that retail prices of voluntary and cooperative chains are significantly lower than those of unaffiliated independent food stores. Actually, the advantage of corporate chains over independents in terms of price is revealed further in a number of other studies.[15]

Inability of independents, including affiliated groups, to meet the retail prices of corporate-chain stores can be attributed to several factors. More efficient wholesaling by corporate chains is one factor leading to lower prices. Another important factor is the manufacturing of merchandise by corporate chains into which only a few affiliated groups have integrated. A third is direct volume buying by chains and volume discounts which result in lower procurement costs. Related to this is the more extensive and successful use of private-label merchandise by corporate chains. In the St. Louis study Hirsch concluded that "consumers buying in the national chain store could have bought food baskets of identical quality (on chain labels) at even greater savings than is indicated in this study." [16]

These findings suggest that (1) affiliated independents are doing a better job than unaffiliated independents, (2) independents affiliated in cooperative chains are performing the wholesaling function more cheaply than are voluntary wholesalers, (3) voluntary wholesalers appear to be performing more services and are more closely integrated with their retailers than are cooperative groups, and (4) corporate chains appear to be performing the wholesaling function more efficiently, are more fully integrated into manufacturing, and have developed their own labels more extensively than have either voluntary or cooperative groups.

Insofar as these relationships continue into the future, we must expect unorganized independents to continue to lose ground to both affiliated independents and chains, and chains to continue to expand relative to both affiliated and unaffiliated independents.

CHAPTER SEVEN

Summary of Changes in Market Structure of Grocery Retailing

INCREASING RELATIVE IMPORTANCE OF GROCERY RETAILING

THE comparisons made below deal only with the changing market structure of grocery retailing. But in interpreting these comparisons, it should be noted that during the past three decades, grocery-store retailing has been encompassing an ever increasing share of all food retailing. For example, in 1929 grocery and combination stores accounted for only 66 per cent of all retail food-store sales. By 1939 this percentage had grown to 77 per cent, by 1948 to 85 per cent, and by 1958 to 89 per cent. The increasing percentage of food marketed through grocery stores has been at the expense of specialty stores such as meat markets, candy stores, and delicatessens.

If we had defined grocery retailing to be only one part of all food retailing, instead of an industry in itself, over-all market concentration would be lower than indicated below, but the rate of increase between 1940 and 1958 would have been greater than our comparisons indicate.

CHANGES IN MARKET CONCENTRATION

NATIONAL LEVEL

Store Concentration.—Grocery retailing remains an industry of large numbers in spite of a pronounced and continuing decline in store numbers since 1940. The 285,000 grocery and combination stores operated in 1958 reflect a decrease of about one-third since 1940 (Table 44).

115

Moreover, most grocery sales were concentrated in a relatively small percentage of stores. In 1958, 30,000 supermarkets (annual sales of over $375,000), while constituting 10.5 per cent of all grocery stores, accounted for 68.2 per cent of all grocery-store sales (Table 6). But while this comparison suggests a high concentration of sales among grocery stores, the number of supermarkets still represents a large absolute number of establishments in comparison with practically any other American industry. For example, in 1954 there were 2,367 establishments in meat packing, the most important (in terms of volume) food-processing industry supplying grocery retailers. Thus we must conclude that concentration in terms of number of retail establishments is still very low relative to the industries supplying food retailers.

Concentration among Chain Firms.—Concentration of sales among firms is a much more significant indication of market structure than concentration among establishments, since a single firm may operate many stores. One broad measure of national concentration measured in these terms is the concentration of sales among firms of various sizes.

On this basis, we found that in 1958 the 790 corporate chains operating 4 or more stores accounted for 43 per cent of all grocery-store sales (Table 8). This represented an increase of over 5 percentage points in the last 10 years. Between 1940 and 1947 the chains' share of sales averaged between about 34 per cent and 38 per cent of total sales. Moreover, not only have chains increased their share of total grocery sales, but the number of chains has been declining quite consistently in recent years. Whereas in 1953 there were 866 chains operating 4 or more stores and 279 with 10 or more stores, by the beginning of 1958 there were only 790 chains with 4 or more stores and 247 with 10 or more stores (Table 9). Hence, a decreasing number of chains are doing an increasing share of the total grocery business.

This increased concentration is best reflected in the increasing share of grocery business done by the country's largest chains.

Significantly, the share of grocery sales of the four largest chains declined from 23 per cent in 1940 to 22.4 per cent in 1958; their share of chain sales decreased from 61.5 per cent in 1940 to 52.1 per cent in 1958. This significant decline in concentration was due mainly to A & P's failure to maintain its share of national sales during this period. Its share of chain sales fell from 35.8 per cent to 26.6 per cent (Table 41).

The share of grocery sales of the fifth to eighth largest grocery chains climbed from 3.2 per cent in 1940 to 6.1 per cent in 1958; their share of chain sales climbed from 8.6 per cent to 14.1 per cent.

The 9th to 20th largest chains experienced the most dramatic increase in market shares. They more than doubled their 1940 share of 3 per cent of grocery sales by 1958, when they accounted for 7.2 per cent; their share of chain sales rose from 8.1 per cent to 16.6 per cent.

Thus, in the aggregate the 20 largest chains of 1958 accounted for 35.6 per cent of grocery-store sales compared to 29.3 per cent for the 20 largest in 1940, and they increased their share of chain sales from 78.2 per cent in 1940 to 82.8 per cent in 1958.

We estimate that the 21st to 50th largest chains accounted for about 3.1 per cent of total grocery-store sales and 7 per cent of grocery-chain sales. Thus, while there were 790 grocery chains with 4 or more stores in 1958, the 50 largest of these accounted for about 90 per cent of chain sales and the remaining 740 accounted for only 10 per cent.

The preceding comparisons indicate that total grocery sales are becoming increasingly concentrated among the chain sector of grocery retailing and that, in turn, chain sales are becoming increasingly concentrated among the 20 largest chains.

Concentration among Independent Retailers.—The independent sector of grocery retailing in 1958 was composed of 265,600 stores (Table 44). Independents with fewer than four stores had combined sales accounting for 57 per cent of total grocery-store sales. This was down from 63 per cent in 1940 and from their World War II high of 67 per cent in 1943 (Table 8).

Unaffiliated independents still accounted for the largest number of firms in food retailing, 173,600, but accounted for only 27 per cent (Table 45) of the sales of independents and 15.4 per cent of total grocery-store sales. This represents a significant drop in their share of sales since 1940, when they still accounted for about 54 per cent of independent grocery-store sales.

The increased concentration of sales within the chain sector of grocery retailing has been paralleled by a similar trend within the affiliated independent sector. The number of voluntary and cooperative chains has grown quite consistently since 1939. Whereas according to one source, there were 521 voluntary chains in 1939, there were 584[1] by 1956; and whereas there were 161 cooperative chains in 1939, there were 240 by 1956 (Table 16). And while the number of retailers affiliated with these groups was virtually the same in 1956 as 1939, such affiliates so increased in size that their share of total independent retailer sales rose from 46 per cent in 1940 to 73 per cent by 1958; their share of total grocery-store sales increased from 29 per cent in 1940 to 42 per cent in 1958.

Retailers affiliated with the 20 largest voluntary chains and cooperative chains accounted for an estimated 23 per cent of the total sales of affiliated independents (Table 17). This represented about 15 per cent of total grocery-store sales.

It should be emphasized that the purchases of affiliated retailers through their affiliated voluntary and cooperative wholesalers are considerably less than the above comparisons might suggest. This is true because affiliated independents purchase only about 20 per cent of their products through their affiliated voluntary and cooperative wholesalers. They make their remaining purchases from unaffiliated suppliers. Retailers affiliated with the 20 largest cooperative and voluntary chains purchase about 44 per cent of their requirements from their affiliated wholesalers. Therefore, while affiliated independents make about 42 per cent of all retail grocery-store sales, they purchase through their affiliated wholesalers only about 8.4 per cent of total purchases of all retail grocery stores; and while the 20 largest voluntary cooperative chains account for about 15 per cent of total retail grocery-store sales, their purchases through their affiliated wholesalers make up only 6.6 per cent of total purchases of all retail grocery stores. These represent significantly different concentrations of purchases and sales than those of the 20 largest chains, which accounted for about 36 per cent of total retail grocery sales and 36 per cent of total purchases of retailers. These comparisons indicate that it could be a serious error to conclude that the market structure of affiliated independents is a close kin to that of corporate chains.

In addition to the above affiliations of independents, affiliated independents were indirect members—through their affiliated voluntary and cooperative wholesalers—in a number of national organizations. In 1956 the three largest of these national organizations—Cooperative Food Distributors of America, Independent Grocers Alliance (IGA), and Red & White Corporation—included as indirect members, independent retailers with retail sales of about $10.25 billion, or about 45.1 per cent of total affiliated independent sales and 26.2 per cent of total grocery-store sales. We did not have data needed to determine the exact functions performed by these organizations. However, many of their activities are apparently like those carried on by trade associations. Therefore they may not have a very significant bearing on the market structure of affiliated independents, either in buying or selling. But they are potentially significant in concentrating purchases of various affiliated groups.

Summary of Market Structure at National Level.—In 1958 the market structure of grocery retailing at the national level could still be characterized as an industry of large numbers and relatively low market concentration. There were still about 263,000 retail firms: 790 corporate chains with over three stores accounted for 43 per cent of total grocery sales; independents operating 92,000 stores affiliated with 463 voluntary and cooperative chains accounted for 41.6 per cent of retail grocery sales; unaffiliated independents operating 174,000 stores accounted for about 15.4 per cent of grocery sales. We have estimated the extent of market concentration in 1958 of retail grocery-store sales of the largest corporate, voluntary, and cooperative chains as follows:

These estimates indicate that the 20 largest corporate chains and the retailers affiliated with the 20 largest voluntary and cooperative chains account for about 51 per cent of total retail grocery-store sales.

The buying side of grocery retailing is somewhat less concentrated than the selling side because independents affiliated with the 20 largest voluntary and cooperative chains buy only about 44 per cent of their requirements through their affiliated wholesalers. Hence, concentration on the buying side of grocery retailing is as follows: the 20 largest corporate chains make about 36 per cent of total grocery purchases and independents affiliated with the 20 largest cooperative and voluntary chains make about 6.6 per cent of total grocery-store purchases. Thus the 20 largest corporate chains and 20 largest voluntary and cooperative chains account for about 42 per cent of total grocery-store purchases.

The 40 per cent of retail sales and 60 per cent of purchases not accounted for by these large chains and affiliated independents are accounted for by 770 other corporate chains, 443 voluntary and cooperative chains, and 173,600 unaffiliated independent stores.

CONCENTRATION IN REGIONAL AND LOCAL MARKETS

Market concentration at the national level is an important structural consideration because it indicates the relative absolute size of firms and is important in considering the competitive relationships between retailers and their suppliers which sell in a national market. But in terms of competition among retailers in selling, and between retailers and their suppliers which sell in less than national markets, the market structures of local and regional markets become most relevant.

Market Concentration in Regional Markets.—Although only two corporate chains accounted for 5 per cent or more each of total retail grocery sales in 1958, 17 of the 18 largest corporate chains had retail sales of over 5 per cent of the total retail sales in the regions in which they operated (Table 10). The average for all 18 chains was 10.1 per cent. This indicates that whereas many of these chains are relatively insignificant in terms of national sales, all are relatively important in their operating regions. For example, whereas A & P accounts for 11.4 per cent of national grocery sales and Red Owl for only .4 per cent, A & P accounts for 13.8 per cent of the sales in the regions where it operates and Red Owl for 11.3 per cent.

Unfortunately, data are not available for the relative importance of voluntary and cooperative chains in their operating regions. But since about 55 per cent of such chains operate in only one state, over 82 per cent in two or less states, and only 5.8 per cent in over four states (Table 18), it is obvious that their share of sales and purchases in their operating region is considerably greater than their share of national sales.

It is our judgment that in most important regions in the country, typically the four largest corporate chains and four largest voluntary and/or cooperative chains account for about two-thirds of total retail grocery-store sales. We estimate that they account for nearly as large a percentage of wholesale purchases of products sold in essentially regional markets.

Concentration in Local Markets.—Analysis of the growth of large chains in their local markets suggests that all but 1 of the 14 of the 20 largest chains for which such estimates could be made, experienced an increase in share of sales in cities in which they operated (Table 10). A greater increase in market shares occurred in slow-growing cities than fast-growing ones (Table 43). We estimate that in 1957 each of the 20 largest chains accounted for an average of about 16 per cent of the sales in the cities in which they operated. The chain with the lowest market share averaged 9.1 per cent, and the one with the highest share averaged 24.6 per cent (Table 10).

It was estimated that the largest corporate chain in each of 133 selected cities averaged 25.4 per cent of sales in each city, the two largest grocery retailers averaged 42.2 per cent, and the four largest retailers averaged 58.3 per cent (Table 14). And while reliable estimates of local sales concentration among affiliated independents are not available, it is our judgment that in cities with over 25,000 population, the four largest retail firms and the four largest voluntary and/or cooperative chains typically account for about 75 per cent of total retail grocery-store sales. Since most of the remaining sales are channeled through independent retailers, many of whom are in essentially different economic markets, we conclude that market concentration on the selling side of grocery retailing is very high.

Another significant aspect of the changing structure of local markets is that the 20 largest chains increasingly are competing with one another in the same markets as a result of their geographic expansion (Table 11). Whereas in 1942, 3 or more of the 20 largest chains operated in only 18 per cent of 211 of the country's largest cities, by 1957 this number of chains was operating in 60.8 per cent of these cities; and whereas over 3 of the top 20 chains were operating in only 1.4 per cent of these cities in 1942, by 1957 this percentage was 22.3 (Table 12). These findings indicate that today more large chains are competing with one another in the same market than ever before.

Corporate Chains	Per cent of total grocery-store sales in 1958
4 largest	22.4
5-8 largest	6.0
9-20 largest	7.2
21-50 largest	3.1
182 other chains with over 10 stores	3.0
558 chains with 4-10 stores	1.3
790 corporate chains (19,400 stores)	43.0

Cooperative and Voluntary Chains[2]	
4 largest	7.4
5-8 largest	2.4
9-20 largest	5.3
443 others	26.5
463 total cooperative and voluntary chains (92,000 stores)	41.6
Unaffiliated independents (173,600 stores)	15.4

LEGAL TIES AMONG GROCERY CHAINS

The above discussion of changes in market structure treats all corporate chains as separate legal entities. Actually a number of chains have legal relationships with one another or with third parties which may result in actual or potential joint action among them.

The cases of such legal ties developed in the course of this study are the following.

1. National Food Products has a 31.4 per cent interest in Colonial Stores, the country's 11th largest chain, and 21.1 per cent interest in Bohack, the country's 16th largest chain. In 1958, Bohack and Colonial had combined retail sales of $598 million, which were larger than those of all but six other chains.

2. George Weston, Ltd., has a controlling interest in Loblaw, the country's 13th largest chain, and a 37 per cent interest in National Food, the country's 5th largest chain. In 1958 National Food and Loblaw had

combined sales of over $1 billion, which were greater than those of all but three others.

3. In 1940 Topco Associates was formed as a buying cooperative for chain stores. By 1958 Topco was owned by 29 chains, including 3 of the country's 20 largest chains. Chains affiliated with Topco had total retail sales of $1.5 billion and Topco made wholesale purchases of $150 million for its members.

Insofar as the above legal ties result in collective instead of independent buying and selling decisions, they have a significant effect on market structure; that is, market concentration is greater than our preceding comparisons indicate.

Analysis of the retail market areas of the above concerns indicates that these ties did not have a direct effect on local market structure because these firms did not operate in the same local markets. Of course, these ties could have an indirect effect if they tended to keep these firms from expanding into one another's markets.

To date, however, their main actual and potential effect seems to be in the buying side of the market. But while Topco apparently has eliminated competition among its members in buying some products, the effects of the other instances of legal ties between chains studied were not determinable from available data.

IMPACT OF HORIZONTAL MERGERS ON MARKET STRUCTURE

Firms may expand horizontally through internal or external growth. We are concerned with the importance of external growth, that is, growth by mergers, consolidations, or acquisitions, because industrial experience teaches that extensive use of this method of growth may result in drastic and rapid transformations in industrial structure. The current concern with mergers in food retailing is based on the belief that grocery mergers are resulting, or may result, in a drastic transformation of the structure of grocery retailing. Our findings follow.

We recorded 342 acquisitions of grocery retailers by other grocery retailers between 1940 and 1958 (Table 19). These acquired concerns operated at least 4,061 grocery stores and had estimated retail sales of $3,162 million (expressed in 1957 dollars). This was equal to 7.4 per cent of total retail sales of grocery stores in 1958. We estimate that there were about 625 grocery stores acquired from 1940 to 1958 which were not reported by our sources. Thus we estimate the total sales of all grocery retailers acquired from 1940 to 1958 may have been as much as $3.5 billion (1957 dollars). This is equal to about 8 per cent of total grocery-store sales in 1958.

These aggregate measures of the magnitude of grocery-store acquisitions from 1940 to 1958 do not support the conclusion that, to date, mergers have resulted in a drastic change in the industrial structure of grocery retailing comparable to merger movements in some other leading industries such as explosives, steel, machinery, petroleum, or chemicals.[3] However, it would be incorrect to infer from these aggregate data that mergers in grocery retailing have not had an important impact on market structure. On the contrary, it is our judgment that retail mergers (1) explain much, and perhaps most, of the increased share of total grocery sales of the largest chains, (2) were responsible for much of the increased concentration within the chain sector of food retailing, (3) contributed to increased local market concentration, and (4) played a prominent role in the rapid growth of individual firms.

Firms acquired by the 20 largest grocery retailers of 1958 had sales equal to 65 per cent of all acquired retailers (Table 48). The adjusted sales of these acquired retailers were 4.8 per cent of total grocery-store sales and 10.3 per cent of chain sales in 1958. This is a significantly large percentage in view of the fact that between 1940 and 1958 the top 20 chains' share of total grocery-store sales increased by 6.4 percentage points (Tables 41A and 41B). Hence, the aggregate sales of retailers acquired by the top 20 chains were about 70 per cent as great as the increase in their share of total grocery-store sales. Thus, the increase in these chains' share of national grocery-store sales may be explained largely by the extensive merger activity of some chains. Had none made mergers, it seems probable that the 20 largest chains' share of grocery-store sales would have increased but little. This conclusion is further supported by the fact that only the 3 chains of the top 20 which made no mergers—A & P, First National, and Fisher Bros.—experienced a decline in their share of grocery sales from 1940 to 1958.

The retail mergers of the 20 largest chains also contributed somewhat to the high level of local market concentration existing in 1958. Analysis of the acquisitions of these chains reveals that the acquiring chains operated in 22 per cent of the cities in which acquired firms operated stores (Table 27). This indicates that most mergers did not have an immediate effect on local market concentration. Our analysis of horizontal mergers does not permit precise measurement of their effect on local market concentration; but in the aggregate they had some effect, and in particular cases may have had a significant effect on local market structure. More study is needed of this problem.

Perhaps the most dramatic effect of mergers by the top 20 chains is that they have played a dominant role in transforming some relatively obscure chains to national prominence in a decade or less. The most spectacular example is the ACF-Wrigley Co. In 1940 Wrigley had retail grocery sales of only $2.1 million, or only about .02 per cent of total grocery-store sales (Table 10). By 1958 it had sales of $383 million. About 46 per cent of this growth was the direct result of its acquisitions (Table 24).

Analysis of the growth experience of the 20 largest firms reveals that there is a close relationship between their growth rates and the relative extent to which they used mergers in their growth (Tables 24 and 25). However, this does not prove that mergers were responsible for their different growth rates. For these facts support both the hypotheses that (1) fast-growing firms make most extensive use of mergers and (2) the extensive use of mergers by some firms causes their high growth rates.

In attempting to determine which of these hypotheses most correctly interprets the relationship between mergers and growth rates, we analyzed the changes in the relative sizes of the top 20 firms. This analysis indicates that most of the changes between 1940 and 1958 in the relative sizes of the 20 largest firms were due to their differing rates of internal growth rather than differences in the extent to which they used mergers (Table 26).

This conclusion should be interpreted carefully. First, we cite in the text a number of qualifications to it. Second, we do not infer from these findings that mergers are unimportant in firm growth or market structure. Actually, we believe that our over-all analysis of the importance of horizontal mergers demonstrates that they have played a prominent part in the growth of many large retail firms and that their net effect has been to increase national market concentration significantly above that which would have occurred had none of these firms used mergers.

The public should be concerned over the future pace of merger activity because of the effect to the market structure if the merger movement continues. If the 20 largest chains average annually as many acquisitions during the years 1959 to 1967 as they did annually from 1955 to 1958, by the end of 1967 they will have acquired stores with sales greater than the combined sales of the other 770 chains operating in the beginning of 1958.

Early in 1959 the Federal Trade Commission charged that mergers by Kroger and National Food violated section 7 of the Clayton Act, as well as constituting unfair competition and business practices under the Federal Trade Commission Act. Since these actions were initiated, the extent of merger activity of large chains apparently had decreased considerably.[4] The final decisions in these two antitrust cases may have a profound impact on the market structure which emerges in grocery retailing in the next decade.

SUMMARY OF VERTICAL INTEGRATION OF GROCERY RETAILERS

INTEGRATION BY CORPORATE CHAINS

Vertical integration by grocery chains dates back over 50 years. By 1920, 5 of the largest chains operated a total of 37 manufacturing plants. During the 1920's many additional chains entered manufacturing; and by 1930, 25 chains operated 1 or more grocery-manufacturing plants. Additional chains entered food manufacturing between 1930 and 1958, when 62 grocery chains operated a total of 326 food-manufacturing plants. In 1958, chain-owned plants manufactured products with a wholesale value of $1.3 billion; 85 per cent of these products were sold through the chains' own stores (Table 28).

Meat and dairy products, coffee, and baked and canned goods were the leading products manufactured by chains in 1958. In terms of relative importance, baked goods, coffee, and concentrated milk led all others. We estimated that in 1958 the chains manufactured 39 per cent of their baked-goods needs, 38 per cent of their coffee needs, and 47 per cent of their concentrated-milk needs. On the other hand, they manufactured only about 5 per cent of their meat products, 8.9 per cent of their dairy products (other than concentrated milk), 6.8 per cent of their canned products, and 1.2 per cent of their processed poultry products (Table 29).

All chain-manufactured products sold through chain stores accounted for about 7.6 per cent of total grocery chain-store sales.

Significantly, this was not much different from the percentage of chain-manufactured products sold through chains in 1930, when chains made about 11 per cent of their own products. The most significant change in vertical integration by chains in the past 30 years is that more chains have become integrated and chains have entered more fields of grocery manufacturing.

VERTICAL INTEGRATION OF 20 LARGEST CHAINS

In 1958 the country's 20 largest corporate chains operated over 90 per cent of all chain manufacturing plants. And the top 4 chains operated more grocery plants than all other chains combined (Table 49).

There is a clear relationship between chain size and the extent of vertical integration. Whereas by 1957 the top 4 chains on the average had integrated into 10.5 of 17 grocery manufacturing industries, the 5th to 8th largest chains had integrated into 4.6 of these industries, and the 9th to 20th largest chains on the average had integrated into only 1.9 of these (Table 30).

Perhaps the most striking change since 1940 in the vertical integration variable of market structure is the increase in the number of potential integrators into various fields. The most crucial factor determining whether a chain is capable of integrating into a particular industry is its size. Consequently, one effect of the increased horizontal integration of many chains since 1940 has been to place increasing numbers of chains in the position to integrate into many fields. Our analysis of the number of *potential* integrators into 16 different grocery-manufacturing industries in 1940 and 1957 indicated the magnitude of this change. For example, whereas in 1940, only 14 out of the 40 largest corporate chains were large enough to have integrated into the field of baking, by 1957 all 40 were large enough to do so (Table 31).

The comparable numbers of potential chain integrators in 1940 and 1957 for some other important fields were as follows: poultry dressing, 14 and 40; ice cream, 10 and 32; meat packing, 8 and 31; cheese, 5 and 12; evaporated milk, 4 and 12; biscuits and crackers, 1 and 5. These findings indicate that an ever growing number of chains are becoming potential integrators into grocery manufacturing.

The reason chains are able to integrate into so many fields is that they are in the unique position of being able to overcome the main barrier which makes entry difficult or impossible for other firms; that is, the product differentiation barrier. As chains become large they are able to develop consumer acceptance of their own brands. And if they become large enough to sell the output of an efficiently sized plant under their own brand, they are in the position of being able to integrate into such industries by either buying a going concern or by building their own plant. Thus the main determinants of whether a chain can integrate into a particular field are (1) the development of its own brand, and (2) the expansion to a size adequate to operate and utilize the output of efficiently sized plants manufacturing various products.

Motives for Integration into Manufacturing

There are various technical, market structure, and miscellaneous reasons why chains integrate into manufacturing. This study did not attempt an exhaustive empirical analysis of all these reasons. However, we did test the market structure hypothesis for vertical integration.

This hypothesis explains ownership integration in terms of the market structure of vertically related industries. Applied to grocery retailing, this hypothesis states that retailers have the greatest incentive to integrate into those grocery-manufacturing industries in which sellers have the greatest amount of market power in selling their products.

We tested this hypothesis by correlating statistically the market concentration ratios of various grocery-manufacturing industries with an index of chain integration into these industries. This index was a measure of the percentage of actual chain integrators to the potential chain integrators. This correlation indicated a highly significant statistical relationship between the market concentration of various food-manufacturing industries and the extent to which chains integrated into them.

Analysis of the integration experience of large chains in the last five years further supports this hypothesis. Chains definitely are integrating into the more concentrated grocery-manufacturing industries at a higher rate than into the less concentrated ones.

Although our analysis does not permit precise prediction of future vertical integration trends by grocery chains, we may expect continued integration by more chains into the most concentrated industries and, perhaps, some decrease in the relative importance of their integration into less concentrated manufacturing industries.

NONOWNERSHIP INTEGRATION

Chains may enjoy many advantages of vertical integration without actually entering, through ownership, vertically related industries. The unifying economic result of these less complete forms of integration is that certain decisions of chains and their suppliers are made jointly rather than individually; that is, firms in different stages of the marketing system coordinate certain operations through formal or informal agreements rather than rely on open markets—and the prices generated therein—to coordinate their operations.

This study dealt with only two aspects of nonownership forms of integration—specification buying and private labeling by chains. These two phenomena are intricately related. They are the outgrowth of the decisions of retailers to increase control over their selling policies and decrease their procurement costs.

As early as 1930 about 45 per cent of all grocery chains sold some groceries under their own brands. By 1958 most chains in all size categories sold some groceries under their own brands. Even independents operating from 1 to 3 supermarkets sold about 5 per cent of their dry groceries under their own labels, and about 12 per cent of the dry-grocery sales of retailers operating from 11 to 100 stores were of their own brands. We estimate that as much as 50 per cent of the food sales of some very large chains are of their brands.

The basic motive for using chain private labels is that they increase profits. Brands or labels are one form of product differentiation; and when such differentiation is pronounced, firms are able to follow selling policies which are partially independent of other firms. As discussed above, when retailers buy from manufacturers with market power built on successful product differentiation, chains have an incentive to integrate into such industries. But chains have an incentive to develop their own brand even for products not produced by firms with market power. By developing their own brands for such products they may achieve some "original" market advantage.

There is an important distinction between retailer branding of products bought from firms in oligopolistic market structures and competitive ones; in the former type of market structure retailers may prefer, or are forced, to produce the product in their own plant whereas in the latter they may generally prefer to buy it from existing producers. The reason is that firms operating in competitive industries are likely to earn lower returns than chains. Consequently, chains may enjoy the advantages of selling a differentiated product bought from firms which do not enjoy market power based on product differentiation.

Once chains develop their own labels, they almost inevitably embark on a policy of specification buying. For once they no longer buy on a brand basis, they must prescribe physical specifications for their product. And since they have a vital interest in maintaining consumer acceptance of their private brands, their specifications will be designed to assure them of an adequate product.

A similar situation exists in the field of fresh fruits and vegetables. Here many chains have integrated their wholesaling and retailing operations through direct buying, and to some extent they buy on a specification basis.

VERTICAL INTEGRATION BY AFFILIATED INDEPENDENTS

Independent retailers have attempted to obtain the advantages of corporate chain operations by affiliating with one another in voluntary and cooperative chains. Such action involves both horizontal and vertical integration: horizontal integration insofar as it integrates certain of their selling and buying decisions, and vertical integration insofar as through joint action they integrate the retailing, wholesaling, and manufacturing functions. We summarized the over-all extent of affiliated independent operations above in our discussion of horizontal integration of grocery retailers. Here we shall summarize only the degree to which affiliated independent retailers have integrated retailing, wholesaling, and manufacturing.

Our analysis of the operations of affiliated independents revealed that few, if any, were as closely integrated as corporate chains. However, an increasing number of affiliated wholesalers are providing their members with quite complete lines of products, management aids, and financial and other assistance in building new stores. According to reports, about half are providing members with a full line of private-label products.

By 1958 wholesalers associated with independents had integrated into manufacturing on a very limited scale (Table 59). Voluntary wholesalers owned 44 food-manufacturing plants with combined sales of $42.8 million, and 7 cooperatives owned 9 plants with total sales of $12.9 million. The manufacturing plants of voluntary and cooperative chains had combined sales only 4.3 per cent as great as those owned by corporate chains.

Several studies of voluntary and cooperative chains reveal that customarily their prices are higher than those of corporate chains. This apparently is due largely to their higher wholesaling costs; and also they have not integrated into manufacturing as extensively as have corporate chains.

Cooperative chains have lower wholesaling costs than voluntary chains. However, their relative efficiency in this respect has been lower in recent years than it was in the 1930's.

VERTICAL MERGERS OF GROCERY CHAINS

From 1940 to 1958 grocery retailers made at least 81 vertical acquisitions into grocery manufacturing (Table 51); 68 of these were made by the 20 largest chains (Table 52).

Between 1948 and 1958 voluntary chains also acquired eight manufacturing plants and cooperative chains acquired two manufacturing plants.

The greatest number of vertical mergers were made during World War II, when 34 mergers occurred from 1943 to 1945 (Table 51). Analysis of these vertical mergers reveals that chains used mergers extensively to enter new fields. However, once they had entered a new field, chains customarily grew by internal means.

These findings suggest that chains used vertical mergers in preference to internal growth because it provided the easiest means of overcoming the technical and management know-how barriers to entry.

SUMMARY OF VERTICAL INTEGRATION BY RETAILERS

Today, a large number of grocery retailers are integrated into a wide variety of grocery-manufacturing industries. Moreover, most chains, including affiliated independents, are distributing products under their own brands as well as manufacturers' brands.

These developments have had a dramatic impact on the market structure of food distribution. Its main effect has been to transform the traditional relationship between retailers, wholesalers, and grocery manufacturers. Historically, the preponderant percentage of retailers was concerned almost exclusively with performing the retailing function. Such firms competed with other retailers in buying and selling. And whereas some retailers may have had some market power in selling because of high seller concentration in local markets, there were so many retailers that none had any significant market power in buying products produced in national or even regional markets.

However, as retailers expanded horizontally and were able to develop consumer acceptance of products sold under their own brands or labels, they were able to manufacture and sell their own products rather than rely entirely on manufacturer or wholesaler brands. Hence, their horizontal integration placed them in the unique position of being able to overcome the entry barriers confronting other prospective entrants. Chains, therefore, have integrated into a large number of industries, especially into those with high seller concentration.

Even more often, chains buy from manufacturers for sale under their own retailer labels. The effect on market structure is essentially the same: Grocery retailers are now in competition with grocery manufacturers which sell under their own brands.

It should be noted that vertical integration by grocery retailers is not new. Even in the 1920's a number of chains were quite fully integrated into manufacturing and were selling many products manufactured by others under their labels. Similarly, the largest chains had already developed direct buying of fresh fruits and vegetables by the mid-1930's. The most significant change in the vertical integration variable of market structure is that many more chains have experienced sufficient horizontal expansion since 1940 so that many chains are able to do today what only a relatively few chains could do previously.

Chapter VIII analyzes the implication for firm behavior and industrial performance of these and the other changes in market structure discussed in this report.

Entry of Grocery Wholesalers and Manufacturers into Retailing

Although grocery retailers had integrated into manufacturing for over 50 years, a recent development significant to market structure has been the integration of grocery suppliers into grocery retailing. Since 1948, 5 grocery-manufacturing firms have acquired control of 40 retail firms with sales of $1,109 million at the time of purchase (Table 36). Moreover, at least 9 grocery wholesalers also made retail acquisitions from 1948 to 1958; these included 131 retail stores with combined 1958 sales of $63.2 million. In addition several manufacturers and wholesalers are known to have expanded into grocery retailing through internal growth.

Although complete data of these developments are not available, we estimate that by 1958 grocery manufacturers and grocery wholesalers controlled chain grocery outlets with sales of at least $1.5 billion, or about 8 per cent of the total sales of all chains with 11 or more stores.

Moreover, there reportedly are various, more subtle financial ties between chains and manufacturers. These may involve loans or other financial assistance from manufacturers to chains or outright selling of chain shelf and display space to suppliers. However, we were unable to document the extent or exact nature of such practices which actually constitute forms of vertical integration.

The developments of the last decade indicate a significant reaction to past vertical integration in food distribution. And if the current pace of food manufacturer and wholesaler integration into retailing continues, food manufacturers will soon control more of food retailing than retailers control of food manufacturing.

In addition to the horizontal and vertical mergers discussed above, between 1940 and 1958 at least 16 grocery firms with combined sales of $446 million were acquired by 5 firms not previously engaged in any phase of the grocery industry. These mergers, which might appropriately be called conglomerate mergers, did not have any immediate effect on the degree of either horizontal or vertical structure of grocery retailing.

Implication of Changing Market Structure for Competitive Behavior and Industrial Performance

THE frame of reference of this study has been that of market structure analysis. Economic theory suggests that the competitive behavior of firms is determined, in large part, by the types of market structures in which they operate. Therefore, we have attempted to determine the changing nature of certain relevant variables of market structure, especially (1) numbers of firms, (2) market concentration, (3) nature of barriers to entry, and (4) product differentiation. Here we shall discuss what we think are the theoretical implications for competitive behavior of existing and prospective market structures in food retailing and allied industries. And while this study is primarily an analysis of changes in the above market structure variables, rather than an attempt to measure empirically changes in competitive behavior and industrial performance, we shall introduce some empirical data in this section. However, we wish to emphasize that the data introduced here are not offered as conclusive proof of actual performance. Such proof must be developed in subsequent studies.

IMPLICATIONS OF LOCAL MARKET STRUCTURES

The structure of local markets in grocery retailing approximates oligopoly models. Typically, a relatively few large firms account for the bulk of sales with a fringe of small independent firms accounting for the remainder. Moreover, the existing rivals often enjoy considerable spatial separation, so that very large cities actually contain a number of submarkets rather than a single large one.

Economic theory suggests that when the number of sellers in the relevant market is small, or where a few firms account for a considerable share of sales, rivals tend to behave in an interdependent manner.[1] Market structures of small numbers of rivals tend to create an atmosphere and opportunity conducive to outright collusion. But even in the absence of collusion, firms may tacitly agree to avoid price competition, although still engaging in a variety of nonprice forms. In grocery retailing nonprice competition may assume the form of product and/or service differentiation and extensive local advertising. This does not mean that all the symptoms of price competition disappear, or that some products will not be priced near, at, or below costs. Such pricing may become a common part of a package of special inducements to encourage customers to shop in a particular store. But intensive price competition would not be expected to prevail in local markets in grocery retailing if sales are concentrated in a few firms, except in instances where large horizontally integrated firms choose to operate their stores in a particular city below costs in order to enter a new market.

The extent to which retail prices actually are maintained above costs would be expected to depend upon both existing and prospective market structures. If entry into a market is very easy, high profits would encourage additional entrants, which would tend to diminish the future profits of existing firms. To prevent this, existing firms would tend to charge below what short-run market conditions would warrant. In this respect, one of the main stimulants to competition in the past decade may have been the geographic expansion of medium and large chains into one another's market areas. This tended to place large, presumably efficient, rivals in competition with one another. Of course, insofar as they used mergers to enter one another's market, they tended to minimize the price and nonprice rivalry which would ordinarily result as one large firm tries to enter another's market through internal growth. Thus, while many retail mergers may not have increased market concentration greatly, they may well have reduced considerable potential rivalry among large chains. Moreover, if local market structures become more concentrated, we may expect a further diminution in price competition, although nonprice competition may actually increase. Economic experience in other industries indicates that nonprice competition—especially advertising and selling efforts—often becomes more intensive as concentration increases. There is evidence that this development is already underway in grocery retailing.

According to internal revenue records, the advertising expenses of corporate food retailers increased from $49 million in 1947 to $233 million in 1957, or from .48 per cent of their sales to .92 per cent of sales

(Table 37). Between 1947 and 1952 advertising expenditures as a per cent of sales remained relatively stable. But between 1952 and 1957 they increased from .54 per cent to .92 per cent, or by three-fourths in only four years.[2]

A key determinant of future market structure and competitive behavior in local markets is the success with which affiliated independents are able to achieve the economies of corporate chains, and the extent to which small and medium-sized corporate chains are able to survive and grow. Recent trends and performance suggest that affiliated independents as a group are not able to operate as efficiently as corporate chains,

TABLE 37
Advertising Expenditures of Food Retailers
(In Millions of Dollars)

Year	Advertising expenses	Advertising expenses as per cent of total food store sales
1947	$ 49.4*	.48*
1948	57.0	.48
1949	66.5	.54
1950	74.3	.55
1951	86.4	.55
1952	96.2	.54
1953	114.6	.61
1954	134.7	.68
1955	171.8	.76
1956	211.9	.85
1957	$ 233.5	.92

*U.S. Treasury Department, Internal Revenue Service, Statistics of Income, various editions. These data are for corporate food retailers filing corporate income tax returns. Roberta Lamb, Agricultural Economist in the Marketing Economics Research Division of the Agricultural Marketing Service, has estimated that if advertising expenditures on nonfood sales are excluded (by assuming that advertising expenditures of food retailers are divided between their food and nonfood products in proportion to the relative importance of each), retailers' advertising expenditures on food products amounted to $41.5 million in 1947 and $183.4 million in 1957. Her estimates do not affect the third column in this table.

and that consequently, corporate chains will continue to expand their share of grocery sales. The extent to which small and medium chains continue to offer competition to large chains will largely depend on the extent to which large chains continue, or are permitted to continue, to use mergers in their expansion. If the 20 largest chains average as many acquisitions from 1959 to 1967 as they did annually from 1955 to 1958, by the end of 1967 they will have acquired stores with sales greater than the total sales of the 770 other chains with 4 or more stores operating in the beginning of 1958.

We have not attempted to develop any empirical evidence of competitive behavior at the local level to determine whether it currently approximates that which economic theory suggests. But our conversations with retailers suggest that they think largely in terms of nonprice rivalry with other chains. And casual observation suggests that currently such nonprice rivalry is extremely keen in many areas. However, a recent indictment against leading grocery retailers in the San Diego area illustrates how retailers allegedly have combined to avoid nonprice as well as price competition. The indictment charges, among other things, that the grocery retailers in this area agreed "to establish and maintain minimum prices and uniform terms and conditions, including uniform charges for cashing checks, in sales of groceries to consumers in the San Diego area."[3] This suggests that under certain circumstances, grocery retailers in local markets may go so far as to avoid nonprice as well as price competition.

The contention sometimes made in the trade that A & P's policy of low margins has limited the profits of other food retailers suggests that grocery retailers do have considerable potential market power in local markets. The *Wall Street Journal,* in a recent feature article on A & P, expressed this view as follows: "If only this one principle of A & P behavior (its policy of low margins) were modified—as some family stockholders desire—it could affect the entire food industry, at both retailing and manufacturing levels, and thereby also the consumers."[4] If this is a correct representation of A & P's ability to hold down market margins, it suggests that A & P operates in a market structure which permits marketing margins to be determined largely by managerial decision rather than by competitive market forces. Insofar as other chains act similarly, the result is administered pricing. Some evidence suggests that even other large firms follow A & P's lead in selling. In analyzing Kroger's pricing policy, Kaplan, Dirlam, and Lanzillotti report, "Its pricing is, as for so many other operators, largely a matter of finding out what A & P charges on the most important food items and then coming very close to A & P's prices."[5]

The preceding comments are not offered as conclusive proof that local retail market structures have, in fact, resulted in market behavior consistent with that which economic theory implies. Rather, we report it here simply to illustrate that scattered evidence suggests that such behavior may indeed exist. Actually, however, additional research is needed to give a conclusive picture of the type of competitive behavior actually extant in local markets.

Implications of Absolute Size of Grocery Chains on Local Market Behavior.— The market power conferred on firms as a result of their absolute size, rather than only their relative size in particular markets, has not been incorporated in most theories of competitive behavior. However, the absolute size of firms influences greatly the kind of competitive practices they are able to follow in particular markets. As Edwards points out, a firm that "operates across many markets need not regard a particular market as a separate unit for purposes of determining business policy. It may possess power in a particular market not only by virtue of its place in the organization of that market but also by virtue of the scope and character of its activities elsewhere. It may be able to exploit, extend, or defend its power by tactics other than those that are traditionally associated with the idea of monopoly." [6]

This concept of the market advantages conferred by large size would seem to have important implications for competitive behavior in local retail grocery markets. Even though a very large regional or national chain may not have the largest sales in a particular local market, it may nonetheless be a much more important factor in the market than its local market sales alone suggest. Because of its ability to sustain losses in a particular market out of its operations elsewhere, it has the potential power to expand its market share at the expense of other firms. Moreover, once it has established its position in a market, it may be able to induce local retailers to follow its pricing policy, because of its potential ability to engage successfully in any price wars which might develop, should others not follow its lead. Edwards states it succinctly when he says, "The large company is in a position to hurt without being hurt."

There is some evidence that the large size of some chains has permitted them to follow the practices that Edwards suggests. The record in the A & P case cited many cities in which company units operated at a loss over long periods, for example, Boston and Providence, 1934–41; Toledo, 1932–38; Indianapolis, 1932–35 and 1937–38; Detroit and Cincinnati, 1932–37. [7]

In a recent antitrust case involving Safeway Stores, the country's second largest grocery chain, the Department of Justice charged that Safeway operated some of its districts below costs for the purpose of discouraging competition.[8] Safeway pleaded *nolo contendere* and was fined.

Edwards cites another market characteristic of very big firms which may have important implications for competitive behavior in local markets. He points out the differences in competitive attitudes which emerge when large firms come into contact with one another in many local markets. As Edwards puts it:

> The interests of great enterprises are likely to touch at many points, and it would be possible for each to mobilize at any one of these points a considerable aggregate of resources. The anticipated gain to such a concern from unmitigated competitive attack upon another large enterprise at one point of contact is likely to be slight as compared with the possible loss from retaliatory action by that enterprise at many other points of contact. . . . Hence there is an incentive to live and let live, to cultivate a cooperative spirit, and to recognize priorities of interest in the hope of reciprocal recognition.[9]

This conception of competitive conduct among large firms has important implications for the future, as well as some relevance today. As grocery chains become ever larger and meet one another in more and more markets, we might expect the emergence of a "live and let live" policy which Edwards implies results from such industrial characteristics.

IMPLICATIONS OF REGIONAL AND NATIONAL MARKET STRUCTURE

Market structure theory suggests that the relative market power of firms derives from their relative share of particular markets, over-all market concentration, the extent of their product differentiation, the degree to which other firms can enter their markets, and the structure of markets from which they buy their inputs and to which they sell their outputs. Here we shall analyze each of these structural variables as they apply to the buying side of grocery retailing, and determine the kinds of market behavior they imply.

On the buying side of grocery retailing, the relevant market typically is much larger than it is in selling. In some products—such as many canned fruits and vegetables and concentrated milk and butter—retailers buy and manufacturers sell in essentially national markets. But in some products—for example, fluid milk, bread, and locally produced fruits and vegetables—the relevant markets vary from essentially local markets to rather large regional ones. We have not attempted to develop data on the structure of regional markets for all agricultural products sold to grocery retailers. Consequently, the competitive performance of grocery retailers in buying products sold in local or regional markets will be treated as a variation of their behavior in buying products in national markets.

Despite the increased concentration which occurred in national markets from 1940 to 1958, grocery retailing in 1958 still was *much less concentrated* than most other important American industries. The 20 largest corporate chains accounted for only 36 per cent of all grocery-store purchases from the industries supplying food retailers; organized independents bought through their 463 affiliated wholesalers another 8.4 per cent, and the remainder was purchased by about 770 small and medium corporate chains and 174,000 unaffiliated independents. Thus, for products sold nationally or in large regional markets, the structure of the buying side of grocery retailing appears to be characterized by a fairly large number of large and medium-sized chains or affiliations of independents, and a very large number of smaller firms. Economic theory suggests that such market structures limit severely interdependent pricing behavior; that is, this large number of firms would encourage very many buyers to behave as if their individual market behavior had an insignificant effect on market conditions. Even 'A & P, which purchases about 11 per cent of all products sold through grocery retailers, does not buy enough of products sold in national markets to control arbitrarily the general price level received by suppliers of such products.

According to the classification of market concentration developed by Bain, the buying side of grocery retailing represents a form of "low-grade" oligopsony.[10] (An "oligopsony" refers to few buyers in an industry.) Bain predicts that on purely structural criteria we would expect in such markets a very small amount of interdependence in market behavior. In other words, firms in such markets behave more like competitors than oligopsonists.

Caution must be exercised in interpreting the implications of certain market conduct of large chains as prima facie evidence that they have market power in buying. It is frequently observed that some large chain acts as a price leader in certain supply markets. Care must be taken, however, in determining the exact type of price leadership exercised by such a chain.

The term "price leadership" is used to describe any pricing policy where one firm takes the initiative in making price changes in a market. Often there is a tendency for observers to infer that the mere existence of such a policy indicates that the resulting prices approximate monopolistic (or in the case of a single buyer, "monopsonistic") prices. But economic theory and industrial experience indicate that there are a variety of types of price leadership, and that, depending upon the market structure in which the price leader operates, the resulting prices range all the way from monopolistic to competitive levels. It is imperative, therefore, to do more than establish that such a policy exists; it must be analyzed to determine its unique competitive type.

It is our judgment that the price leadership policies most likely to emerge on the buying side of grocery retailing, conform to the "barometric" type[11] of price leadership. The theoretical explanation of this kind of price leadership is that the leader is chosen or accepted because of his superior ability to assess market conditions. As Stigler puts it, the barometric firm "commands adherence of rivals to his price only because, and to the extent that, his price reflects market conditions with tolerable promptness."[12] In other words, the leading firm plays the role of an industry's price barometer, and others in the industry are willing to let it play this part as long as it performs it well.

The price which the barometric price leader sets may be competitive, monopolistic, or somewhere in between. Thus, it is possible to have a competitive or monopolistic barometric price leader. To discover which it is in a particular industry requires thorough investigation. However, certain types of market structure are most conducive to competitive behavior and others to monopolistic, and certain patterns of action may be taken as implicit evidence of competitive pricing.

The leading structural determinant of the type of barometric price leader which emerges is the number and size distribution of firms. If the leader has too many rivals to make some fairly well disciplined form of collusion or tacit understanding workable, the barometric leader may be forced to indicate prices near or at competitive levels. A more profitable price (to the leader), would be in constant danger of being shaded by some of his rivals because they felt their individual actions had an insignificant effect on the general price level.

We believe that on strictly market structure grounds, the price leadership practiced in buying products sold in national and large regional markets is essentially of the competitive barometric type.[13] However, in local and small regional markets the market structure of grocery retailing may become conducive to a less competitive type of barometric price leadership.

It should be emphasized that the above discussion deals only with the theoretical implications of these market structures. More empirical work must be done to determine the forms of price leadership actually practiced by grocery retailers in different markets.

The above conclusions concerning the kind of competitive behavior implied by the market structure of the buying side of grocery retailing should be qualified in several important respects.

First, they apply only to products sold in essentially national and large regional markets. In smaller markets it seems likely that market concentration in buying is great enough to confer potential power on grocery retailers in their relationship with their suppliers.

Second, these generalizations apply only to the relative market power these structures confer upon retailers in buying from firms which have no significant degree of market power in selling; that is, suppliers which operate in competitive market structures in selling. Of course, retailers may have some market advantages in buying in such markets if they are buying from relatively uninformed sellers. But this advantage is not a function of market concentration but of superior market information.

Third, the above influences are based only on the relative size and market concentration variables of market structure. Even though they lack market power based on market concentration, large grocery retailers may still improve their market position vis-à-vis their suppliers because of their ability to manipulate to their advantage the vertical integration and product differentiation variables of market structure. It is our hypothesis that much of the "shift in the balance of power" between retailers and their suppliers is not the result of increased market concentration but rather is directly attributable to the increasing ease with which grocery retailers can integrate into grocery manufacturing and can develop their own brands. The remainder of this discussion will (1) deal with the theoretical implications which actual or potential integration by chains has for competitive behavior in grocery retailing and manufacturing and (2) test empirically some of these implications.

MARKET POSITION OF GROCERY RETAILERS VERSUS GROCERY MANUFACTURERS

In analyzing the competitive position of retailers versus their suppliers, it is necessary to consider both the market structure of the grocery-retailing and grocery-manufacturing industries. The relevant structural variables include market concentration, product differentiation, and ease of entry.

The grocery-manufacturing industries are considerably more concentrated in national markets than is grocery retailing. In 1954 there were 38,476 firms in the 49 industries manufacturing food and related products.[14] Thus, there were fewer firms in *all* of the industries manufacturing food and related products than in grocery retailing with its over 200,000 firms.

In 1954 market concentration at the national level, measured in terms of the four largest firms, was greater in 41 (83 per cent) of these 49 grocery-manufacturing industries than it was in grocery retailing. Similarly, whereas in 1954 the 20 largest grocery retailers accounted for just under 32 per cent of all grocery-store purchases, in 47 of the 49 grocery-manufacturing industries, the 20 largest firms accounted for over 32 per cent of their industry's sales. In fact, in 29, or about 60 per cent, of these industries the 20 largest manufacturers accounted for over 70 per cent of their industry's sales (Table 38).

TABLE 38
Industry Sales by the Largest
Manufacturers in 49 Food-manufacturing Industries, 1954

Concentration ratios for industry	Size class of firm		
	Four largest	Eight largest	Twenty largest
0-9	0	0	0
10-19	5	1	0
20-29	10	7	1
30-39	6	6	6
40-49	8	4	4
50-59	5	6	6
60-69	5	7	3
70-79	5	4	6
80-89	5	6	6
90-100	0	8	17
Total	49	49	49

Source: Concentration in American Industry, Report of Sub-committee on Antitrust and Monopoly, 85th Cong., 1st sess. (1957), Table 42. Includes all S.I.C. four-digit industries including food and kindred products, tobacco, salt and soap.

These comparisons indicate that the grocery-manufacturing industries generally are considerably more concentrated in selling than are grocery retailers in buying. Moreover, these comparisons tend to understate the relative differences in concentration between these industries. First, many grocery manufacturers sell significant quantities of their products to other than grocery retailers. In some cases they sell directly to the consumer as in the case of home-delivered milk. Institutions and restaurants buy canned vegetables and dairy and meat products. Other types of food stores buy from the grocery manufacturer; for example, meat is sold to meat markets and flour to retail bake shops. Another market is other food manufacturers—sugar is sold directly to confectioners, fruit canners, and ice-cream makers. We have not attempted to estimate the extent of sales of grocery manufacturers to other than grocery retailers. But in 1954 grocery stores accounted for about 86.4 per cent of the sales of all food stores, and sales of manufacturers to other than food retailers are quite substantial in some items. It is our judgment that in 1954 the 20 largest chains accounted for about 25 per cent or less of the markets of the total sales of grocery manufacturers. Of course, in some items these chains represented more than 25 per cent of the markets and in other items less.

Furthermore, because the industry classifications upon which Table 38 is based often are very broad, market concentration in particular products produced in these industries often is considerably greater. For example, whereas the four largest canners account for 28 per cent of all canned fruit and vegetable products, the four largest soup makers account for 89 per cent of all canned-soup sales. Table 39 summarizes the 1954 market concentration in the manufacture of 98 grocery products. This summary reveals that in all of these products the 20 largest manufacturers accounted for a higher percentage of sales than did the 20 largest chains. In fact, in 80 (82 per cent) of these products the 20 largest manufacturers accounted for over 50 per cent of product sales and in 40 (41 per cent) for over 80 per cent of product sales.

TABLE 39
Per Cent of Sales of Food and
Related Products by the Largest Manufacturers, 1954

Concentration ratios	Size class of firm		
for industry	Four largest	Eight largest	Twenty largest
0-9	0	0	0
10-19	6	0	0
20-29	21	8	0
30-39	15	18	6
40-49	23	13	12
50-59	7	15	13
60-69	10	15	11
70-79	6	5	16
80-89	10	12	11
90-100	0	12	29
Total	98	98	98

Source: <u>Concentration in American Industry</u>, Report of Sub-committee on Antitrust and Monopoly, 85th Cong., 1st sess. (1957), Table 37, includes all five-digit product classes in food and kindred product industries, cigarette industries, and salt.

What is the significance of this high degree of market concentration in most food-manufacturing industries? On the basis of market structure theory we would expect that such structures give sellers some discretion over their selling policies. The extent of such discretion would vary considerably from industry to industry.

According to Bain's classification of market structures, nearly one-third of the manufacturing industries summarized in Table 39 are "highly concentrated" industries. Bain predicts that in such industries "oligopolistic interdependence among the largest six to eight firms . . . must still be very strong."[15]

Another 10 per cent of these industries fall into what Bain defines as industries with "high-moderate" concentration.[16] Bain predicts that although these are sufficiently concentrated to "produce a substantial degree of oligopolistic interdependence among the few largest firms, a significant share of the market is supplied by a substantial number of smaller firms."[17]

Almost a third more of the food-manufacturing industries fit Bain's definition of "low-moderate" concentration.[18] Bain states that according to structural criteria "there is still some oligopoly in these industries. . . ." However, such industries may be expected to perform in a fairly competitive manner, although "neither theory nor observation" is conclusive as to the extent of competition likely to develop in such industries. Bain suggests that individual studies be made to determine actual behavior in such industries.

The remaining industries summarized in Table 39 fall into what Bain calls "low-grade" oligopolies, that is, industries in which the four largest sellers do less than 35 per cent of their industry's business. In such industries we expect a very low degree of oligopolistic interdependence, especially if the industry has a very large number of firms.

Significantly, the buying side of grocery retailing is considerably less concentrated than in all but a handful of food-manufacturing industries. Since the 20 largest grocery chains account for only 36 per cent of all grocery-store purchases, the buying side of grocery retailing clearly falls into Bain's definition of an industry with "low-grade" concentration.

The above comparisons are based on market concentration in national markets. Actually, of course, some grocery suppliers operate in essentially regional markets. In such markets both processor and retailer market-concentration ratios are higher than the above. But as a generalization we may assume that food-processing industries are more concentrated than grocery retailing in both regional and national markets. Moreover, in most manufactured food products the relevant market is essentially a national or very large regional market; hence, the above concentration ratios are fairly good indicators of relative market concentration.

If only the market concentration variable of market structure is considered, economic theory suggests that manufacturers would have significantly greater bargaining power in selling than would retailers in buying. The relatively high degree of concentration among sellers of many products would be conducive to noncompetitive behavior in selling; and the relatively low concentration and large number of retailers, which tends to encourage competitive behavior in buying, would prevent a situation approximating bilateral oligopoly from arising. Hence, many manufacturers would have the potential ability to charge noncompetitive prices and retailers would be forced to accept them. Of course, the fact that some buyers represented large accounts would tend to encourage some sellers to give them special discounts. Such price discrimination would be more common in the least concentrated manufacturing industries because large retail accounts become relatively more important as seller concentration decreases. For example, in industries where four firms accounted for over 80 per cent of sales, all the large manufacturers would have sales greatly exceeding those of all but the largest grocery retailers (in 1958 only three chains had sales exceeding 2 per cent of total grocery-store sales and only nine had sales exceeding 1 per cent). But in manufacturing industries where concentration was low, the purchases of some large chains would be larger than the individual sales of practically all manufacturers. In the latter case we could expect that although market concentration among chains is not very great, manufacturers would compete quite aggressively for the accounts of the largest chains with the result that manufacturers' prices would be pushed down toward competitive levels. But in the most concentrated manufacturing industries we would not expect manufacturers to engage in much price discrimination motivated by a desire to get the accounts of large chains.[19] Each seller would realize that others might retaliate, with a consequent general erosion of the industry's price level.

That we would expect the least price discrimination for the above reasons in highly concentrated manufacturing industries is borne out by the experiences A & P and other large chains had with cigarette manufacturers. Nicholls found that whereas A & P received discriminatory advertising allowances from cigarette makers from 1930 to 1933, thereafter it did not.[20] Similarly, Dirlam and Kahn found that A & P was never very successful in getting price concessions from powerful, profitable oligopolist suppliers in soap, biscuits, and evaporated milk.[21]

Consequently, based solely on the relative degree of market concentration in grocery buying and selling, economic theory suggests that in most industries the balance of bargaining power would rest with manufacturers, but that in the less concentrated industries the largest chains would be able to induce suppliers to grant them discriminatory prices—in the absence of effective enforcement of the Robinson-Patman Act. But if such price discrimination were extended to more and more buyers, it would soon become so commonplace that it would force a readjustment in prices quoted to all buyers. Hence, in the less concentrated manufacturing industries large retailers might have little market advantage in their dealings with grocery manufacturers.

Unfortunately, available empirical evidence is too scanty to permit generalization as to the precise nature, extent, and impact of price discrimination. But insofar as price discrimination in favor of particular retailers is persistent rather than temporary, it places other retailers at a competitive disadvantage, and therefore ultimately influences the effectiveness of industrial performance. This is therefore an area which warrants further study and continuing public concern.

Vertical Integration and Private Labeling by Retailers

Relative market concentration data suggest that in most products, grocery manufacturers have much more market power in selling than retailers have in buying. However, relative market concentration is only one factor influencing the relative market power of buyers and sellers. Vertical integration by grocery retailers is another factor.

As our analysis of the motives of vertical integration indicated, grocery retailers theoretically may integrate for many reasons. On the basis of economic theory and empirical evidence we conclude that the primary reasons for retailer integration into manufacturing are to be found in the market structure of grocery manufacturing. As shown above, many grocery-manufacturing industries are highly concentrated. Insofar as this results in market power which, in turn, results in relatively high manufacturing profits, chains have an incentive to integrate into such industries. Moreover, insofar as the high concentration and profits of such industry result from product differentiation based on high advertising expenditures, chains with acceptable brands of their own may be able to save some of these advertising expenses should they make the product themselves. Both of these reasons, especially the first, act as a strong stimulant to chain integration into manufacturing; the second advantage, saving of advertising expenditures, may be enjoyed by chains without actually making their own products by simply placing their brand on products made by others.

If the above hypothesis is a primary explanation of chain integration, we would expect the greatest relative amount of chain integration into those manufacturing industries with the greatest amount of market power. Our empirical analysis of chain integration supports this hypothesis. Although other factors also encourage chain integration, our analysis of its implications for competitive behavior shall deal mainly with market-structure-motivated vertical integration.

Grocery retailers have integrated into manufacturing in two ways: (1) by actually operating their own manufacturing plants and (2) by developing their own labels. Let us consider the impact of each type of integration on market structure and industrial performance.

IMPLICATIONS OF CHAIN MANUFACTURING

Traditionally, retailers specialized in the retailing function, food processors specialized in manufacturing, and retailers and processors dealt with one another through intermediary firms performing the wholesaling function. Although their local market structure gave retailers some power in selling, in buying they were at a relative disadvantage in their dealings with grocery manufacturers, whether they bought from firms directly or through wholesalers.

Often the main source of high concentration in grocery manufacturing was that some firms had successfully differentiated their products; this made it difficult for other manufacturing firms to enter such industries. Integration into certain fields of production became relatively easy for grocery retailers developing their own brands after sales of their brands equaled the output of efficient-sized manufacturing plants making these products. In other words, they were able to overcome the product-differentiation barrier to entry which kept many other potential entrants out.

As long as only one or a few of the largest chains are able to integrate into an industry, we would not expect this to affect drastically the structure or behavior of the manufacturing industry. The main immediate effect would be that the initial integrators could share in any oligopolistic profits of such industries. It is important to note the true source of the added profits of an integrating chain. Its integration does not give it market power as a result of its market position as a retailer, but rather permits it to become one of the oligopolists in manufacturing.

As more and more chains become large enough to integrate into particular products, their integration may begin to affect significantly the number and market shares of firms making such products. As a result, we would expect that extensive chain integration into manufacturing, or even extensive potential integration, would have the effect of making the affected manufacturing industry behave in a more competitive manner than market concentration data alone suggest. However, on strictly theoretical grounds,[22] integration by chains into manufacturing would not necessarily drive prices all the way down to competitive levels; for once earnings of grocery manufacturers fell to the point where earnings on marginal investments of chains in grocery manufacturing were less than additional investments in grocery retailing, chains would no longer have an incentive to integrate into grocery manufacturing. Thus, the entry-forestalling price of grocery manufacturers would tend to be something above competitive levels as long as the earnings of grocery chains were above competitive levels.

Data developed in this study as to the extent of actual and potential vertical integration by chains into leading grocery-manufacturing industries demonstrate that there has been a pronounced change in the importance of the vertical integration variable of market structure since 1940. The significant point to remember is that this structural change has come about because of the increase in the absolute horizontal size of many chains from 1940 to 1958, and it is not due to market power resulting from increased market concentration. This increased horizontal integration of many chains has given them the ability to do what a few decades ago only a few large chains could accomplish. As shown above, market structure theory suggests that the effect of this increased integration is to increase somewhat competition in grocery manufacturing.

IMPLICATIONS OF PRIVATE-LABEL SELLING BY CHAINS

When chains become large enough to develop their own brands, they are in the position of integrating into food manufacturing as discussed above; but they may gain some, or all, of the advantages of actually integrating into manufacturing by having food manufacturers pack their product under chain labels. When this is done, chains, in effect, have integrated into grocery manufacturing; for now their private-label products are in competition with products sold under manufacturers' brands. Such "integration" into manufacturing would change the structure of the manufacturing industry. If, as we believe, the main source of market power in most food-manufacturing industries is successful product differentiation, firms selling to chains on a private-label basis may not have much market power on such sales since they are selling undifferentiated products. For if manufacturing firms which originally had market power continued to price above competitive levels they would induce entry of new firms or encourage expansion of those firms which were willing to sell on a private-label basis. Entry of new firms would be induced because the main barrier to entry, product differentiation, would not bar the entry of new firms willing to sell on a private-label basis. Actually, entry would not be necessary to bring about competitive results if some firms—most likely small or moderately sized ones—which had not successfully differentiated their products, were willing to sell to chains on a private-label basis. But even large manufacturers would sell private-label products to chains at near competitive prices if they feared the alternative was that smaller firms would supply the product. Consequently, we conclude on the basis of market structure theory that extensive private-label selling by grocery manufacturers would encourage very competitive behavior in their sales to chains. And though concentration in manufacturing remains high in such industries, even the largest firms may lose much of the main source of their original market power—successful product differentiation.

It is important to note this important difference between the results of actual integration by chains into manufacturing and extensive private-label buying by many chains. As noted above theoretically, actual or threatened chain integration into manufacturing would not necessarily drive prices down to competitive levels since manufacturers' prices would only have to drop sufficiently to forestall chains from entering manufacturing. This would be true because, by definition, only large chains are in the unique position of being able to hurdle the entry barrier. However, in the case of extensive private-label buying by many chains, the entry-forestalling price of manufacturers would have to be low enough to forestall entry of additional manufacturing firms as well as chains. Therefore, unless other barriers beside product differentiation limited entry, the entry-forestalling price would have to be near competitive levels to prevent new manufacturing firms from entering the industry. Special analysis of the barriers to entry surrounding each industry affected must be made before it is possible to determine the level of the entry-forestalling price.

Insofar as some manufacturers are able to develop and maintain brands with considerably more consumer appeal than chain brands, even extensive chain-label selling will not necessarily undermine the market power of all manufacturing firms. But if such firms had to spend ever increasing amounts on advertising to maintain their brands, they would not necessarily be assured of high profits.

Also, in cases where market power of grocery manufacturers results from high market concentration due to things other than product differentiation—such as economies of large-scale plants, special production processes, or product and process patents—we would not expect chains to share in or eliminate such profits of manufacturers simply because chains had developed their own label. Chains might have to integrate into these industries themselves, if they could, unless some manufacturers would give them discriminatory prices to forestall such integration.

In general, however, we would expect that the main effect of extensive chain integration into manufacturing through operating their own plants and/or through partial integration by developing their own brands or labels, would be to change the structure and behavior of manufacturing industries so as to induce them to operate in a much more competitive manner than relative market-concentration data suggest. Such behavior would presumably be reflected in profits. Profits of the affected grocery-manufacturing industries would decline relative to grocery retailing. Available empirical data support this hypothesis.

Estimating corporate profit rates is a precarious procedure at best;[23] however, comparison of profits of different industries over a period of time provides a fairly satisfactory indication of *relative* if not *absolute* profitability. Therefore, comparisons of the earnings in food retailing and in several food-manufacturing industries provide a fairly satisfactory indication of the relative changes in profitability of these industries during the period studied.

Chart V compares chain earnings with those of several industries into which chains have integrated most extensively—baking, dairy, and meat packing. This comparison reveals that during the period covered by this study, 1940–58, there has been a gradual deterioration of earnings in these industries relative to the chain earnings. Baking, dairy, and meat-packing firms improved significantly their relative profitability during World War II, but thereafter all lost ground relative to their pre-war position.

The series of earnings of "other" food industries reveals a similar trend during this period.

These findings of the changing relative profitability of these grocery-supply industries are consistent with the hypothesis that increasing vertical integration by chains during this period has had the effect of increasing competition in these industries. More detailed analysis of these industries is necessary, however, before we can say conclusively that these declining earnings are due to the changing structure of grocery retailing. Another important area requiring additional work is the way these lower profits in manufacturing are distributed among firms of different sizes. Theoretically, depending on the assumptions we make, large firms could lose either more or less than medium firms.

The above data suggesting that grocery manufacturing has become less profitable than food retailing are consistent with our earlier finding that the relative extent of chain manufacturing was not significantly greater in 1958 than in 1929. Although we were unable to obtain data of the relative extent of chain manufacturing in various products in the intervening years, it seems probable that since the 1930's some chains

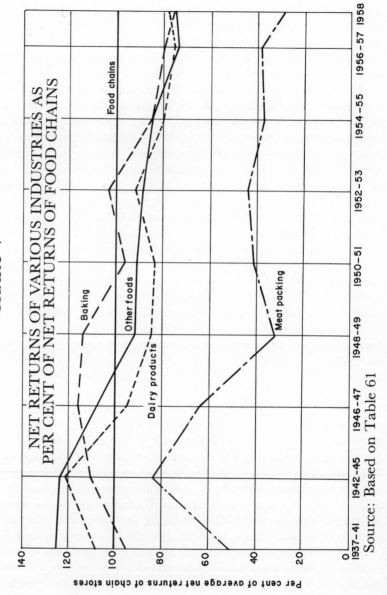

CHART V

NET RETURNS OF VARIOUS INDUSTRIES AS
PER CENT OF NET RETURNS OF FOOD CHAINS

Source: Based on Table 61

150

have decreased the relative amounts of certain products manufactured in their own plants. Certainly the above comparisons of changes in relative profits in manufacturing and retailing suggest that they had an incentive to get out of certain manufacturing industries in favor of buying from others on a private-label basis.

There are important exceptions to this generalization. Profits in some manufacturing industries very likely have not been affected adversely by chain integration because not any, or only a few, chains have integrated into them. Also, it is possible that in certain cases where chains face concentrated market structures, even though manufacturers do not make very large profits, they still are unwilling to sell to chains on a private-label basis at prices as low as chains could enjoy if they manufactured the product. A possible example of this is bread baking. Although chains are extensively integrated into the field of baking—19 of the top 20 chains—large nonchain bakeries may still be unwilling to become "captive suppliers" of chains because bakeries have relatively few market alternatives. Consequently, although large baking firms may not be making very large profits because of excess capacity brought about by chain integration, they may try to maintain or improve their market position through increased advertising, hoping thereby to induce the chains to stock some of their baked goods as well as the chains' own manufactured products. As a result, the chains still have an incentive to integrate into baking even though profits of other baking concerns are low.[24]

This result of extensive chain integration is less likely to occur when chains buy in national markets. In such markets manufacturing firms are more likely to be willing to sell on a private-label basis because the structure of the buying side of retailing results in quite competitive bidding among chains. Thus, a manufacturing firm has a relatively large number of alternative buyers and may expect to receive something at least approximating long-run competitive prices for its private-label products. On the other hand, a firm with only a few potential buyers in a market is placed at a serious bargaining disadvantage if it becomes entirely dependent on one buyer.

Another theoretical implication of the higher earnings in retailing relative to manufacturing is that while chains have less incentive to integrate into some manufacturing industries today than they did previously, many manufacturers now have a strong profit incentive to integrate into retailing.

This implication of changing structure and performance brought about by chain integration is supported by recent experience. A number of food manufacturers and wholesalers have integrated into retailing in the past few years. And as long as earnings in retailing continue higher than in much of food manufacturing, many manufacturers will have an incentive to integrate into retailing even though to do so is more difficult than for chains to integrate into manufacturing.

The chief barriers restricting a food manufacturer's integration into food retailing are (1) the relatively large capital investments required in retailing to obtain outlets for a significant portion of the manufacturer's products and (2) the marketing problems such integration may create. Let us consider each of these in turn.

If a diversified-dairy processing firm wished to sell $10 million worth of its products through its own retail grocery stores, it would have to control a grocery chain with sales of over $100 million. If a meat-packing firm wished to sell a similar volume through its own retail grocery outlets, it would have to control a grocery chain with sales of about $50 million. Since meat and dairy products are the most important items sold through grocery stores, manufacturers of other food products would have to control much larger chains to market a similar volume of their products.[25]

Another serious obstacle to manufacturer integration into food retailing is the possibility of jeopardizing existing retail accounts; because retailers would likely consider such integrated manufacturers as competitors in retailing, they would favor other suppliers.

Both of the above considerations create especially serious obstacles to integration by the largest food manufacturers. Moreover, insofar as the largest firms have developed differentiated products which compete most successfully with chain brands, their incentive to integrate into food retailing is not as great as is that of food manufacturers generally.

Food manufacturers having the greatest incentive and opportunity to integrate into retailing are medium-sized, multiproduct firms which have not successfully developed differentiated products. The more diversified such firms are, the greater is their incentive to develop captive retail outlets. Therefore, processing firms would have an incentive to diversify, presumably through merger, into various grocery products in order to gain a broader base for such integration. This is exactly what Consolidated Foods did prior to its entry into food retailing on an extensive scale since 1956.[26] Similarly, George Weston Associates acquired control of a number of food-manufacturing firms prior to and since acquiring control of National Food and Loblaw. Also, the chief owners of P & C Foods are farmer cooperatives marketing dairy, livestock, and other products.

As indicated in this study, by 1958 food wholesalers and manufacturing interests controlled grocery chains with about 8 per cent of total grocery-chain-store sales. This was almost equal to the extent of chain integration into grocery manufacturing. But whereas extensive chain integration into grocery manufacturing dates from the 1920's, practically all manufacturer integration in grocery retailing occurred since 1950.

An important factor affecting the future extent of integration by manufacturers into retailing is the outcome of the current efforts of leading meat packers to modify a 1920 antitrust consent decree. This decree prohibits Swift and Company, Armour and Company, Cudahy Packing Company, and Wilson and Company from (1) manufacturing 144 selected grocery items, (2) handling fluid milk and cream, and (3) operating retail stores. Should this decree be modified to permit these packers to integrate into retailing, one or more might do so. As pointed out above, because meats are the leading item sold in stores, packers have a greater incentive to integrate than producers of other products. Moreover, their relatively low profits give them an added incentive to get into the more profitable field of retailing. On the other hand, should a national packer enter grocery retailing, this almost certainly would jeopardize some of its sales to other retailers because they would resent the packer's intrusion into food retailing. Consequently, a packer would probably have to enter retailing on an extensive scale to make it pay.

To date very few grocery manufacturers have integrated into retailing. But if many additional ones do so, the entire structure of grocery distribution could be transformed drastically. Moreover, the effect could be cumulative. Some manufacturing firms originally not integrating into retailing might feel compelled to do so for defensive reasons.

The ultimate effect of such integration on industrial performance is not entirely clear. A major determinant of this behavior will be its effect on market concentration in grocery retailing. Extensive manufacturer integration into retailing would not necessarily increase market concentration, unless food manufacturers integrate into retailing by acquiring a number of medium and small chains, as did Consolidated Foods.

It is conceivable, however, that the immediate effect on performance of further manufacturer and wholesaler integration into retailing will be an intensification of rivalry among retailers. If additional chains are formed, and if they attempt to expand their market position, their expansive behavior will intensify competitive rivalry. This could cut all profit margins for a time, which would likely place many independents in an even more precarious position than they are today.

The long-run effect on behavior of these structural developments is even more difficult to predict. This is an area which deserves continuing study.

CONCLUDING COMMENTS ON INDUSTRIAL PERFORMANCE

The primary purpose of this study has been to measure changes in the market structure of grocery retailing and to determine the implications of these changes for competitive behavior among retailers and between retailers and their suppliers. We are interested in market structure and competitive behavior because of our belief that these factors influence, in part, the economic and social performance of industries in a market economy.

Conceptually, there are many criteria by which industrial performance may be judged, all of which are difficult to measure empirically.

For example, one criterion of performance is the profit component of marketing margins. The rationale underlying this criterion is that if the profit portion of food-marketing margins declines, the economic welfare of consumers and farmers is improved.

As indicated previously, certain changes in the structure of food retailing apparently have intensified competition in grocery manufacturing and consequently have reduced profits in some of these industries. Chart VI illustrates the effect this decline in earnings has had upon earnings as a per cent of sales of several grocery-manufacturing industries. These comparisons indicate a generally downward trend in profit margins in these industries since prewar and postwar years. Moreover, profit margins of chains have not increased during this period even though grocery retailers are performing more functions than previously. This suggests that the food-retailing industry is also performing in an improved manner.

Insofar as profit margins are a legitimate measure of industrial performance, these data suggest that these food industries are performing in a more satisfactory manner today than in prewar years. But this limited evidence is by no means conclusive proof of improved performance. Profit margins may change for many reasons, for example, changes in marketing technology, which are completely unrelated to competitive behavior, and increased advertising expenditures.

Another important aspect of industrial performance is the effects of recent structural changes on promotional expenses of manufacturers and retailers. As noted above, the increasing market concentration of retail grocery sales in local markets has tended to intensify nonprice competition. One major result has been that chains are increasing their promotion efforts. This has been reflected in rising advertising expenditures by grocery retailers (Table 37).

Similarly, many food manufacturers have responded to growing integration and private-label selling of chains by expanding their promotion efforts in hopes of improving their consumer franchise. President Charles S. Bridges of Libby, McNeill & Libby, in commenting on the

CHART VI

NET PROFITS AS PER CENT OF SALES OF LEADING
FOOD MANUFACTURING FIRMS AND FOOD-CHAIN FIRMS

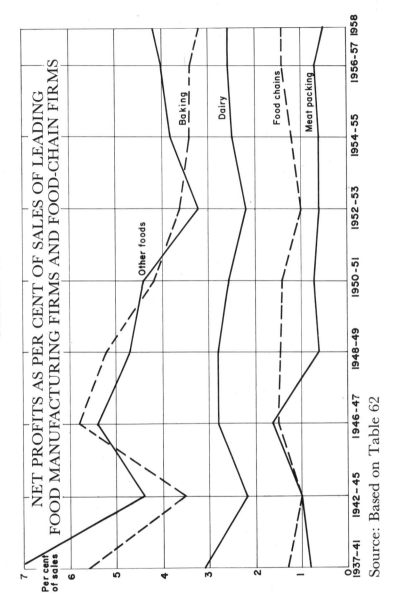

Source: Based on Table 62

155

expansion of chain labels, recently said, "This obviously has increased the pressure on the advertised brands, necessitating larger expenditures for advertising to hold their share of the consumer's business." [27]

The result has been a great expansion of advertising expenses in an industry which already was the country's leader in this field. According to internal revenue records, food-manufacturing corporations spent $337 million in 1947, which equaled 1.11 per cent of their sales (Table 40). By 1957, food processors spent $808 million on advertising, which equaled 2.03 per cent of their sales.[28] Thus, their advertising expenditures, as a per cent of their sales, increased by 83 per cent in just four years. This compared with an increase of only 33 per cent for all other manufacturing industries.

If this trend continues, food processors and retailers may spend

TABLE 40
Advertising Expenditures of Food Manufacturers
(In Millions of Dollars)

Year	Advertising expenditures	Advertising as a per cent of sales
1947	$ 337.0	1.11
1948	366.9	1.17
1949	400.2	1.35
1950	462.2	1.45
1951	497.2	1.39
1952	560.5	1.56
1953	598.1	1.68
1954	656.8	1.80
1955	743.3	1.96
1956	774.3	2.00
1957	$ 808.1	2.03

Source: U.S. Treasury Department, Internal Revenue Service, Statistics of Income, various years. These data are for corporate food manufacturers filing corporate income tax returns. Roberta Lamb, Agricultural Marketing Service, has estimated that in 1947, $17 million and in 1957, $46 million of the above advertising expenditures were for non-food products (animal feeds).

nearly $1,250 million on advertising in 1960. And advertising represents only the most obvious selling cost in our modern food-distribution system. Evidence on nonadvertising promotional cost is scanty, and is usually buried in broad, vaguely defined categories of a firm's operating statement.[29] For example, some food manufacturers spend considerable amounts on point-of-sale promotion which may not show up as advertising expenses. Similarly, entertainment and other miscellaneous expenses incurred by salesmen are not recorded among advertising expenses. Also, much that is officially classified as product development costs may actually involve only superficial product and packaging changes aimed at increasing consumer acceptance of an otherwise unchanged product. It may not be unreasonable to expect that nonadvertising promotional efforts of many food processors are as great as or greater than their advertising expenses.

Why all this concern over the size of selling expenditures? Clearly, not all selling efforts involve social waste of resources. Many are informational in character; in a private-enterprise economy this is the means of informing potential buyers of the availability, prices, and quality of a manufacturer's wares. However, today much, and perhaps most, advertising by food processors and an increasing amount by food retailers is concerned with persuading rather than informing the consumer.[30]

In judging advertising as a component of industrial performance, it is of more than passing interest to compare its magnitude with the size of expenditures for research. After all, these are alternative forms of competition; in truth, a growing number of economists have come to believe that the main and most fruitful competition in modern American capitalism is the drive to develop better products and processes.

One measure of this performance characteristic is the amount of resources firms devote to research aimed at product and process discovery and development. In 1956 manufacturers of food and kindred products spent an estimated $76 million on research;[31] this was equal to about .2 per cent of their total sales. This compared with 1956 advertising expenditures of about $774 million. Thus food manufacturers spent ten dollars for advertising for every dollar spent on research. In 1960, food manufacturers will spend an estimated $96 million on research[32] compared to nearly one billion dollars on advertising.

These facts suggest that when measured against the advertising component of industrial performance some of the recent changes in the market structure of grocery retailing have tended to lower rather than raise the level of industrial performance.

The preceding comments are not intended to demonstrate empirically whether the net result of the recent structural changes in retailing has been to raise or lower the level of performance of the food industries. More thorough analysis is required of the criteria we have mentioned here, and, of course, these are only two of many criteria. Additional performance criteria must be tested before a conclusive answer can be given to the question, Are the current and prospective market structures of grocery retailing encouraging desirable industrial performance? Among the most important aspects of performance requiring study are (1) the effects of recent structural changes on the efforts of manufacturers and retailers to make real or superficial product innovations, and (2) the effects on other aspects of their production and marketing efficiency.

In his excellent critique on workable competition concepts, Sosnick has catalogued a number of other criteria which might be applied in evaluating industrial performance.[33] However, it was not within the scope of the present study to undertake such an analysis. A number of specific food-industry studies currently underway may be better able to undertake this task.

Although we have not attempted here an exhaustive study of the performance of the grocery-retailing industry, we do believe that economic theory, buttressed by industrial experience in other industries, warrants this generalization: The future performance of grocery retailing will depend, in large part, on the extent to which market concentration continues to increase, especially at the local level.

It is our judgment that one of the leading structural elements causing intense rivalry among retailers in local markets in recent years has been the efforts of large chains to enter one another's markets. But we question whether society can be certain that this cause for rivalry will continue indefinitely. If market concentration increases and big chains meet as rivals in many markets, their appetite for aggressive competitive rivalry may diminish. It is more difficult to predict when market structure will have changed enough to permit and encourage such performance than to predict that it will occur. Much will depend upon public policy toward maintaining effectively competitive market structures through placing certain restraints on growth via merger by large retailers.

REFERENCE MATTER

Sources of Data on Mergers among Grocery Retailers

DATA on mergers among grocery retailers were derived from the following sources: *Moody's Industrials, Chain Store Age, Progressive Grocer, Supermarket News,* and other miscellaneous sources. The first three sources were used to obtain data for the years 1940–58, whereas *Supermarket News* and the miscellaneous sources were used beginning with 1953.

The net numbers of retail firms and stores acquired by retailers, as reported by the above sources, are given in the accompanying table.

	Number of firms acquired					Number of stores acquired†				
Source of data	20 largest chains		Others			20 largest chains		Others		
	1940-52	1953-58	1940-52	1953-58	Total	1940-52	1953-58	1940-52	1953-58	Total
Moody's	18	71	1	30	120	1,301	1,407	6	388	3,102
Chain Store Age	3*	4	23	25	55	54	12	67	67	200
Progressive Grocer	1	2	5	6	14	31	32	57	11	131
Supermarket News	0 (4)†	15	0 (53)	112	127 (57)	0 (58)	61	0 (126)	453	514 (184)
Miscellaneous sources	0 (3)	9	0 (8)	17	26 (11)	0 (17)	23	0 (20)	91	114 (37)
Total (actual)	22	101	29	190	342	1,386	1,535	130	1,010	4,061
Total (actual and estimated)	29	101	90	190	410	1,461	1,535	276	1,010	4,282

*This is the number of acquisitions reported in Chain Store Age which had not been reported in Moody's. Net number of acquisitions reported in other sources was obtained in the same way.
†Figures in parentheses are estimates based on the assumption that if these sources had been consulted for 1940–52, they would have listed the same percentage of net mergers as they did from 1953 to 1958.
‡These are the stores operated by the acquired firms.

These data indicate that from 1953 to 1958 *Supermarket News* and the miscellaneous sources accounted for 153 of the 291 firms and 628 of the 2,545 stores reported as being acquired by all five sources during this period. This indicates that the three sources used from 1940 to 1958 understated significantly the number of mergers occurring from 1953 to 1958. If we assume that these three sources underreported mergers by the same percentage from 1940 to 1952 as they did from 1953 to 1958, the number of retail mergers occurring from 1940 to 1958 was 410 instead of 342, and the number of retail stores acquired was 4,282 instead of 4,061.

It should be noted that most acquisitions which were reported in *Supermarket News* and the miscellaneous sources but not in *Moody's, Chain Store Age,* and *Progressive Grocer,* were acquired by small retailers. From 1953 to 1958, *Supermarket News* and the miscellaneous sources reported only 24 firms operating 84 stores which were not reported by our other sources as being acquired by the top 20 chains.

A recent census survey of mergers in the food industries permitted us to check on the completeness of our data.[1] Census agents compared the grocery retail mergers reported in the census survey and those reported in the sources used in this study. This comparison revealed that for 1952–57, 2.4 per cent of the mergers recorded in the census survey were not reported by the sources used here.[2] These acquired firms accounted for 9.4 per cent of the total employment of all acquired firms reported in the census survey.

A similar comparison was made of just the 16 largest retail chains common to both studies. This comparison revealed that our sources understated the number of retail firms acquired by these large chains by 1.7 per cent and the number of retail stores they acquired by 3.8 per cent. Thus our sources are most accurate in the case of large chains.

If we assume that our secondary sources understated over-all retail grocery merger activity by 2.4 per cent for the entire period from 1940 to 1958, 420 retail grocery firms were acquired during this period.

If we assume a perfect correlation between the number of employees of retail grocery firms and the number of stores they operate, we understated the number of stores acquired by 9.4 per cent. Thus, 4,685 retail grocery stores were acquired from 1940 to 1958.

TABLE 41A
Per Cent of Grocery Sales by the 20 Largest Chains

					Per cent of total grocery-store sales					
Year	A&P	Safeway	Kroger	American	Total of four largest	Second four*	Next 12*	Total of top 20 chains	Other chains†	All chains
1929	14.3	2.9	3.9	2.0	23.1	3.6	...	...	...	...
1935	13.7	4.6	3.6	1.8	23.7	3.6	...	...	...	...
1940	13.4	4.8	3.1	1.7†	23.0	3.2	3.0	29.2	8.2	37.4
1941	14.4	4.9	3.2	1.8†	24.3	3.4	2.8	30.5	8.6	39.1
1942	12.1	5.0	3.2	1.7	22.0	3.4	2.6	28.0	9.5	37.5
1943	9.9	4.4	3.2	1.6	19.1	3.0	2.5	24.6	8.2	32.8
1944	10.3	4.1	3.3	1.7	19.4	3.1	2.7	25.2	9.3	34.5
1945	10.0	4.6	3.2	1.6	19.4	3.2	3.1	25.7	7.6	33.3
1946	10.3	4.6	3.1	1.7	19.7	3.5	3.2	26.4	7.7	34.1
1947	11.4	5.0	3.4	1.7	21.5	3.7	3.3	28.5	9.3	37.8
1948	11.5	5.2	3.3	1.7	21.7	3.8	3.3	28.8	8.8	37.6
1949	11.7	4.8	3.3	1.7	21.5	3.9	3.7	29.1	9.7	38.8
1950	12.0	4.6	3.3	1.7	21.7	4.1	4.1	29.9	8.6	38.5
1951	11.2	4.8	3.3	1.7	21.0	4.1	4.1	29.2	6.9	36.1
1952	11.7	5.1	3.3	1.6	21.7	4.2	4.5	30.4	7.2	37.6
1953	11.9	5.2	3.2	1.8	22.0	4.5	4.8	31.3	7.7	39.0
1954	11.8	5.2	3.2	1.8	22.0	4.8	5.1	31.9	8.2	40.1
1955	11.7	5.2	3.3	1.8	22.0	5.3	5.8	33.1	7.9	41.0
1956	11.4	5.1	3.8	2.0	22.3	5.6	6.6	34.5	7.5	42.0
1957	11.2	5.0	3.9	2.0	22.1	5.7	6.8	34.6	7.4	42.0
1958	11.4	5.0	4.0	2.0	22.4	6.0	7.2	35.6	7.4	43.0

*These include the chains falling into these size classes in the respective years.

†First National was the fourth largest chain in 1940 and 1941.

‡Firms with four or more stores.

Source: U.S. grocery and combination store sales from U.S. Department of Commerce, Statistical Abstracts; sales of individual chains from Moody's Industrials.

163

TABLE 41B
Per Cent of Chain Grocery-Sales by the 20 Largest Chains

Year	A&P	Safeway	Kroger	American	Per cent of total chain-grocery sales				
					Total of four largest	Second four*	Next 12*	Total of top 20 largest	Other chains‡
1929	37.2	7.5	10.1	5.1	59.9	9.4	...	...	...
1935	35.4	12.0	9.3	4.7	61.4	9.4	...	...	21.8
1940	35.8	12.8	8.3	4.6†	61.5†	8.6	8.1	78.2	21.7
1941	36.8	12.7	8.1	4.7†	62.3†	8.8	7.2	78.3	21.7
1942	32.3	13.4	8.5	4.6	58.8	9.0	6.9	74.7	25.3
1943	30.1	13.5	9.7	4.9	58.2	9.2	7.6	75.0	25.0
1944	29.8	13.9	9.5	4.8	58.0	9.1	7.9	75.0	25.0
1945	30.1	13.9	9.6	4.9	58.5	9.5	9.3	77.3	22.7
1946	30.4	13.5	9.0	5.0	57.9	10.2	9.3	77.4	22.6
1947	30.2	13.2	8.9	4.6	56.9	9.8	8.6	75.3	24.7
1948	30.5	13.7	8.9	4.5	57.6	10.2	8.9	76.7	23.3
1949	30.2	12.5	8.4	4.3	55.4	10.0	9.5	74.9	25.1
1950	31.4	11.9	8.5	4.6	56.4	10.7	10.6	77.7	22.3
1951	29.3	12.6	8.6	4.5	55.0	10.7	10.7	76.4	23.6
1952	31.1	13.6	8.7	4.3	57.7	11.2	12.0	80.9	19.1
1953	30.4	13.4	8.1	4.6	56.5	11.4	12.4	80.3	19.7
1954	29.6	13.0	7.9	4.5	55.0	12.0	12.7	79.7	20.3
1955	28.5	12.8	8.1	4.3	53.7	13.0	14.1	80.7	19.3
1956	27.2	12.1	9.1	4.7	53.1	13.3	15.7	82.1	17.9
1957	26.8	11.9	9.4	4.7	52.8	13.7	16.3	82.8	17.2
1958	26.6	11.6	9.3	4.6	52.1	14.1	16.6	82.8	17.2

*These include the chains falling into these size classes in the respective years.
†First National was the fourth largest chain in 1940 and 1941.
‡Firms with four or more stores.

Source: U.S. grocery and combination store sales from U.S. Department of Commerce, Statistical Abstracts; sales of individual chains from Moody's Industrials.

164

TABLE 42
Estimated Per Cent of Food Sales
by the 20 Largest Chains of 1957 in 201 Cities

City size*	Number of cities	Per cent of U.S. population		Average sales concentration†		
		1942	1957	1942	1957	Per cent Increase
Under 35,000	32	0.71	0.81	19.60	36.40	85.7
35,000-59,999	51	1.74	1.84	20.85	37.67	80.7
60,000-99,999	46	2.57	3.00	22.16	41.19	85.9
100,000-249,999	43	4.73	4.94	23.66	37.92	60.3
250,000-499,999	17	4.72	4.72	24.36	40.82	67.6
500,000 and over	12	9.46	8.26	28.62	43.53	52.1
Total	201‡	23.93	23.57			
Average				22.31	38.94	74.5

*Based on 1942 population ranking. Smallest city in 1942 had a population of 18,000. Corporate city population based on Consumer Markets, Standard Rate and Data Service, Evanston, Illinois, 1943 and 1958.

†The sales of each chain in a city were computed by assuming that each of its stores in the city had sales equal to the average sales of all its stores in that year.

‡These are the 201 largest cities in the United States in 1942 for which the necessary information was available to make these estimates.

Source: Computed from Editor and Publisher, Market Guides, 1943 and 1958 editions; and Sales Management, 1943 and 1958 editions.

165

TABLE 43

Changes in Sales Concentration
of the Three Largest Chains in Fast-growing and Slow-growing Cities

Size*	Chain	Slow population increase				Rapid population increase				All cities	
		No. of cities	Average share of sales 1942	1957	Per cent change	No. of cities	Average share of sales 1942	1957	Per cent change	Average share of sales 1942	1957
Under 60,000†	A&P	34	10.7	12.6	17.4	27	9.2	10.8	17.6	10.0	11.8
	Safeway	11	19.6	20.0	2.0	10	20.7	17.1	-17.1	20.1	18.6
	Kroger	16	10.2	14.6	43.0	18	9.6	11.8	22.3	9.9	13.1
	Average‡		13.5	15.7	16.5		13.2	13.2	0.6	13.3	14.5
60,000 to 249,999	A&P	40	10.9	16.8	54.1	33	11.9	10.5	-11.7	11.4	14.0
	Safeway	10	20.8	19.9	-4.2	8	31.9	18.1	-43.3	25.7	19.1
	Kroger	13	10.7	16.3	53.3	9	9.5	16.4	74.0	10.2	16.4
	Average		14.1	17.7	25.3		17.7	15.0	-15.4	15.7	16.5
250,000 and over	A&P	11	12.0	14.3	19.5	11	6.7	8.8	30.6	9.4	11.6
	Safeway	4	24.2	23.8	-1.7	4	25.2	22.3	-11.5	24.7	23.1
	Kroger	5	5.5	11.2	101.4	6	20.9	21.1	0.8	13.9	16.6
	Average		13.9	16.4	18.1		17.6	17.4	-1.3	16.0	17.1
All cities	A&P	85	11.0	14.8	34.9	71	10.1	10.4	2.9	10.6	12.8
	Safeway	25	20.8	20.5	-1.2	22	25.6	18.4	-28.0	23.0	19.5
	Kroger	34	9.7	14.8	53.0	33	11.6	14.7	26.7	10.6	14.7
	Average		12.4	15.8	27.6		13.2	12.9	-2.0	12.8	14.4

*Population in 1942.

†These are the cities among those referred to in Table 14 in which these chains operated in both 1942 and 1957 and for which the data necessary to make these comparisons were available.

‡All averages are weighted averages.

166

TABLE 44
Estimated Number of Grocery Stores

		Independents			Total all stores	Per cent of total stores		
Year	Chains	Affiliated	Unaffiliated	Total independent		Chain	Affiliated independent	Other independent
1940	39,950	108,750	296,250	405,000	444,950	8.98	24.44	66.58
1941	38,450	108,750	296,250	405,000	443,450	8.67	24.52	66.80
1942	35,000	100,000	284,000	384,000	419,000	8.35	23.87	67.78
1943	33,000	92,000	258,000	350,000	383,000	8.62	24.02	67.36
1944	33,000	92,000	258,000	350,000	383,000	8.62	24.02	67.36
1945	32,000	94,000	271,000	365,000	397,000	8.06	23.68	68.26
1946	32,000	93,000	282,000	375,500	407,500	7.85	22.82	69.20
1947	28,500	95,000	280,500	375,500	404,000	7.05	23.51	69.43
1948	27,700	115,000	260,500	375,500	403,200	6.87	28.52	64.61
1949	26,500	115,000	255,000	370,000	396,500	6.68	29.00	64.31
1950	25,700	122,000	253,000	375,000	400,700	6.41	30.45	63.14
1951	24,000	122,000	248,000	370,000	394,000	6.09	30.96	62.94
1952	22,396	117,000	238,000	355,000	377,396	5.93	31.00	63.06
1953	23,224	100,000	239,376	339,376	362,600	6.40	27.58	66.02
1954	22,869	97,600	234,171	331,771	354,640	6.45	27.52	66.03
1955	22,365	101,000	219,935	320,935	343,300	6.51	29.42	64.06
1956	22,167	90,000	197,833	287,833	310,000	7.15	29.03	63.82
1957	21,949	88,000	188,851	276,851	298,800	7.34	29.45	63.20
1958	19,400	92,000	173,600	265,600	285,000	6.81	32.28	60.91

Source: Facts in Grocery Distribution, Progressive Grocer, various editions.

TABLE 45
Comparisons of the Total Stores and Sales
of Affiliated and Unaffiliated Independents

	Affiliated independents		Unaffiliated independents	
	Per cent of	Per cent of	Per cent of	Per cent of
	independent	independent	independent	independent
Year	stores	sales	stores	sales
1940	26.7	46.2	73.3	53.8
1941	26.3	46.8	73.7	53.2
1942	26.1	46.8	73.9	53.2
1943	26.3	46.3	73.7	53.7
1944	26.3	47.0	73.7	53.0
1945	26.1	47.0	73.9	53.0
1946	25.0	45.3	75.0	54.7
1947	25.0	46.8	75.0	54.2
1948	30.1	51.6	69.9	48.4
1949	31.2	51.6	68.8	48.4
1950	32.3	52.4	67.7	47.6
1951	33.0	54.8	67.0	45.2
1952	33.0	54.7	67.0	45.3
1953	28.7	54.7	71.3	45.3
1954	28.7	56.2	71.3	43.8
1955	30.8	61.9	69.2	38.1
1956	30.8	69.8	69.2	30.2
1957	31.2	71.0	68.8	29.0
1958	34.6	73.0	65.4	27.0

Source: Computed from Facts in Grocery Distribution
(Progressive Grocer, various editions). Prior to 1951 this
source defined independents as firms operating less than
four retail stores. Beginning with 1951 it defined independents as those operating one to ten stores.

TABLE 46

Comparison of Retail Sales* of 25 of the Largest Voluntary and Cooperative Groups
(In Millions of Dollars)

| Group | Annual retail sales | | Type of chain |
	1955	1953	
Certified Grocers of California, Ltd., Los Angeles	$1,400	$1,000	Cooperative
United Grocers, Sponsored by United Grocers, Ltd., San Francisco	600	450	Cooperative
Orange Empire Stores, Sponsored by Alfred M. Lewis, Inc., Riverside	425	350	Voluntary
Spartan Stores, Sponsored by Spartan Grocers, Inc., Los Angeles	293	260	Cooperative
A.W. and Thrif-Tee Stores, Sponsored by Abner A. Wolf, Inc., Detroit	288	192	Voluntary
Super Valu and U-Save Food Stores, Sponsored by Super Valu Stores, Inc., Minneapolis	250	175	Voluntary
M & H Cooperative Stores, Sponsored by Malone and Hyde, Inc., Memphis	175	170	Voluntary
Fairway Stores, Sponsored by Fairway Foods, Inc., St. Paul	177	161	Cooperative
I.G.A. Stores and Buy-Way Stores, Sponsored by the Fleming Company, Topeka	156	142	Voluntary
Shop-Rite Food Centers, Sponsored by West Coast Grocery Co., Tacoma	145	135	Voluntary
Spartan Stores, Sponsored by Grand Rapids Wholesale Grocery Co., Grand Rapids	164	135	Cooperative
A-G and Thriftway Stores, Sponsored by Associated Grocers, Inc., Seattle	150	132	Cooperative
Unity-Frankford Stores, Sponsored by Frankford Grocery Co., Inc., Philadelphia	113	110	Cooperative
AG Stores, Sponsored by Associated Food Stores, Inc., Salt Lake City	110	100	Cooperative
Red and White Stores and Super Duper, Sponsored by S.M. Flickinger Co., Inc., Buffalo	105	100	Voluntary
Associated Food Stores, Sponsored by Associated Food Stores, Inc., Jamaica, N.Y.	115	85	Cooperative
I.G.A. Stores, Sponsored by Grainger Bros. Co., Lincoln	71	67	Voluntary
Liberty Food Stores, Sponsored by Schuylkill Valley Grocery Co., Bridgeport, Pa.	78	65	Voluntary
Red and White Stores, Sponsored by Sweeny and Co., Inc., San Antonio	63	59	Voluntary
I.G.A. Stores, Sponsored by the McLain Grocery Co., Massillon	60	50	Voluntary
I.G.A. Stores and Sentry Stores, Sponsored by Godfrey Co., Milwaukee	57	51	Voluntary
Pioneer Stores and American Family Super Markets, Sponsored by William Montgomery Co., Philadelphia	53	50	Voluntary
New England Food Markets, Sponsored by New England Grocer Supply Co., Worcester	55	50	Voluntary
Tom-Boy Stores, Sponsored by Tom-Boy Inc., St. Louis	52	40	Voluntary
U.R.M. Stores, Sponsored by U.R.M. Stores, Inc., Spokane	50	39	Cooperative
Total	$5,205	$4,168	

*Estimated in round figures.

Source: Voluntary and Cooperative Groups (April, 1956), pp. 39, 40.

169

TABLE 47
Per Cent of Stores Acquired
to Total Grocery Stores and Grocery Chains

Year	Total number stores acquired	Acquired stores as per cent of total grocery stores*	Acquired stores as per cent of chain stores
1940	22	0.005	0.055
1941	745	.168	1.938
1942	6	.001	0.017
1943	47	.012	0.142
1944	17	.004	0.052
1945	40	.010	0.125
1946	135	.033	0.422
1947	62	.015	0.218
1948	52	.013	0.188
1949	49	.012	0.185
1950	10	.002	0.039
1951	97	.025	0.404
1952	234	.062	1.045
1953	103	.028	0.444
1954	89	.025	0.389
1955	876	.255	3.917
1956	435	.140	1.962
1957	387	.130	1.763
1958	655	0.230	3.376
Total	4,061		
Average		0.062	0.878

*This percentage is computed by dividing the number of stores acquired each year by the number of stores operating during the year.

TABLE 48
Estimated Sales of Acquired Stores and Per Cent of Sales to Total Chain and Grocery-Store Sales
(000 omitted)

Year	Sales of stores acquired by 20 largest chains in 1958		Sales of all other acquired stores		Total sales of all acquired stores		20 chains as per cent of total chain	20 chains as per cent of total grocery	Total as per cent grocery sales
	Current dollars	1957 dollars	Current dollars	1957 dollars	Current dollars	1957 dollars			
1940	$ 19,281	$ 45,118	$ 6,802	$ 15,916	$ 26,083	$ 61,033	0.62	0.23	0.31
1941	106,849	227,297	5,234	11,134	112,083	238,431	2.86	1.11	1.17
1942	2,633	4,777	...	...	2,633	4,777	0.06	0.02	0.02
1943	19,568	31,799	870	1,413	20,438	33,212	0.45	0.15	0.15
1944	15,429	25,425	...	...	15,429	25,425	0.33	0.11	0.11
1945	14,569	23,675	4,230	6,873	18,799	30,548	0.30	0.10	0.13
1946	35,000	50,245	2,171	3,116	37,171	53,362	0.56	0.19	0.20
1947	39,876	46,422	654	761	40,529	47,184	0.47	0.18	0.18
1948	1,377	1,491	34,416	37,284	35,792	38,775	0.01	0.01	0.14
1949	33,166	37,492	2,101	2,398	35,267	39,890	0.34	0.13	0.14
1950	...	...	7,210	8,150	7,210	8,150	...	...	0.03
1951	59,800	60,840	4,016	4,086	63,816	64,926	0.55	0.20	0.21
1952	45,377	44,803	4,272	4,217	49,649	49,020	0.37	0.14	0.15
1953	57,766	59,027	35,760	36,541	93,526	95,568	0.44	0.17	0.28
1954	53,459	54,866	46,357	47,577	99,816	102,443	0.38	0.15	0.28
1955	512,230	532,752	162,298	168,790	674,528	701,542	3.38	1.39	1.83
1956	207,967	215,322	223,958	231,823	431,925	447,144	1.26	0.53	1.10
1957	211,297	211,297	247,247	247,247	458,544	458,544	1.18	0.05	1.08
1958	375,047	371,601	297,850	290,712	672,897	662,313	2.01	0.87	1.54
Total	1,810,691	2,044,248	1,085,446	1,118,038	2,896,135	3,162,287			
Average	$ 100,594	$ 113,569	$ 63,850	$ 65,767	$ 152,428	$ 166,436	0.86	0.32	0.48

171

TABLE 49
Manufacturing Plants Operated by the Largest Chains*

1957 rank	Food chains	1920	1930	1940	1945	1950	1955	1957
1	A&P	8	70	64	65	65	65	65¶
2	Safeway	†	20	48	56	65	124	120
3	Kroger	14	25	34	33	36	37	37
4	American Stores	5	11	10	12	14	11	12
5	National Food	...	5	10	13	12	14	16
6	Food Fair	...	...	0	2	1	6	11
7	Winn Dixie	...	...	0	0	0	6	6
8	First National	...	11	8	10	9	8	8
9	Colonial Stores	...	2	3	1	1	1	1
10	Grand Union	8	2	3	3	3	3	4
11	Jewel Tea	...	...	6	6	6	6	6
12	ACF-Wrigley	...	...	0	0	0	0	2
13	Loblaw	...	...	0	0	0	0	1
14	Fitzsimmons	...	...	0	0	0	0	2
15	Stop & Shop	...	...	1	1	1	1	1
16	Penn Fruit	...	...	...	0	0	0	0
17	H.C. Bohack	...	3	3	4	4	3	3
18	Red Owl	...	...	0	3	2	2	4
19	Lucky Stores	...	...	0	0	2	2	2
20	Weingarten	...	...	4	4	4	5	5
	Total	35	149	192	213	225	294	306

*All garages, warehouses, gas stations, and power and re-
frigeration plants are excluded.
†Where there is a blank, information is not available.
¶A&P also operated 18 subsidiary companies from 1940 to
1957 but the nature of their operations is not disclosed in
Moody's

Sources: Computed from Moody's Industrials, 1941–58.
Data for A&P for 1920 and 1930 from Chain-Store Manufacturing,
Senate Document No. 13, 73rd Cong., 1st sess. (1934), pp. 13–14.
Data for other chains for 1920 and 1930 from H.E. Hardy, "The
Integration of Manufacturing and Chain Distribution—with Spec-
ial Reference to Food Products," unpublished Ph.D. thesis
(University of Minnesota, November, 1947).

TABLE 50
Vertical Integration by the 20 Largest Food Chains of 1957*

Commodities	1940	1941	1942	1943	1944	1945	1946	1947	1948	1949	1950	1951	1952	1953	1954	1955	1956	1957
Bread and Related Items:																		
firms	11	11	11	11	11	12	13	13	13	13	13	13	13	15	15	15	15	15
plants	86[3]	86[2]	87[3]	87[3]	86	88[4]	87[4]	87[4]	88[4]	89[4]	89[4]	89[4]	91[4]	91[4]	93[3]	94[4]	97[4]	95[4]
Coffee roasting:																		
firms	7	7	7	7	8	8	8	8	8	8	8	8	9	9	9	9	9	10
plants	23[1]	23[1]	23[1]	23[1]	24[1]	24[1]	24[1]	24[1]	24[1]	24[1]	24[1]	24[1]	25[1]	25[1]	25[1]	25[1]	25[1]	26[1]
Meat Packing and Distribution:																		
chains	3	3	4	6	6	7	8	7	6	6	6	6	6	7	7	7	7	7
plants	8	7	9	14	18	20	39	19	16	15	17	16	18	17	25	18	16	17
Salad dressing:																		
firms	3	3	3	3	3	3	4	4	3	3	3	3	4	5	5	5	5	5
plants	6[1]	6[1]	6[1]	6[1]	6[1]	6[1]	7[1]	7[1]	6[2]	6[2]	6[2]	6[2]	7[2]	8[2]	8[2]	8[2]	8	7[1]
Jam and Jelly manufacture:																		
firms	4	4	4	4	4	4	6	6	6	6	6	6	6	6	6	6	6	6
plants	4[3]	4[3]	4[3]	4[3]	4[3]	4[3]	6[3]	6[4]	6[4]	6[4]	6[4]	6[4]	6[4]	9[4]	9[4]	9[4]	9[4]	9[2]
Evaporated and condensed milk:																		
firms			3	3	4	4	4	4	5	5	5	5	5	5	5	5	5	5
plants			3	3	5	5	5	5	6	6	6	6	6	6	6	6	6	6
Bottled soft drinks:																		
firms	3	3	3	3	3	3	3	4	4	4	4	4	4	4	4	4	4	4
plants	3[3]	3[3]	3[3]	3[3]	3[3]	3[3]	3[3]	4[3]	4[3]	5[3]	6[3]	6[3]	6[3]	6[3]	6[3]	6[3]	5[3]	5[3]

173

TABLE 50
(Continued)

Commodities	1940	1941	1942	1943	1944	1945	1946	1947	1948	1949	1950	1951	1952	1953	1954	1955	1956	1957
Butter:																		
firms	1	1	1	1	3	4	4	5	4	4	4	4	4	4	4	4	5	4
plants	1	1	1	1	3	9	10	10	9	9	9	9	9	9	9	9	7	6
Ice cream:																		
firms	. . .	. . .	. . .	. . .	. . .	. . .	. . .	. . .	. . .	. . .	1	2	2	3	3	3	3	3
plants	. . .	. . .	. . .	. . .	. . .	. . .	. . .	. . .	. . .	. . .	1	3	5	9	11	13	16	16
Fluid milk:																		
firms	2	2	2	2	2	2	2	2	2	2	2	2	2	2	2	2	2	3
plants	12	12	12	12	12	12	12	12	13	13	13	10[1]	14	15	15	15	14	15
Fruit and Vegetable Canning:																		
firms	3	3	3	2	2	2	2	2	2	2	2	2	2	2	2	3	3	3
plants	3	3	3	2	2	2	2	3	5	4	4	4	4	4	4	5	5	5
Soap and detergent:																		
firms	2	2	2	2	2	2	2	2	3	3	3	3	3	3	3	3	3	3
plants	2	2	2	2	2	2	2	2	3[1]	3[1]	3[1]	3[1]	3[1]	3[1]	3[1]	3[1]	3[1]	3
Cheese:																		
firms	2	2	2	2	1	2	3	3	3	3	3	3	3	3	3	2	2	2
plants	10	10	10	10	3	4	4	15	5[1]	5[1]	5[1]	5[1]	5[1]	7	7	6	6	6
Candy:																		
firms	2	2	2	2	2	2	2	2	2	2	2	2	2	2	2	2	2	2
plants	2[1]	2[1]	2[1]	2[1]	2[1]	2[1]	2[1]	2[1]	2[1]	2[1]	2[1]	2[1]	2[1]	2[1]	2[1]	2[1]	2[1]	2[1]
Egg candling:																		
firms	1	1	1	1	1	1	1	1	1	1	1	1	1	2	2	2	2	2
plants	1[1]	1	1[1]	1[1]	1[1]	1[1]	1[1]	1[1]	1[1]	1[1]	1[1]	1[1]	3	30	27	29	30	28

174

TABLE 50
(Continued)

Commodities	1940	1941	1942	1943	1944	1945	1946	1947	1948	1949	1950	1951	1952	1953	1954	1955	1956	1957
Biscuit and crackers:																		
firms	...	...	...	1	1	1	1	1	1	1	1	1	1	1	1	1	1	2
plants	...	...	...	1	1	1	1	1	1	1	1	1	1	2	2	2	2	3
Poultry dressing:																		
firms	1	1	1	1	1	1	1	1	2	2	2	2	2	2	2	2	1	1
plants	1	1	1	1	1	1	1	1	4	4	3	2¹	2	2	2	2	1	1
Canned fish:																		
firms	1	1	1	1	1	2	2	2	3	3	2	2	2	1	1	2	1	1
plants	4	4	4	4	4	5	5	5	6	6	5	5	5	4	4	5	4	4
Unclassified manufacturing plants:																		
firms	4	4	4	4	4	4	5	5	3	3	3	3	3	4	5	4	4	5
plants	9	9	9	9	9	9	10	10	8	8	8	8	8	9	11	10	13	14
Miscellaneous commodities:																		
firms	6	6	6	7	7	7	9	9	8	8	7	7	7	8	8	8	8	10
plants†	14	17	17	17	17	15	16	16	19	17	16	19	19	22	24	27	33	38
Total plants	192	193	197	202	203	213	237	230	226	224	225	225	239	280	293	294	302	306

* Excluding gas stations, power and refrigeration plants, garages and repair stations, equipment depots, and warehouses. Raised digit (e.g., 4*) is the number of chains which did not disclose number of plants operated. We counted one plant for each time a chain did not give us this information.

† In 1940, the miscellaneous category consisted of one chain manufacturing household goods, three operating spices and extract plants, two laundries, two printing plants, and two peanut-butter plants; in 1957, this category included three chains owning stamp firms, one a magazine firm, one operating a wine-bottling plant, one each manufacturing household goods, bleach, margarine, leavening compounds, and cereals. One chain operated a plant for freezing fruits and vegetables, one a produce-packing plant, two operated gelatin-dessert plants, two operated laundries, two operated printing plants, four operated peanut-butter plants, and five operated spices and extract plants.

Source: Computed from Moody's Industrials, 1941-58.

TABLE 51
Vertical Acquisitions by Grocery Retailers

Year	Meat packing and slaughter	Butter	Cheese	Fluid milk	Ice cream	Evaporated, condensed milk	Bakery products	Food products wholesalers	Canners	Misc.	Total
1940	...	...	...	...	...	...	...	1	...	...	1
1941	...	...	...	...	...	...	...	...	...	...	0
1942	1	...	...	...	...	...	...	...	...	...	1
1943	3	...	...	...	...	...	1	...	...	2*	6
1944	5	...	1	...	...	...	2	2	...	1†	11
1945	7	6	...	...	...	...	1	...	1	2‡	17
1946	...	1	...	...	...	...	...	...	...	...	1
1947	...	...	...	1	...	...	...	...	...	1§	2
1948	...	...	...	...	...	...	...	...	...	2¶	2
1949	...	...	...	...	...	...	...	...	...	...	0
1950	...	...	...	...	...	...	...	...	...	1§	1
1951	...	...	...	...	1	1	...	...	...	...	2
1952	1	...	...	...	...	...	...	...	...	1**	2
1953	...	...	...	1	1	...	...	...	...	...	2
1954	...	...	...	...	...	...	1	...	...	6††	7
1955	1	...	...	...	...	...	1	4	1	4‡‡	11
1956	...	...	...	...	...	...	...	1	1	...	2
1957	...	...	...	1	...	...	3	4	...	2§§	10
1958	...	...	...	...	...	...	...	1	...	2§§	3
Total	18	7	1	3	2	1	9	13	3	24	81

*Insurance company, gelatin dessert plant. †Warehouse and fish company. ‡Warehouse equipment firm. §Soap company, salmon canner. ¶Magazine publisher. **Potato warehouse. ††Coffee roaster, variety stores, soluble oils, potato chip and pretzel plant, two warehouses. ‡‡Salmon cannery, institutional meat distributor, two stamp companies. ¶¶Salad-dressing plant, warehouse. §§Department store with sales of from $15 to 20 million and a confectionery company.

Source: Moody's Industrials and various trade journals.

TABLE 52
Vertical Mergers by the Largest Grocery Chains of 1958

Chains	Meat packing and slaughter	Dairy products	Baking	Misc.	Total
Safeway	12	10	3	6	31
National Food	4	. . .	1	5	10
ACF-Wrigley	. . .	. . .	1	3	4
Kroger	. . .	1	. . .	2	3
American	2	1	. . .	. . .	3
Red Owl	. . .	. . .	2	1	3
Food Fair	. . .	. . .	1	3	4
A&P	. . .	. . .	. . .	2	2
Lucky	. . .	1	. . .	1	2
Thriftimart (Fitzsimmons)	. . .	1	. . .	1	2
Winn Dixie	. . .	. . .	. . .	2	2
First National	. . .	. . .	. . .	1	1
Stop & Shop	. . .	. . .	. . .	1	1
Total	18	14	8	28	68

Source: <u>Moody's Industrials</u> and various trade journals.

177

TABLE 53
Services Provided to Retail Members by Sponsors and Cooperative Groups, 1958

Service rendered	Number providing services				Retail stores receiving services			
	Number		Per cent		Number		Per cent	
	Cooperatives	Wholesale sponsors	Cooperatives (144=100)	Wholesale sponsors (319=100)	Cooperatives	Wholesale sponsors	Cooperatives (34,329=100)	Wholesale sponsors (34,809=100)
Purchasing								
dry groceries	142	288	98.6	90.3	33,497	34,809	97.6	89.8
Advertising	122	288	84.7	90.3	20,685	27,999	60.2	80.4
Warehousing	104	210	72.2	65.8	27,376	26,614	79.7	76.4
Purchasing nonfoods	103	193	71.5	60.5	21,564	23,361	62.8	67.1
Purchasing frozen foods	84	129	58.3	40.4	20,718	15,878	60.4	45.6
Delivery, f.o.b.	70	105	48.6	32.9	13,133	14,710	38.2	42.2
Purchasing dairy items	64	73	44.4	22.9	13,884	10,646	40.4	30.6
Managerial advice	63	186	43.7	58.3	12,589	19,319	36.7	55.5
Delivery, free	61	170	42.4	53.3	15,257	19,834	44.4	57.0
Store engineering	55	186	38.2	58.3	9,325	14,759	27.2	42.4
Purchasing produce	42	72	29.2	22.6	9,351	8,009	27.2	23.0
Floor display	32	132	22.2	41.4	7,286	11,414	21.2	32.8
Purchasing meat	28	78	19.4	24.4	6,282	6,112	18.3	17.6
Accounting system	15	87	10.4	27.3	3,476	4,712	10.1	13.5
Record-keeping aids	14	88	9.7	27.6	5,229	7,239	15.2	20.8
Pricing information	3	. . *	2.1	. . *	890	. . *	2.6	. . *
Baked goods	1	. . †	.7	. . †	405	. . †	1.2	. . †
Servicing nonfood racks	1	. . †	.7	. . †	2,697	. . †	7.8	. . †

*Not given.
†Less than 1 per cent.

Source: Federal Trade Commission, Economic Inquiry into Food Marketing, 1959.

TABLE 54
Type of Merchandise
Supplied Affiliated Independents, 1956

Merchandise	Voluntary chains		Retailer cooperatives	
	Number	Per cent	Number	Per cent
Frozen foods	283	92.79	114	92.68
Fresh fruits and vegetables	235	77.05	75	60.98
Fresh meats	184	60.33	48	39.02
Milk and dairy products	119	39.02	48	39.02
Bakery products	74	24.26	29	23.58
Delicatessen	32	10.49	17	13.82
Total reporting	305		123	

Source: Computed from Index to Voluntary Chains and Retailer Cooperatives (New York: American Institute of Food Distribution, 1957).

TABLE 55
Private-label Products
of Voluntary and Cooperative Chains, 1956

Policies	Voluntary chains		Retailer cooperatives	
	Number	Per cent	Number	Per cent
Full-line private labels	229	50.89	71	39.66
Limited-line private labels	150	33.33	78	43.58
No private labels	71	15.78	30	16.76
Total reporting	450	100.00	179	100.00

Source: Computed from Index to Voluntary Chains and Retailer Cooperatives (New York: American Institute of Food Distribution, 1957).

179

TABLE 56
Number of Products Provided by Different-sized Voluntary and Cooperative Groups, 1956

Number of products handled*	Type of group	Number of stores in group							
		1-99		100-299		Over 300		Total	
		Number	Per cent	Number	Per cent	Number	Per cent	Number	Per cent
One	Voluntary	32	14.04	11	19.30	8	32.00	51	16.45
	Cooperative	11	22.92	13	26.00	8	30.77	32	25.82
	Total	43	15.58	24	22.43	16	31.38	83	19.12
Two	Voluntary	55	24.12	11	19.30	3	12.00	69	22.26
	Cooperative	7	14.58	18	36.00	6	23.08	31	25.00
	Total	62	22.46	29	27.11	9	17.65	100	23.04
Three	Voluntary	65	28.51	9	15.79	5	20.00	79	25.48
	Cooperative	10	20.83	9	18.00	5	19.23	24	19.35
	Total	75	27.18	18	16.82	10	19.61	103	23.73
Four	Voluntary	29	12.72	12	21.05	2	8.00	43	13.87
	Cooperative	14	29.17	7	14.00	3	11.54	24	19.35
	Total	43	15.58	19	17.76	5	9.80	67	15.44
Five	Voluntary	35	15.35	14	24.56	5	20.00	54	17.42
	Cooperative	3	6.25	2	4.00	2	7.69	7	5.64
	Total	38	13.77	16	14.95	7	13.72	61	14.06
Six	Voluntary	12	5.26	1		2	8.00	14	4.52
	Cooperative	3	6.25	1	2.00	2	7.69	6	4.84
	Total	15	5.43	1	.93	4	7.84	20	4.61
Total	Voluntary	228	100.00	57	100.00	25	100.00	310	100.00
	Cooperative	48	100.00	50	100.00	26	100.00	124	100.00
	Total	276	100.00	107	100.00	51	100.00	434	100.00

*These are the six product classes listed in Table 54.

Source: Computed from Index to Voluntary Chains and Retailer Cooperatives (New York: American Institute of Food Distribution, 1957).

TABLE 57
Summary of Buying and Selling
  Policies of Affiliated Independents, 1956

Type of service	Voluntary chains		Retailer cooperatives	
	Number	Per cent	Number	Per cent
Retailer features and displays weekly specials	323	71.14	93	58.86
Stocks brands promoted by central group	329	72.47	100	63.29
Displays under group's labels	227	50.00	68	43.04
Total reporting	454		158	

Source: Computed from Index to Voluntary Chains and
Retailer Cooperatives (New York: American Institute of
Food Distribution, 1957).

TABLE 58
Assistance by Wholesalers
to Independent Retailers, 1958

Type of assistance	Voluntary group wholesalers	Cooperative wholesalers	Unaffiliated wholesalers
	Per cent of wholesalers		
Select site	61	90	30
Give extended credit	52	78	32
Hold mortgage	17	6	6
Guarantee loans	28	20	10
Assist in obtaining lease	60	63	25
Take lease, sublet to retailer	29	11	9

Source: Facts in Grocery Distribution (Progressive Grocer, 1959), p. F-19.

TABLE 59
Food Manufacturing by Voluntary Sponsors and Cooperative Chains

Product and year	Voluntary chains			Cooperative chains			Total		
	No. of chains	No. of plants	Shipment value (000 omitted)	No. of chains	No. of plants	Shipment value (000 omitted)	No. of chains	No. of plants	Shipment value (000 omitted)
Coffee									
1954	...	20	...	5	5	$ 4,706	...	25	...
1958	...	20	...	5	5	2,864	...	25	...
Dairy products									
1954	...	3	...	0	0		...	3	...
1958	...	10	...	2	4	10,069	...	14	...
Bread									
1954	...	3	...	...	...	...	...	3	...
1958	...	4	...	...	...	...	...	4	...
Canning									
1954	...	3	...	...	...	...	...	3	...
1958	...	6	...	...	...	...	...	6	...
Misc.									
1954	...	4	...	...	...	...	...	4	...
1958	...	4	...	...	...	...	...	4	...
Total									
1954	29	33	40,068	5	5	4,706	34	38	44,781
1958	29	44	$42,802	7	9	$12,933	36	53	$ 55,735

Source: Federal Trade Commission, Economic Inquiry into Food Marketing, Cooperatives, Table 3, Voluntary group, Table 2, 1959.

183

TABLE 60
Operating Expenses of Grocery Wholesalers

Type of wholesale organization	Total operating expenses as per cent of sales			
	1935	1939	1948	1954
Voluntary chains	10.1	10.6	8.3	7.4
Retailer cooperatives	5.2	5.2	4.6	4.4
Full service	8.9	9.6	8.7	8.9

Source: U.S. Department of Commerce, Census of Business, Wholesale Trade, 1954, Table 1A, pp. 1-4; Table 1B, pp. 1-10.

TABLE 61
Comparison of Net Rates of Return of Various Industries to Those of Chain Food Stores

Year	Food chains		Baking		Dairy products		Meat packing		Other foods	
	Av. rate of ret. (%)	% of chain earnings	Av. rate of ret. (%)	% of chain earnings	Av. rate of ret. (%)	% of chain earnings	Av. rate of ret. (%)	% of chain earnings	Av. rate of ret. (%)	% of chain earnings
1937–41	8.4	100.0	8.0	95.2	9.1	108.3	4.3	51.2	10.5	125.0
1942–45	8.7	100.0	9.6	110.3	10.7	123.0	7.3	83.9	10.8	124.1
1946–47	18.1	100.0	21.0	116.0	17.2	95.0	11.4	63.0	19.5	107.7
1948–49	17.2	100.0	19.6	114.0	14.6	84.9	5.5	32.0	15.9	92.4
1950–51	14.8	100.0	14.2	95.9	12.4	83.8	6.0	40.5	13.6	91.9
1952–53	11.7	100.0	12.1	103.4	10.8	92.3	5.2	44.4	10.4	88.9
1954–55	13.6	100.0	11.6	85.3	12.2	89.7	5.0	36.8	11.5	84.6
1956–57	15.6	100.0	12.4	79.5	12.2	78.2	6.0	38.5	11.6	74.4
1958	15.2	100.0	11.5	75.6	11.8	77.6	4.4	28.9	11.4	75.0

Source: Computed from the First National City Bank of New York's series of net rates of return in these industries. Rates of return are computed as a percentage of the net assets of these corporations.

TABLE 62
Average Net Profit Margins of Leading Manufacturing
  Corporations
  (In Cents Per Sales Dollar)

Year	Food chains	Baking	Dairy products	Meat packing	Other foods
1937–41	1.3	5.6	3.1	0.8	7.2
1942–45	1.0	3.5	2.2	1.0	4.4
1946–47	1.5	5.8	2.8	1.6	5.4
1948–49	1.4	5.2	2.8	0.6	4.7
1950–51	1.4	4.2	2.6	0.7	4.4
1952–53	1.0	3.6	2.2	0.6	3.2
1954–55	1.2	3.4	2.5	0.6	3.8
1956–57	1.4	3.4	2.6	0.7	4.0
1958	1.4	3.2	2.6	0.5	4.2

Source: Computed from First National City Bank
of New York's series, "Net Profit Margins in
Cents Per Sales Dollar."

TABLE 63
Membership in Largest Organizations of Affiliated Groups

Year	CFDA*		I.G.A.		Red & White		Clover Farms	
	Wholesalers	Retailers	Wholesalers	Retailers	Wholesalers	Retailers	Wholesalers	Retailers
1936	89	16,751- 17,000	64	6,001- 6,250	42	6,001- 6,250	30	2,001- 2,250
1939	91	15,751- 16,000	58	5,501- 5,750	41	6,261- 6,500	33	2,251- 2,500
1950	95	22,251- 22,500	47	5,501- 5,750	31	4,751- 5,000	29	2,751- 3,000
1956	91	22,001- 22,250	67	5,251- 5,500	54	3,251- 3,500	34	2,251- 2,500

*Cooperative Food Distributors of America.

Source: Index to Voluntary Chains and Retailer Cooperatives (New York: American Institute of Food Distribution, 1957), p. xxv.

TABLE 64
Percentage of Voluntary Chain Groups Providing Members with One or More Types of Merchandise*, 1956

Size of group (number stores)	One		Two		Three		Four		Five		Six		Not reporting this information
	No.	Per cent	No.	Per cent	No.	Per cent	No.	Per cent	No.	Per cent	No.	Per cent	
1-25	11	12.2	24	26.7	22	24.5	11	12.2	13	14.4	9	10.0	30
26-50	8	13.6	14	23.7	20	33.9	4	6.8	10	17.0	3	5.0	...
51-100	13	16.5	17	21.5	23	29.1	14	17.7	12	15.2	...	...	37
101-200	7	16.3	7	16.3	8	18.6	9	20.9	12	27.9	...	...	41
201-300	4	26.7	4	26.7	1	6.6	3	20.0	2	13.3	1	6.6	18
301-400	3	60.0	1	20.0	...	...	...	...	...	...	1	20.0	5
401-500	1	11.1	...	...	3	33.3	...	...	5	55.6	...	...	6
501-1000	4	50.0	...	...	2	25.0	2	25.0	...	...	...	...	5
Over 1000	...	...	2	100.0	...	...	...	...	...	...	...	...	1

*These are the six product classes appearing in Table 45.

Source: Computed from Index to Voluntary Chains and Retailer Cooperatives (New York: American Institute of Food Distribution, 1957).

TABLE 65
Comparison of the Percentage of Supermarkets, Superettes, and Small Stores, 1956

Size of group	Voluntary chains					Retailer cooperatives				
	Total groups	Number reporting	Per cent supermarkets reporting	Per cent superettes reporting	Per cent small stores reporting	Total groups	Number reporting	Per cent supermarkets reporting	Per cent superettes reporting	Per cent small stores reporting
1-25	138	90	36.4	32.0	31.6	29	13	23.1	42.7	34.2
26-50	118	60	18.6	29.3	52.1	38	23	20.6	20.5	58.9
51-100	132	69	15.3	29.6	55.1	55	28	14.6	23.5	61.9
101-200	105	41	18.4	27.2	54.4	59	33	11.9	32.4	55.7
201-300	38	20	11.8	30.7	57.5	23	13	11.7	25.6	62.7
301-400	13	3	9.7	36.3	54.0	11	8	11.7	30.5	57.8
401-500	13	6	9.5	13.7	76.8	9	7	8.4	17.0	75.6
501-1000	17	7	13.4	21.9	64.7	12	4	15.7	42.3	42.0
Over 1000	5	1	10.0	40.0	50.0	5	2	40.0	41.0	19.0
Not disclosed	5	...	...	...	...	241	...	...	...	...
Total	584	297					131			
Weighted average			15.1	27.3	57.6			15.5	30.0	54.5

Source: Computed from Index to Voluntary Chains and Retailer Cooperatives (New York: American Institute of Food Distribution, 1957).

189

TABLE 66
Number and Percentage
of Affiliated Independent Groups, 1956

Group size	Voluntary chains	Retailer cooperatives	Buying groups
1-25:			
Number	138	29	5
Per Cent	23.6	12.0	50.0
26-50:			
Number	118	38	1
Per Cent	20.2	15.8	10.0
51-100:			
Number	132	55	3
Per Cent	22.6	22.8	30.0
101-200:			
Number	105	59	1
Per Cent	18.0	24.5	10.0
201-300:			
Number	38	23	. . .
Per Cent	6.5	9.5	. . .
301-400:			
Number	13	11	. . .
Per Cent	2.2	4.6	. . .
401-500:			
Number	13	9	. . .
Per Cent	2.2	3.7	. . .
501-1,000:			
Number	17	12	. . .
Per Cent	2.9	5.0	. . .
Over 1,000:			
Number	5	5	. . .
Per Cent	.9	2.1	. . .
Not disclosed:			
Number	5	. . .	. . .
Per Cent	.9	. . .	. . .
Total groups	584	241	10

Source: Computed from Index to Voluntary
Chains and Retailer Cooperatives (New York:
American Institute of Food Distribution, 1957).

TABLE 67
Food-Store Acquisitions
(Sales in Thousands of Dollars)

Year of acquisition	Number of acquiring companies	Number of acquisitions	Number of stores acquired	Annual sales when acquired	Number of stores				Sales in 1958 of stores in operation
					Closed				
					Replaced	Not replaced	Sold	Still in operation	
1949	6	6	72	66,180	15	12	12	33	$ 51,978
1950	5	5	5	3,889	0	0	1	4	3,204
1951	10	12	69	27,829	29	17	1	22	19,715
1952	5	10	273	67,343	152	8	64	49	37,042
1953	11	12	71	86,617	9	8	2	52	68,676
1954	17	20	70	60,580	4	11	7	48	66,128
1955	23	48	455	434,166	38	52	23	342	368,471
1956	36	70	439	397,325	24	93	24	298	345,749
1957	34	54	363	322,520	10	34	17	302	305,732
1958	38	78	421	450,003	1	11	9	400	372,309†
Total	83*	315	2,238	$1,916,452	282	246	160	1,550	$1,639,004

*Column does not add as some companies made acquisitions in more than one year.
†Does not represent a full year's sales for the 400 stores, as acquiring companies reported 1958 sales for only that portion of the year in which they had control.

Source: Federal Trade Commission, Economic Inquiry into Food Marketing, Interim Report, Chains, Table 6, 1959.

TABLE 68
Food-Store Acquisitions by 10 Large Food Chains, 1949-58
(Sales in Thousands of Dollars)

Company	Number of acquisitions	Number of stores acquired	Annual sales when acquired	Number of stores				Sales in 1958 of stores in operation
				Closed		Sold	Still in operation	
				Replaced	Not replaced			
American Stores Co.	5	93	$ 34,442	4	43	0	46	$ 27,273
Colonial Stores, Inc.	10	99	121,906	4	5	0	90	98,467
Food Fair Stores, Inc.	6	67	107,731	2	0	4	61	104,397
The Grand Union Co.	15	128	128,417	24	11	1	92	84,924
Jewel Tea Co., Inc.	2	43	56,234	4	4	0	35	50,852
The Kroger Co.	5	130	174,064	7	10	0	113	167,162
Lucky Stores, Inc.	4	56	72,612	2	4	6	44	61,956
National Food Co.	24	485	251,612	167	40	68	210	178,474
Safeway Stores, Inc.	25	67	33,016	2	3	0	62	31,955
Winn Dixie Stores, Inc.	11	306	221,070	39	65	15	187	190,519
Total	107	1,474	$1,201,104	255	185	94	940	$995,979

Source: Federal Trade Commission, Economic Inquiry into Food Marketing, Interim Report, Chains, Table 6a, 1959.

192

TABLE 69
Per Cent of Increase in Sales
from 1953 to 1958 by Source of Growth

Stores in chain on Dec. 31, 1958	Number of companies	Stores in operation in 1953	New stores opened since 1953	Stores acquired since 1953	All stores
501 and over	6	+ 10.4	+ 20.2	+ 4.7	+ 35.3
101–500	13	18.9	62.1	33.0	114.0
51–100	18	9.5	54.4	27.4	91.3
26–50	45	12.5	62.4	7.4	82.3
11–25	69	19.3	46.8	21.6	87.7
Total	151	+ 12.2	+ 33.1	+ 11.0	+ 56.3

Source: Federal Trade Commission, Economic Inquiry into Food Marketing, Interim Report, Chains, Table 5a, 1959.

193

TABLE 70
Total Store Sales of Chains
(Sales in Thousands of Dollars)

Stores in chain on Dec. 31, 1958	Number of companies	1953 sales of all stores	1958 Sales			
			Stores in operation in 1953	New stores opened since 1953	Stores acquired since 1953	All stores
501 and over	6	$7,881,600	$ 8,697,900	$1,592,800	$ 371,500	$10,662,200
101–500	13	1,636,800	1,945,600	1,017,100	540,800	3,503,500
51–100	18	645,100	701,900	349,200	175,700	1,226,800
26–50	45	1,062,700	1,193,700	662,500	78,900	1,935,100
11–25	69	618,500	731,200	286,800	132,400	1,150,400
Total	151	$11,844,700	$13,270,300	$3,908,400	$1,299,300	$18,478,000

Source: Federal Trade Commission, Economic Inquiry into Food Marketing, Interim Report, Chains, Table 5, 1959.

TABLE 71
Sales of Large Chains Operating in 1940 and 1958
(In Millions of Dollars)

Chain	1940	1945	1950	1955	1958
A&P	$ 1,116	$ 1,435	$ 3,180	$ 4,305	$ 5,095
Safeway	339	665	1,210	1,932	2,225
Kroger	258	457	861	1,219	1,776
First National	143	182	372	492	551¶¶
American	125	234	470	655	875
National Food	62	107	315	576	794
Colonial	46	99	179	380	437
Grand Union	35	55	161	283	504
Jewel Tea	29	64	189	300	444
Food Fair	29	60	206	475	718§§
H.C. Bohack	26	65	99	140	161
Fisher Brothers	23	38	69	86	102
Loblaw	23	32	94	212	285
Stop and Shop	23	33	56	98	194
Daniel Reeves*	22	. . .	. . .	. . .	. . .
C. Thomas Stores†	20	. . .	. . .	. . .	. . .
Southern Grocers‡	19	. . .	. . .	. . .	. . .
Weingarten	13	26	52	85	140¶¶
Red Owl	13	27	58	95	166¶
Winn Dixie§	12	41	165	421	631
Albers**	10	26	57	. . .	. . .
Thorofare	7	11	28	82	109
Thriftimart††	6	12	35	100	169
Market Basket	6	10	28	66	93
Lucky	5	18	33	45	142
ACF-Wrigley‡‡	$ 2	$ 9	32	157	383
Penn Fruit	n.a.	n.a.	48	109	162
Mayfair	n.a.	n.a.	$ 28	$ 67	$ 117

*Acquired by Safeway in 1941. †Acquired by National Food in
1943. ‡Acquired by Colonial in 1940. ¶Retail sales only. §1940
and 1950 sales are for Winn and Lovett; Dixie Home merged with
Winn and Lovett in 1955. **Acquired by Colonial in 1955.
††Formerly known as Fitzsimmons. ‡‡Sales prior to 1955 are
for Wrigley stores. ¶¶Estimated for 1958. §§Estimate including
its 1958 acquisitions.

Source: This table includes chains which in at least one year
from 1940 to 1958 were among the 20 largest chains reported in
Moody's Industrials.

Notes

CHAPTER ONE

1 George Mehren, "The Changing Structure of the Food Market," *Journal of Farm Economics* (May, 1957), p. 353.

2 J. S. Bain, *Industrial Organization* (New York: John Wiley & Sons, 1959), p. 7.

3 Willard Cochrane, "The Market as a Unit of Inquiry," *Journal of Farm Economics* (February, 1957), p. 29.

4 J. S. Bain, "Relation of Profit Rate to Industry Concentration," *Quarterly Journal of Economics* (August, 1951) pp. 293–324.

5 J. S. Bain, *Barriers to New Competition* (Cambridge: Harvard University Press, 1956).

6 Robert L. Clodius, Darrell F. Fienup, and R. Larry Kristjanson, *Procurement Policies and Practices of a Selected Group of Dairy Processing Firms,* Research Bulletin 193, University of Wisconsin (January, 1956); Homer C. Evans, *The Nature of Competition among Apple Processors in the Appalachian Area,* West Virginia Agricultural Experiment Station Bulletin 405 (June, 1957); Norman R. Collins, Willard F. Mueller, and Eleanor M. Birch, *Grower-Processor Integration in the California Canning-Tomato Industry,* California Agricultural Experiment Station Bulletin No. 768 (October, 1959).

7 Edward Mason must be credited with the original published ideas on this subject: "Monopoly in Law and Economics," *Yale Law Review* (November, 1937);

197

but it remained for J. M. Clark to formalize the concept in "Toward a Concept of Workable Competition," *American Economic Review* (June, 1940), pp. 241–56.

8 Stephen Sosnick, "A Critique of Concepts of Workable Competition," *Quarterly Journal of Economics* (August, 1958), p. 386.

9 A study is underway currently at the University of Nebraska on the changing market structure and performance of the baking industry. The University of Wisconsin is conducting a study analyzing the interrelationship between the changing market structure of food retailing and the fruit and vegetable processing industries.

10 This is the method employed by Paul E. Nelson, Jr., in *Ownership Changes by Purchases and Mergers in Selected Food Industries,* Marketing Research Report No. 369, Agricultural Marketing Service, U.S. Department of Agriculture (Washington, D.C., October, 1959).

11 Federal Trade Commission, *Economic Inquiry into Food Marketing,* Interim Report, June 30, 1959.

CHAPTER TWO

1 Other writers on the subject have divided the development and growth of grocery firms into various time periods. For instance, A. C. Hoffman, *Large-Scale Organization in the Food Industries,* Temporary National Economic Committee Monograph No. 35 (Washington, D.C., 1940), pp. 5–6, divides the span of years into three periods. The period from 1860 to 1899 is termed the "pioneering" period, 1900 to 1917 the development period, and 1918 to the date of his publication the period of rapid increase. Harold E. Hardy does essentially the same thing. He divides the years into spans encompassing the later nineteenth century, the period to the 1930's and the recent years, in "The Integration of Manufacturing and Chain Distribution—with Special Reference to Food Products," unpublished Ph.D. thesis (University of Minnesota, November, 1947), pp. 152–81.

For present purposes, however, the evolution of the institutions in food retailing presents a more desirable means of analysis since the selection of definite time periods may be unjustifiably arbitrary.

2 M. M. Zimmerman, *The Super Market* (New York: McGraw-Hill, 1955), p. 24.

3 Clarence Saunders, Memphis, Tennessee, is often given credit for the self-service type of food store. In 1916 he designed a special store floor plan requiring customers to pass through a turnstile and to follow a prescribed path. The implications are that self-service stores embody more than the elimination of clerk service.

4 Godfrey M. Lebhar, *Chain Stores in America, 1859–1950* (New York: Chain Store Publishing Corp., 1952), p. 27.

5 Zimmerman, *The Super Market,* pp. 16–30, 57–58.

6 *Ibid.,* p. 18.

7 Strictly defined, nonfood items often constitute over 20 per cent of grocery-store sales. For example, the following items which are not included in Table 4 repre-

sent the following shares of a typical supermarket's sales: cigarettes, 5.03 per cent; beverages, 5.42 per cent; soaps and detergents, 2.01 per cent; paper products, 2.11 per cent; household and laundry supplies, 2.56 per cent; candy, 1.85 per cent.—*Super Valu Study* (New York: *Progressive Grocer,* 1958). However, all of the above are grocery items which have been handled by most grocery stores for many years. The items listed in Table 4, on the other hand, have been common grocery items only since about World War II.

8 J. H. Handler, *Selling the Supermarket* (Fairchild publications, 1956), p. 31.

9 Lebhar, *Chain Stores,* p. 22.

10 U.S. Department of Commerce, Bureau of Census, *1929 Census.* Reliable information is not available on the number of chains operating in earlier periods, but the Federal Trade Commission reported that of the 315 grocery chains it studied in 1928, only 21 were operating in 1900 and only six in 1890.—*Chain Stores: Growth and Development of Chain Stores,* Senate Document No. 100, 72nd Cong., 1st sess. (1932), p. 80.

11 These should not be confused with retail cooperative stores which are consumer-owned. Consumer-owned retail food stores have always been much less significant in the United States than in many European countries. In 1954 the census of retailing reported that there were only 475 consumer-owned grocery stores, with combined sales of $104 million. This represented .3 per cent of total food-store sales. Since consumer cooperatives constitute a very small part of grocery retailing in the United States, we shall not deal separately with them here. Consumer cooperatives are included among the independent stores in this study.

CHAPTER THREE

1 This is the definition commonly used today by students of market structure. Cf. Andreas G. Papandreou and John T. Wheeler, *Competition and Its Regulation* (New York: Prentice-Hall, Inc., 1954), p. 307. Some economists would define it to include only growth involving the addition of new facilities or the combination with other firms. However, since we are interested in the effects of such growth, we shall define all methods of expansion of existing functions as horizontal integration.

2 See Jesse Markham, "Changing Structure of the American Economy; Its Implications for Performance," *Journal of Farm Economics* (May, 1959), pp. 349–61.

3 These were the 20 largest chains reported in *Moody's Industrials* for that year. The following comparisons always involve the largest chains operating in particular years. Hence, if a chain drops out of the top 20, its replacement is counted in its stead.

4 Definitions of nonfood sales vary considerably. Most sources do not include cigarettes, soaps and detergents, and other standard nonfood grocery items among nonfoods.

5 Data on the number of stores operated by these chains in 1942 and 1957 in each of the country's 258 largest cities (based on their 1942 population) were obtained from *Editor and Publisher, Market Guides,* 1943 and 1958 issues. Food sales for these cities were obtained from *Sales Management* magazine.

6 Our estimates of the average local market share of eight chains approximate closely those made by another source based on a smaller sample of cities. Below are our estimates and those made by *Supermarket News* for the eight chains which were reported as operating in 10 or more cities of a sample of 133 cities.

| | Supermarket News | | Our estimate |
Chain	Average per cent of sales	No. of cities	Average per cent of sales
A & P	15.2	100	15.6
Safeway	20.6	37	22.6
Kroger	14.3	46	15.7
American	17.7	14	19.6
Winn Dixie	20.3	14	22.9
First National	19.9	10	18.2
National Food	8.4	19	9.1
Colonial	15.5	23	14.4

7 This is an unweighted average of the market shares in all cities.

8 This seems like a reasonable estimate since these chains did about 35 per cent of the country's grocery-store business in 1957. However, the estimate of their share of 1942 sales seems low, since in that year they did about 28 per cent of the total grocery-store business.

9 The growth of other chains was not analyzed on this basis because they did not operate in enough cities in both periods to permit statistically reliable comparisons and because many achieved much of their growth during this period through external growth (mergers), and consequently are less likely to be affected by the rate at which their local market expands. As shown below, from 1940 to 1957 none of A & P's growth was due to mergers, only 11 per cent of Safeway's was due to mergers, and only 9.9 per cent of Kroger's was due to mergers.

10 These cities were not divided evenly between the fastest- and slowest-growing cities. Instead, the division was made where a significant gap existed in growth rates of the cities in the group.

11 See pp. 28–29.

12 Eleven of the 12 cities from which A & P withdrew between 1942 and 1957 were west of the Mississippi. The sole exception was St. Paul.

13 The original sample of the 258 largest cities in the U.S. was reduced to 211 cities because only in these cities was information given for each year studied.

14 *Distribution of Food Store Sales in 133 Cities* (*Supermarket News*, 1958).

15 These were the four largest retailers, whether independent or chain. If total food sales of these markets had been used instead of grocery sales in estimating market shares, the resulting market shares would have been about 12 per

cent less. We believe the *Supermarket News* estimates tend to overstate concentration somewhat in certain markets. However, these data are very useful indicators of the high degree of local concentration, the relative extent to which concentration varies among cities of different sizes, and the extent of variation among cities of the same size.

16 *Moody's Industrials,* 1958.

17 *Ibid.*

18 *Ibid.*

19 Topco Associates, Inc., *Fact Sheet* (Chicago, undated).

20 *Ibid.,* pp. 3–4.

21 "A Place for the Private Label," *Business Week,* February 23, 1957.

22 *Food Field Reporter,* April 4, 1959, p. 19.

23 *Ibid.*

24 As pointed out below, about 13 per cent of the voluntary and cooperative groups cited as operating in 1956 by the source used to compute Table 16, had either gone out of business by 1959 or did not perform any buying services for their members.

25 See Chapter VI for a discussion of the operations of these national organizations.

26 See Table 63 for the number of wholesalers and retailers affiliated with the four largest national organizations in 1936, 1939, 1950, and 1956.

27 *Chains (This Week,* 1957), p. 102.

28 "The I.G.A. Story," *Meat and Food Merchandising* (Fall edition, 1957).

29 *Chains,* p. 112.

30 While Table 46 does not include all of the largest voluntary and cooperative chains, we believe it to include the bulk of them. One large voluntary chain not included here is Consolidated Foods Corporation, which in 1956 sponsored several voluntary chains with about 2,500 affiliated independents.

31 *Chains,* p. 105.

32 *Minnesota Homemaker Survey No. 11 (Minneapolis Star and Tribune,* 1958), p. 2.

33 An undisclosed number of these consisted of small chains. We estimate that small chains constituted less than 10 per cent of all affiliated retailers. Small chains are more often members of cooperative chains than of voluntary chains. On the basis of conversations with industry representatives, we estimate that perhaps as many as one out of five small chains are members of cooperative chains.

34 The sales of these voluntaries included sales to nonaffiliated independents (Table 18).

35 Estimated by assuming that the average retail margin of affiliated independents was 25 per cent.

36 This comparison excludes the sales of voluntary wholesalers to nonmembers.

37 Estimated on the basis of the volume of wholesale and retail sales of 20 of the largest voluntary and cooperative chains reported in *The Big Challenge in Food Marketing (This Week,* 1959), pp. 78 and 83.

38 See Chapter VI for a discussion of the functions performed by voluntary and cooperative chains.

39 *Wall Street Journal,* March 30, 1959, p. 19.
40 *Index to Voluntary and Retailer Cooperatives* (New York: American Institute of Food Distribution, Inc., January, 1957), p. 95.
41 Federal Trade Commission, *Economic Inquiry into Food Marketing,* Interim Report, June 30, 1959, Voluntary Group, Table 2. These are the sales of the 109 stores which were still operated by the acquirers in 1958.

CHAPTER FOUR

1 This terminology has been developed by J. Fred Weston, *The Role of Mergers in the Growth of Large Firms* (Berkeley: University of California Press, 1953), p. 3. This definition of external and internal growth should not be confused with the terminology often used to distinguish between the sources of a firm's capital which it uses in its growth. As used herein, acquisitions are considered as external growth irrespective of whether they are purchased with borrowed funds, accumulated earnings, or exchange of stock.
2 National Association of Retail Grocers, *The Merger Movement in Retail Food Distribution, 1955–58* (Chicago, 1959), pp. 25–27.
3 *Ibid.,* p. 26; Hugh M. McNeil, "Certain Tax Aspects of Mergers and Acquisitions," *Legal, Financial, and Tax Aspects of Mergers and Acquisitions,* Financial Management Series No. 114 (New York: American Management Association, 1957), pp. 40–41.
4 The Federal Trade Commission on June 30, 1959, released its *Economic Inquiry into Food Marketing,* Interim Report. This study deals in part with acquisitions by grocery chains from 1949 to 1958 and therefore provides a basis for checking on the relative completeness of the merger data used in this study.

The FTC study reported that from 1949 to 1958 grocery chains acquired 315 retail grocery firms operating 2,238 stores with combined sales of $1,916 million when acquired (Table 67). The secondary sources used in this study reported that from 1948 to 1958 grocery retailers acquired 310 grocery firms operating 2,935 stores with estimated sales of $2,589 million when acquired. The FTC study reported five more acquisitions from 1949 to 1958 than did our secondary sources; however, it reported 24 per cent fewer acquired stores and 26 per cent smaller total sales. This indicates that several relatively large acquisitions were not recorded in the FTC study.

Some of the difference in the total amount of merger activity reported by the two studies is that the FTC recorded only mergers by food chains with over 10 stores whereas this study includes mergers by retailers of all sizes. However, as shown in Table 26, at least 85 per cent of all acquired stores were acquired by retailers with sales of over $25 million. Thus nonchains did not account for a very large percentage of the acquisitions reported in secondary sources.

5 The FTC study very likely also understates the number of actual mergers by at least these percentages.
6 The total number of acquisitions reported here differs from that reported by other sources for several reasons.

First, whenever two retail firms merge, we assume that the smaller firm is acquired by the larger irrespective of the actual legal arrangements involved. The most important example of this is the acquisition of control of National Food, operating 768 stores in 1955, by George Weston, Ltd., which also controlled the 153-store chain of Loblaw, Inc. This acquisition was treated as if Loblaw rather than National Food was acquired.

Second, since we are concerned here with the impact of horizontal mergers on the market structure of food retailing, not all initial acquisitions of retailers by nonretailers were included among our horizontal acquisitions. (These are considered in Chapter V dealing with vertical and conglomerate mergers.) Only subsequent retail acquisitions by such firms are included here. Included in this category were initial acquisitions (and stores involved) of Consolidated Foods (34); Chicasha Cotton Oil Co. (18); Magic Chef (6); Perloff Bros. (4); Williams-McWilliams, Inc. (52); Groce-Weardon Co. (6); Hale-Halsell Grocery Co. (2); Founders Corporation (61); Robinson-Hobbs, Inc. (51); and ACF-Brill Motors (60).

Third, acquisitions of Canadian grocery retailers by American firms (acquisition of Carrolls, Ltd., 31-unit chain, by Grand Union, in 1953), and initial acquisitions of American grocery retailers by Canadian firms were excluded. Among the latter were the 1953 acquisitions of Loblaw, Inc. (153) by Loblaw Groceteria Co., a Canadian subsidiary of George Weston; Dominion Store acquisition of Thrift Stores (77) in 1955.

7 Statistical correlation of the number of retail mergers and the number of mergers in all of manufacturing results in a correlation coefficient of .73. A correlation coefficient of this size is statistically significant at the 1 per cent level. This means that a correlation coefficient of this size would be obtained only one chance in 100 in random samples from a population in which the two variables are uncorrelated.

8 Penn Fruit was among the 20 largest chains in 1958 but was excluded because its sales data were not available prior to 1944. Mayfair, the 21st largest chain, likewise was excluded because information on its sales was not available prior to 1951. Therefore, we considered Fisher Bros., the 22nd largest chain in 1958, as the 20th largest.

9 Bernard A. Kemp, "The Merger Component in the Growth of a Firm," unpublished Ph.D. dissertation (Vanderbilt University, 1957).

10 Weston, *The Role of Mergers.* Elsewhere one of the authors has attempted to measure indirect as well as direct effects of mergers on growth.—Willard F. Mueller, "The Role of Mergers in the Growth of Agricultural Cooperatives," to be published as an Agricultural Experiment Station bulletin of the University of California.

11 Simple correlation of the sales growth and the per cent of growth due to merger results in a correlation coefficient of .39. Correlation coefficients in a sample of this size are statistically significant at the 5 per cent level if they exceed .38. By this we mean that a value of the correlation coefficient as large as .38 would be obtained only 5 chances in 100 in random samples from a population in which the two variables are uncorrelated. A correlation coefficient of

.39 means that only about 16 per cent of the differences in growth rates among these chains is explained statistically by differences in the per cent of their growth due to mergers.

12 Simple correlation results in a correlation coefficient of .987. This means that about 97 per cent of the differences in growth rates among these chains is explained statistically by differences in the per cent of their growth due to mergers.

CHAPTER FIVE

1 Willard F. Mueller and Norman R. Collins, "Grower-Processor Integration in Fruit and Vegetable Marketing," *Journal of Farm Economics* (December, 1957), pp. 1471–83.

2 F. Lavington, "Technological Influences on Vertical Integration," *Economia* (March, 1927), p. 28; George Stigler, "The Division of Labor Is Limited by the Extent of the Market," *Journal of Political Economy* (June, 1951), p. 189.

3 *Ibid.* Stigler points out further that in a new industry the revenue possibilities are too small to support a specialized firm or firms performing a particular function. Then, a firm in the new industry may have to perform all or most of the production and marketing functions involved in making and selling the product.

4 Mueller and Collins, "Grower-Processor Integration," p. 1472.

5 Differences in the average earnings of successive industries are not sufficient proof that firms in the industry with lower earnings have an incentive to integrate for the above reasons. First, differences in profit rates may be due to many things besides differences in competitive conditions. Second, strictly speaking, it is the anticipated marginal rates of return rather than average rates which are significant.

6 The term "private label" refers to arrangements whereby a processor packs his product under someone else's label.

7 An alternative way of viewing the structural transformation brought about by private labeling by retailers is to view firms in industry *B* as having originally integrated into industry *A* via their successful product differentiation, thereby preventing firm *A* from following its own merchandising policy in selling *B*'s products to its retail customers. Then, when firm *A* develops its own brands, it in effect enters in competition with the brands established by firms in industry *B*. Whether viewed in this manner or that presented in the text, the structural change brought about by *A*'s actions is to bring its brands in competition with those of firms in industry *B*.

8 Adelman has suggested that vertical integration may be due entirely to chance. He also cites the Robinson-Patman Act as a stimulant to vertical integration because it thwarts the translation of cost differences into price differences.— M. A. Adelman, "Bases and Bounds of Integration of Firms and Functions," *Frontiers of Marketing Thought and Science,* ed. Frank M. Bass (1958), pp. 183–84. Other writers give many other reasons for vertical integration, but most of these are simply variations of the reasons given in the text.

9 H. E. Hardy, "The Integration of Manufacturing and Chain Distribution—with Special Reference to Food Products," unpublished Ph.D. dissertation (University of Minnesota, 1947), p. 297.

10 *Chain-Store Manufacturing*, Senate Document No. 13, 73rd Cong., 1st sess. (1934), p. 14.

11 *Ibid.*, p. 25.

12 *Ibid.*

13 According to *Moody's Industrials*, the following five chains have concentrated-milk plants: A & P, Safeway, Kroger, American, and First National.

14 In 1929 A & P and Kroger accounted for 47.3 per cent of total chain sales. By 1958 they accounted for only 36 per cent (Tables 41A and 41B).

15 *Chain-Store Manufacturing*, p. 29.

16 This method of estimating the number of potential integrators involves a number of important assumptions. First, it assumes that a chain's size (as measured by total adjusted retail sales) measures its ability to integrate into a particular industry. Other factors are important as well, of course. All chains of the same size do not have the identical financial and managerial resources required to integrate into a related industry, nor have they developed equally acceptable private labels. This is important because the degree of customers' acceptance of a chain's label determines the volume of its own manufactured product which it may expect to sell. Also, for products which are not readily transportable over long distances, this measure of the ability to integrate assumes that each chain's stores are about equally concentrated geographically. Otherwise, whereas one chain could operate a plant of efficient size (for example, a bakery), another chain of identical size could not if its stores were not sufficiently concentrated geographically to utilize the same manufacturing plant.

These and other factors tend to detract from the accuracy of this measure of the number of potential integrators, but we believe that size is the best single measure of a chain's ability to overcome the main barrier to entering various grocery-manufacturing industries—the product-differentiation barrier. Because most medium-sized and all large chains have developed quite acceptable private labels, the main determinant of the volume of private-label sales is their total sales volume. For example, all chains with annual sales of $100 million may expect to sell about $5 million worth of bakery goods. And the experience of chains which have integrated into baked goods indicates that their own brands will account for the great bulk of their total bakery sales.

17 Federal Trade Commission, *Economic Reports of Investigations of Coffee Prices*, July 30, 1954, p. 197.

18 *Concentration in American Industry*, Report of Subcommittee on Antitrust and Monopoly, 85th Cong., 1st sess. (1957), p. 41.

19 The result of this differentiation is reflected in the price premiums of advertised brands at wholesale. For example, in the years immediately preceding World War II, advertised brands sold at a premium of about 25 cents a case, or about 10 per cent of the average wholesale prices in those years.—Hugh L. Cook and Truman Graf, "Some Data Explaining Relocation of the Wisconsin Evaporated Milk Industry," Department of Agricultural Economics, University of Wisconsin (1955), Figure II (Processed).

20 Federal Trade Commission, *Report on Distribution Methods and Costs*, Part I: *Important Food Products* (1944), p. 91.

21 Computed from *Moody's Industrial Manual.*

22 Federal Trade Commission, *Report on Distribution,* p. 89.

23 *Ibid.,* p. 58.

24 Bain has demonstrated empirically that a significant correlation exists between industry concentration and industry profit rates.—"Relation of Profit Rate to Industry Concentration," *Quarterly Journal of Economics* (August, 1951), pp. 293–324.

25 J. S. Bain, *Barriers to New Competition* (Harvard University Press, 1956).

26 Cf. Jesse Markham, "Changing Structure of the American Economy; Its Implications for Performance," *Journal of Farm Economics* (May, 1959).

27 We have excluded fluid milk from our analysis of the relationship between market concentration and vertical integration because market concentration very probably was not the primary reason for the chain integration into fluid milk reported here. Rather, state milk control legislation in California has made milk bottling an especially attractive venture for chain stores. See D. A. Clarke, Jr., *Fluid Milk Price Control in California,* Agricultural Experiment Station, University of California (June, 1955), pp. 148–49. Significantly, two of the three chains which reportedly entered the manufacture of fluid milk (Table 50) operate in California.

28 It might have been more logical to have used concentration ratios for years prior to the actual integration by chains. However, it was not possible to obtain such estimates for all of the industries studied for any other year than 1954.

29 Correlation coefficients in a sample of this size are statistically significant at the 1 per cent level if they exceed .57. By this we mean that a value of the correlation coefficients as high as .57 would be obtained only by one chance in 100 in random samples from a population in which the two variables are uncorrelated.

30 However, correlation of the relative integration ratios and concentration ratios for the same industries over a period of time suggests that this general relationship remains high over a period of years. Correlating the 1940 relative integration ratios of the 11 industries, appearing in Table 32, which chains had already entered in 1940 with their corresponding 1954 concentration ratios, results in an *r* of .90.

31 Paul A. Baumgart, "Procurement of Supplies for Retailing," *The Frontiers of Marketing Thought and Science,* ed. Frank Bass (1958), p. 201.

32 In 1916 the four largest packers accounted for 54 per cent of sales, but by 1954 their share had fallen to 31 per cent.—Willard Williams, "Structural Changes in the Meat Industry," *Journal of Farm Economics* (May, 1958), p. 319.

33 Baumgart, "Procurement of Supplies," pp. 200–201.

34 The recent FTC study bears this out. Chain manufacturing of prepared meats increased by over 100 per cent between 1954 and 1958.—Federal Trade Commission, *Economic Inquiry into Food Marketing,* Interim Report, June 30, 1959, Chains, Table 7.

35 Total chain meat-packing plants dropped from 39 in 1946 to 17 in 1957 (Table 50).

36 Bain, *Barriers to New Competition,* pp. 216–17.

37 The data on vertical mergers by retailers were derived from the same sources as those on horizontal mergers, and are probably about as accurate in terms of numbers of mergers reported. However, it was not possible to make estimates of the size of these mergers.

38 Federal Trade Commission, *Economic Inquiry into Food Marketing,* Voluntary Group, Table 2; Cooperatives, Table 2.

39 The main exceptions to this generalization occurred during World War II when wartime-created shortages made internal growth extremely difficult. Consequently, several chains not only entered new fields by mergers but made subsequent acquisitions as they expanded their operations. The leading example is Safeway's acquisition of packing plants from 1942 to 1945.

40 Norman R. Collins and John A. Jamison, "Mass Merchandising and the Agricultural Producers," *Journal of Marketing* (April, 1958), p. 364.

41 The struggle between retailer and national brands has been referred to as recently as 1957 as "The Third Revolution in Distribution" by M. M. Zimmerman in a paper by this name published by Super Market Publishing Co., New York 36, New York, p. 3.

42 *Chain Store Private Brands,* Senate Document No. 142, 72nd Cong., 2nd sess. (1933).

43 *Ibid.,* p. xvi.

44 *Ibid.,* p. 20.

45 *Ibid.,* Table 3, p. 20.

46 Another 36.8 per cent indicated that they plan to keep about the same number of items and 1.2 per cent gave no answer to this question.

47 *The Big Challenge in Food Marketing (This Week,* 1959), p. 24.

48 *Ibid.*

49 In 1958, 96 per cent of A & P's meat sales reportedly were under its own labels. —*Wall Street Journal,* December 15, 1958, p. 12.

50 Based on an unpublished study by the authors.

51 *Chain Store Private Brands,* p. xvii.

52 *Ibid.,* p. 79.

53 Norman S. Rabb, address to the American Marketing Association, New York City, April 23, 1959, p. 10.

54 *Ibid.,* p. 8.

55 Bain, *Barriers to New Competition,* pp. 216–17.

56 *U.S.* v. *New York Great Atlantic and Pacific Tea Co.,* 67 Federal Supplement 626, p. 639. Another way in which a manufacturer may forestall entry is by giving a chain threatening entry a special price discount on branded products. Of course, such price discrimination is illegal under the Robinson-Patman Act.

57 A. C. Hoffman and L. A. Bevan, *Chain Store Distribution of Fruits and Vegetables in the Northeastern States,* U.S. Department of Agriculture and New Jersey College of Agriculture (November, 1937; mimeographed).

58 William E. Folz, "Merchandising Policies and Practices of Large Chain Supermarkets in Fresh Fruits and Vegetables and Their Implications to Market Structure," *Proceedings, Western Farm Economic Association* (1958), pp. 18–34. A

more complete analysis of the results of this study will be published shortly by William E. Folz and Alden Manchester.

59 *Ibid.*, p. 28.

60 In 1935, A & P's average sales per store were only $58,000. This is much smaller than those of current supermarket operations. And whereas A & P had about 15,000 stores in 1935, in 1936 there were only 1,200 supermarkets (sales over $375,000) operating in the entire country (Table 5).

61 This is a different conclusion from that which Folz comes to in his study. Because he credits supermarkets as the dominant factor determining changes in procurement practices, he concludes, "The extent to which the marketing channels for fresh fruits and vegetables will be changed will depend *in the first instance on the extent to which the supermarket as an institution will continue to grow and to engross within themselves all food retailing.*"—"Merchandising Policies," p. 31.

62 *Wall Street Journal,* March 30, 1959, p. 19.

63 Another possible case of a food manufacturer acquiring a chain is the merger in 1956 of Dolly Madison International Foods, Ltd., and Lucky Stores. Lucky is the country's 19th largest chain and had sales of $142 million in 1958. We have been unable to determine the nature of Dolly Madison's operations prior to this merger, although it reportedly entered dairy manufacturing in 1955.— *New York Times,* November 15, 1956, p. 45. We have not included the Dolly Madison–Lucky Stores merger in Table 36.

64 C. W. Sadd, "Procurement and Pricing Policies for Milk and Ice Cream Followed by P & C Markets," *Proceedings, Fourteenth Annual Midwest Milk Marketing Conference* (1959), College of Agriculture, University of Wisconsin, p. 49.

65 *Ibid.*

66 Corwin Edwards, "The Conglomerate Enterprise," *Business Concentration and Price Policy,* ed. G. J. Stigler (Princeton: Princeton University Press, 1955).

67 *Moody's Industrials,* 1957.

68 Computed by the New York City Bank.

CHAPTER SIX

1 The names and sizes of important national organizations are discussed above in connection with the extent of horizontal integration in grocery retailing.

2 See Cooperative Food Distributors of America, *What Is CFDA?* (Chicago, undated), p. 1.

3 *Ibid.*

4 Cooperative Food Distributors of America, *What CFDA Does for the Retailer-Owned Wholesaler* (Chicago, undated), p. 2.

5 Personal interview with Mr. A. T. MacMath, IGA Headquarters, Chicago.

6 "The IGA Story," *Meat and Food Merchandising* (Fall edition, 1957), p. 16.

7 *The IGA Story,* mimeographed speech supplied by IGA Headquarters (undated), p. 3.

8 *The Red and White Story* (Chicago: Red and White Corporation, undated), p. 3.

9 Federal Trade Commission, *Economic Inquiry into Food Marketing,* Interim Report, June 30, 1959, Voluntary Group, Table 3; Cooperatives, Table 2.

10 *Chain Store Inquiry—Cooperative Grocery Chains,* Senate Document No. 12, 70th Cong. (1928), p. 148.

11 Paul D. Converse, "Prices and Services of Chain and Independent Stores in Champaign-Urbana, 1937," *Journal of Marketing* (January, 1938), p. 194.

12 Richard Millican and Romona J. Rogers, "Price Variability of Nonbranded Food Items among Food Stores in Champaign-Urbana," *Journal of Marketing* (January, 1954), pp. 283–84.

13 Werner Z. Hirsch, "Grocery Chain Store Prices—A Case Study," *Journal of Marketing* (July, 1956), pp. 9–23.

14 *Ibid.,* p. 14.

15 See Edward A. Duddy and Davis A. Revzan, *Marketing,* (2nd ed.; New York: McGraw-Hill, 1953), p. 204.

16 Hirsch, "Grocery Chain Store Prices."

CHAPTER SEVEN

1 The Federal Trade Commission reported that there were only 319 voluntary and 144 cooperative groups operating in 1959. Although the source used in the text overstates the number of these organizations, this is the only source showing the trend in the number of these organizations (Table 18).

2 Estimate based on 1955 data.

3 For example, du Pont did not enter high explosives production until 1880 or smokeless powder production until about 1900. But after making over 50 acquisitions between 1880 and 1905, du Pont produced 72.5 per cent of the country's high explosives and 70.5 per cent of the smokeless powder.—Willard F. Mueller, "Du Pont, a Study in Firm Growth," unpublished Ph.D. dissertation (Vanderbilt, 1955). Similarly, U.S. Steel was organized in 1901 as a combination of 12 companies. After this single consolidation, U.S. Steel produced 43.2 per cent of the nation's pig iron, 65.7 per cent of its steel ingots, 59.8 per cent of its steel rails, and 77.7 per cent of its wire rods.—G. W. Stocking, *Basing Point Pricing and Regional Development* (Chapel Hill: University of North Carolina Press, 1954), p. 20.

4 Only one of the top 10 chains reportedly made any mergers in 1959, and this involved a two-store firm.—*Supermarket News,* January 4, 1960, p. 1.

CHAPTER EIGHT

1 See Edward H. Chamberlain, *The Theory of Monopolistic Competition* (Cambridge: Harvard University Press, 1933); Joan Robinson, *Economics of Imperfect Competition* (London: Macmillan & Co., Ltd., 1933); William H. Nicholls, *Imperfect Competition within the Agricultural Industries* (Ames: Iowa State College, 1941); and William Fellner, *Competition among the Few* (New York: Knopf, 1949).

2 From 1947 to 1956 all areas of retail trade increased advertising expenditures as a per cent of the sales by only 10 per cent, and between 1952 and 1956 by only .1 per cent.

3 *U.S.* v. *San Diego Grocers Association, et al.,* indictment filed June 5, 1959, U.S. District Court for the Southern District of California.

4 *Wall Street Journal,* December 12, 1958, p. 1.

5 A. D. H. Kaplan, Joel B. Dirlam, and Robert F. Lanzillotti, *Pricing in Big Business* (Washington: Brookings Institution, 1958), p. 206.

6 Corwin Edwards, "The Conglomerate Enterprise," *Business Concentration and Price Policy,* ed. G. J. Stigler (Princeton: Princeton University Press, 1955).

7 For other examples of A & P's policy in this respect, see Robert F. Lanzillotti, "Pricing Objectives in Large Companies: Reply," *American Economic Review* (September, 1959), pp. 679–82.

8 *U.S.* v. *Safeway Stores, Inc.,* U.S. District Court for the Northern District of Texas, December 7, 1957.

9 Edwards, "The Conglomerate Enterprise."

10 J. S. Bain, *Industrial Organization* (New York: John Wiley & Sons, 1959), pp. 131-32. Bain defines a "low-grade" oligopolistic structure as an industry in which the four largest sellers account for less than 35 per cent of industry sales and the eight largest for less than 45 per cent.

11 Jesse Markham, "The Nature and Significance of Price Leadership," *American Economic Review* (December, 1951), pp. 891–905.

12 George Stigler, "The Kinky Oligopoly Demand Curve and Rigid Prices," *Journal of Political Economy* (October, 1957), p. 446.

13 See the following reference for an attempt to determine empirically the kind of barometric price leadership followed among California tomato processors: Norman R. Collins, Willard F. Mueller, and Eleanor M. Birch, *Grower-Processor Integration in the California Canning-Tomato Industry,* California Agricultural Experiment Station Bulletin No. 768 (October, 1959), pp. 54–59.

14 These included all the firms in the census of manufacturing listed as producing food and kindred products, tobacco products, soap, and salt.—*Concentration in American Industry,* Report of the Subcommittee on Antitrust and Monopoly, 85th Cong., 1st sess. (1957), pp. 41 ff.

15 Bain, *Industrial Organization,* p. 128. He defines "highly concentrated" industries as those in which the four largest sellers account for 65 per cent to 75 per cent of sales and the eight largest for 85 per cent to 90 per cent.

16 *Ibid.,* p. 128. He means those industries in which the four largest sellers have between 50 per cent and 65 per cent of sales and the eight largest sellers have between 70 per cent and 85 per cent.

17 *Ibid.,* p. 129.

18 Bain defines these as industries in which the four largest firms account for between 35 per cent and 50 per cent of sales and the eight largest between 45 per cent and 70 per cent.

19 Price discrimination for this reason should be distinguished from the type discussed below which results because a manufacturer fears a chain might enter its industry.

20 William H. Nicholls, *Price Policies in the Cigarette Industry* (Nashville: Vanderbilt University Press, 1951), p. 131.

21 Joel B. Dirlam and Alfred E. Kahn, *Fair Competition: The Law and the Economics* (Ithaca: Cornell University Press, 1954), pp. 233–41.

22 For an excellent theoretical discussion of the importance of product differentia-

tion as a barrier to entry, and the effects of barriers to entry on industrial performance, see J. S. Bain, *Barriers to New Competition* (Cambridge: Harvard University Press, 1956), chapter 1.

23 J. S. Bain, "Profit Rate as a Measure of Monopoly Power," *Quarterly Journal of Economics* (February, 1940), pp. 271–93.

24 Of course, small regional bakeries may feel that they have no alternative to private-label selling. In this event some chains may prefer to buy from such bakers rather than make their own products.

25 For example, whereas dairy products constitute about 10 per cent and meats about 22 per cent of total grocery-store sales, bakery products constitute only about 6 per cent and all canned fruits and vegetables about 4.5 per cent. Other leading manufactured food products constitute a much smaller percentage than these products.

26 By 1954 Consolidated had begun a full line of canned fruits and vegetables, coffee, baked goods, dried fruits and nuts, sugar, raisins, frozen foods, tea, and other products.—*Moody's Industrials,* 1954. It achieved most of its diversification through merger.

27 Quoted in *Food Field Reporter,* March 2, 1959, p. 20.

28 U.S. Treasury Department Internal Revenue Service, *Statistics of Income.*

29 For example, the Quaker Oats Company spent $49,166,990 on "selling, general, and administrative expenses" in 1957. This equaled 16.3 per cent of its total sales—up from 14.3 per cent in 1950. The bulk of these expenses very likely represents selling expenses of one kind or another.

30 Even in food retailing, advertising effort is losing much of its informational value. Increasing amounts of newspaper space are being devoted to persuasive rather than informational advertising. Today most full-page newspaper ads of a typical chain list price and other information on only about 50 items. This represents less than 1 per cent of the items handled in modern supermarkets.

31 McGraw-Hill, Department of Economics, *Business Plans, 1957–60,* p. 12.

32 *Ibid.*

33 Sosnick, "A Critique of Concepts of Workable Competition," *Quarterly Journal of Economics* (August, 1958).

APPENDIX

1 Paul E. Nelson, "Ownership Changes by Purchase and Merger in Selected Food Industries," Marketing Research Report No. 369, Marketing Research Division, Agricultural Marketing Service, U.S. Department of Agriculture (October, 1959).

2 Our secondary sources reported 12 acquisitions not reported by the census survey. These acquisitions were 2.1 per cent as great as the total acquisitions reported by the census survey. For a more complete report of this comparison of the census data and our data see Paul E. Nelson and Willard F. Mueller, "A Note on Merger Research Methodology," unpublished manuscript.

Index

213